LANGUAGES OF THE STAGE

LANGUAGES OF THE STAGE
Essays in the Semiology of the Theatre

Patrice Pavis

PERFORMING ARTS JOURNAL PUBLICATIONS

NEW YORK

To Zajačik-Ušiačik

Books by the same author:

Problèmes de sémiologie théâtrale, Presses de l'université du Québec, Montreal, 1976.

Dictionnaire du théâtre—Termes et concepts de l'analyse théâtrale, Editions Sociales, Paris, 1980.

Voix et Images de la scène, Presses Universitaires de Lille, 1982.

ACKNOWLEDGEMENTS

The English translation of these few essays in the semiology of theatre does not owe its publication to any grant for research, documentation, translation, typing or editing. However, it is certain that it would not have come into existence without the friendly complicity and generous help of several people to whom I would like to express my gratitude.

First of all, I wish to thank all those who were involved in translating or even sometimes adapting these articles, as the French technical terms often had no equivalents in English or American criticism: Susan Melrose, who had the difficult task of translating most of the articles (II, i and III, i, ii, iii, iv), Susan Bassnett-McGuire (I, i), Tjaart Potgieter (I, ii), Marguerite Oerlemans Bunn (IV, i), Jill Daugherty (IV, ii and Postface). I am very grateful to Susan Melrose and Barbara Behar for their help in translating and "rewriting" II, ii.

Susan Imhoff, Jill Daugherty, David Trott and Michael Hays, themselves engaged in theatre research, assisted me with great devotion in preparing the final draft of the manuscript. I am particularly indebted to Jill Daugherty who proofread very carefully the whole manuscript and helped me reformulate many passages from the original text.

My stay as visiting professor in the Department of Theatre at the University of California at San Diego furnished me with the right surroundings for rereading and correcting these essays, and I especially appreciated the friendliness and companionship of Barbara Behar, Susan Imhoff, Frantisek Deák, Robert Israel and Floyd Gaffney.

Gilberte Billa and Teri Lamothe typed the manuscript of this book with a patience and perspicacity worthy of semiologists studying hieroglyphics.

Finally, I wish to acknowledge my intellectual debt to all the research workers, too numerous to be named here, who are nevertheless present and, I think, discernible between the lines of my own text, and especially to my colleague at the *Institut d'Etudes Théâtrales de la Sorbonne Nouvelle*, Anne Ubersfeld, whose own work and intellectual curiosity are a constant source of inspiration for us all.

Library of Congress Cataloging in Publication Data
Languages of the Stage
Library of Congress Catalog Card No.: 82-80613
ISBN: 0-933826-14-1
ISBN: 0-933826-15-X (p)

Design: Gautam Dasgupta

Printed in the United States of America

90000427

Publication of this book has been made possible in part by a grant from the National Endowment for the Arts, Washington, D.C., a federal agency, and public funds received from the New York State Council on the Arts.

CONTENTS

Foreword

The subtitle alone—"Essays in the Semiology of Theatre" (for "Essays," read "Attempts")—indicates clearly the change in perspective of my research since my *Problèmes de sémiologie théâtrale* appeared. Not that I now think, moved by the spirit of the essay/attempt, that "scientific method" should give way to the unchecked speculation of the essayist—for how could we construct a theory without some minimal requirements of coherence and exemplarity? Rather, recent developments in theatre studies have made a global treatise on semiology, if not out of place, at least extremely problematical, if it is not to take on the disquieting proportions of a multi-voiced encyclopedia.

Less than ten years ago the now rhetorical question of the possiblilty of a semiology of theatre not yet incongruous. Those were the days—(oh, nostalgia!)—of nocturnal raids into linguistic territory and of the clandestine piecing together of models which, while borrowing heavily from the science of language, managed to mask their origins and offer the student of theatre practicable tools. It was a period of great theoretical effervescence, which, while sometimes lacking the support of men of science and art, nevertheless prepared the way for studies which are now more firmly rooted in stage practice.

Today, there is still no agreement on *the* model of *a* semiology of dramatic art. To see this as a failure would be wrong; rather, there exists a healthy state of suspicion about any universal model and a concomitant desire to make "attempts" on specific objects—a *mise en scène*, a decor, an acting style—using methods inspired by semiology. So, far from enclosing itself in abstruse doctrines, semiology as applied to an art allows us to broaden our understanding of other critical attitudes such as dramaturgy, systems of *mise en scène*, aesthetics of theatrical forms of the act of reviewing a performance.

This book is thus quite naturally situated mid-way between the application and adaptation of theatre semiology. It concentrates on a few of the aspects of a semiology of theatre. This transmutation of theoretical space into a narrower pragmatic one, which is also freer and more playful, explains the apparent disparity of these articles: they are to be considered "first attempts." Without limiting myself to one particular area, I thought it appropriate to deal in each of the four chapters with a precise and illustrated example from the general theory or from a particular performance.

The articles were written almost exactly in the order in which they appear here; their genesis and combination would therefore reflect the movement, the deepening grasp and the verification of a program of research which has led from a theoretical inventory to a study of the actor's body and gestures and, finally, to a reflection on that which determines semiology: the reception of the work of art. Such examples of *mise en scène* serve both as a culmination of these debates and as the sounding-board for a new theoretization, so that one might legitimately be led, at the end of the "voyage," to restate the eternal "present state of the research."

In short, the method should emerge from its own discourse, and what remains is a hope that the comment of the theoretician Polonius to the practician Hamlet will be equally applicable to the present undertaking: "Though this be madness, yet there is method in it."

I. PRESENT SITUATION OF SEMIOLOGY

A Possible Definition
of
Theatre Semiology

This article is the entry under *sémiologie théâtrale* in my *Dictionnaire du théâtre: Termes et concepts de analyse théâtrale,* Paris, Editions Sociales, 1980. An English translation was published in *Theatre Quarterly,* vol. X, no. 40, 1980, pp. 74-78.

A method of analyzing text and/or performance that focuses on the formal organization of the text or the show as a whole, on the internal organization of those signifying systems that make up both text and performance, on the dynamics of the processes of meaning and establishment of sense through the participation of theatre practitioners and audience.

Very loosely, we could follow Michel Foucault in agreeing that semiology is "the ensemble of knowledge and technical skills that enables us to perceive where signs might be, to define what constitutes them as signs and to understand the relationship between them and the laws governing their interaction."[1] Semiology does not concern itself with locating meaning (an issue that belongs more properly to *hermeneutics* and to literary criticism) but with the mode of production of that meaning throughout the theatrical process, beginning with the director's reading of the script through to the interpreting task of the spectator. It is a discipline that is both "ancient" and "modern," for the idea of the sign and of meaning is at the heart of all philosophical debate, while semiological study in the strictest sense of the term goes back to Peirce and Saussure.[2]

Saussure defines his vast program in *Course in General Linguistics* as follows: "A science that studies the life of signs in the midst of social life . . . it should demonstrate what signs consist of and what laws govern them." As regards the application of this approach to theatre studies, this can be traced back to the *Prague Linguistic Circle* of the 1930s and to the work of Veltruský, Mukařovský, Honzl, Burian, Bogatyrev.[3] At the present time there is a revival of interest in the work of the Prague group after some forty years.

I. *Semiology or Semiotics?*

The difference is not simply one of words alone, nor is it the result of the French-American terminological dispute between Peirce's *semiotics* and Saussure's *semiology*. The difference lies, more profoundly, in the irreconcilable opposition of two models of the *sign*. Saussure restricts the sign to the relationship between a *signified* and a *signifier*. Peirce adds to these terms (which he calls *representamen* and *interpretant*) the notion of the *referent*, that is to say the reality denoted by the sign.

Curiously enough, in the usage that seems to have become established following the work of Greimas,[4] *semiology* is used to describe Peirce's *semiotics*, while his own work, which can be traced back to Saussure and Hjelmslev, is termed *semiotics*:

> and so the gap widens between semiology, where natural languages can be used as instruments of paraphrase in the desription of semiotic objects, on the one hand, and semiotics, whose prime task is the construction of a metalanguage of the other. . . .

> semiology demands, in a more or less explicit manner, the mediation of natural languages in the process of reading the signifieds that belong to non-linguistic semiotics (painting, architecture, etc.) even when semiotics challenges this.[5]

Much could be said about this blanket disqualification of semiology (such as theatre semiology, for example) which would be no more than a study of theatre discourse. It is certainly legitimate within the Greimasian vision that is primarily concerned with *semio-narrative* (deep) structures and so sees examination of the *discursive* (surface) structures as secondary. Greimas attempts to consider the emergence and development of all meaning, and he concentrates on "releasing the minimal semiotic forms (relationships, unities) common to different visual domains." Consequently the theatre, as a manifestation of external discourse, is not the subject of his interest. But as theatre scholars know, in moving on to describe what is seen on a stage, the connection between signs and their referents must be made (without, however, turning theatre into a more or less iconic imitation of reality and making *iconicity* the criterion of the appreciation of theatre signs).

What will be discussed here in this examination of the theoretical advantages and disadvantages of this method is, therefore, *semiology* and not semiotics. But to talk about *theatre semiology* presupposes that the phenomenon of theatre can be isolated and specified which, in the present context of the splintering of theatre forms, is obviously problematical. However, it does not seem essential to first solve the aesthetic question of the *specificity* or non-specificity of theatre in order to propose a theatre

semiology. What is needed is simply to conceive of this system as "syn-
cretic" (a sign system that "puts into action many languages of
expression"[6] and make it the meeting point for other sign systems [of
space, gesture, music, text, etc.]).

II. *Difficulties and Stumbling Blocks of the First Phase of Semiology*

A first phase, one that has been necessary and should not be despised,
began by considering the bases of theatre semiology and ran up against the
following methodological problems:

A. *The Search for the minimal sign*

Semiologists set out to try and find the *units* necessary for a formal
description of performance following the program of linguists—"all
semiotic study in the strictest sense will consist of identifying the units,
describing their distinctive features and discovering the minutest criteria
that distinguish them."[7] In the case of theatre, however, it would not be
any use to subdivide the continuum of performance into temporal micro-
units according to the transformation of different systems. Such an attempt
would only succeed in breaking up the *mise en scène* and the totality of the
staging. It would be better to isolate an ensemble of *signs* forming a *gestalt*
pattern, with overall significance instead of simply adding signs (minimal
units) together. As for the distinction between fixed signs and moveable
signs (decor vs. actor, stable components vs. moveable ones, etc.), it is no
longer relevant to contemporary practice.

It can thus be seen that the *sign* is not a prior essential for the formation of
a semiology of theatre, and that it can even obstruct progress if the work
begins by trying to define its limits at all costs.

B. *Typology of Signs*

In the same way a typology of signs (whether derived from Peirce or from
elsewhere) is not a prerequisite for the description of performance. Not only
because the degree of iconicity or symbolism is of no relevance when taking
into account the syntax and semantics of signs, but also because typology is
often too general to take into account the complexities of performance.
Rather than types of sign (such as icon, index, symbol, signal), it is now
more common to follow Umberto Eco[8] and talk about the *signifying function*,
where the sign is conceived of as the result of a semiosis, that is of a correlation and a reciprocal presupposition between the level of expression (the
Saussurian signifier) and the level of content (the Saussurian signified).
This correlation is not a given fact from the start, it emerges from the
"readerly" production reading of the director and the "productive"

reading of the spectator. These signifying functions of the work in performance give a dynamic image of the production of meaning, they replace an inventory of signs and a mechanistic idea of codes of substitutions between signified and signifier, they allow for a certain leeway in the delineating of meanings and mark the same signified or signifier throughout the unfolding of the performance.

C. *"Automatisms" of a semiology of communication*

Barthes' analogy,[9] according to which the theatre is "a kind of cybernetic machine . . . that is programmed to send out a certain number of messages to one's address . . . simultaneous messages that nevertheless have different rhythms" so that one receives *at the same time* six or seven pieces of information (settings, costume, lighting, actors' positioning, gestures, dumb show, words) has often been taken literally. Strengthened by this statement, there has been an attempt to apply to theatre the conceptual apparatus of a semiology of communication, trying to define the theatrical exchange as a reciprocal process, to automatically translate a given signifier by a given signified, even going so far as to make the *mise en scène* the signifier. Sometimes the staging has been treated as almost superfluous, and the question has been asked how "to reconcile the presence of multiple signifiers with that of a single signified,"[10] where the signified is taken to be the known, principal element, i.e., the text.

D. *Universality of the semiological model*

After the period of theoretical fermentation, marked by a need to be set apart from linguistics by elaborating a universal semiologoical model, it became clear that if justice were to be done to the diversity of theatre forms, then the descriptive metalanguage would have to be adapted to the type of performance. It is on the level of the semiosis and the ordering of signs and scenic systems that methods can be differentiated. The stage is not considered as a system that imitates the world, but it is important to try and understand through which processes of symbolization the shift from the represented world to the stage world must go. In the same way, the *actantial models* inspired by Propp, Souriau and Greimas[11] have been applied, often in far too schematic and undifferentiated a manner, so that the universes of meaning of plays seem oddly similar. If applied according to the strictly Greimasian spirit, the actantial model retains its abstract non-figurative character: since it is applied specifically to the dramatic universe of a dramatic text and the actants are no longer "a type of syntactic unity, with a properly formal character prior to any semantic and/or ideological investment (of meaning),[12] it is easy to fall back into the old notion of *character* and *plot-line*.

Without dismissing this type of non-figurative *semiotics* altogether, it seems preferable to follow the process of the *reception* by a given public under certain given conditions, thus carrying out a semiological study *in situ*, relating the explicatory patterns to the spectators interpretative patterns:

> Anyone watching a performance does not carry out semiotic analysis in the theoretical sense, although the processes through which he may see, hear and feel become the processes of evaluation and those are always processes of a semiotic nature.[13]

E. *Fetishism of the code*

The frequent confusion between *scenic material*—the real object—and *code*—the object of knowledge, a theoretical, abstract notion—has compelled semiologists to establish a limited list of codes that are specifically theatrical. Frequently, the hierarchy which they suggest (the code of codes) preemptorily fixes the performance and its content to ignore the problem of how the performance works, while affirming that the system of theatrical signs is translatable into an ensemble of codes.

It would be more worthwhile not to search for a taxonomy of codes first of all, but to observe how each performance makes and conceals its own codes, how they develop through the play, how shifts are effected from explicit codes (or conventions) to implicit ones. Instead of considering the code as a system "hidden" within the performance that needs to be brought to light through analysis, it would be fairer to talk about a *process of setting up a code* through its mediator, for it is the interpreter, whether critic or actor, who decides to read a given aspect of the performance according to a freely selected code. The *code*, thus conceived, is more of a method of analysis than a property of the object analyzed.

F. *Limits of "connotation mania"*

An important branch of semiology, following the work of Barthes, focused on pointing out the connotations that a sign could arouse in the receiver. It is easy to adapt this game of associations to the *reading* of a performance: by encouraging the spectator-semiologist to set up a series of signs linked to a central sign. This results in the production of derived meanings, and that production is a legitimate means of analyzing and commenting on a performance.

All the same, it is also necessary to structure the sequences obtained in this way intrinsically and in relation to the different scenic systems, both in relation to a "constructable" meaning starting with the connotations, and in relation to a latent text comparable to the symbolic work in dreams analyzed by Freud and Benveniste. In this way it is possible to go beyond the simple level of minimal units and individual signs and their connotations and to reconstitute some basic patterns of theatre symbolism as realized in the staging.[14]

G. *Relationship between text and performance*

This has never really been clarified, since work is going on both in terms of a semiology of the text and of performance, without however, always bothering to compare the results of the two approaches. All too often, textual semiology has been content to rescue the text from being considered as the fixed, central part of the final performance, or, on the other hand, the text has been trivialized and slotted into a place as just one system among many, without any consideration of its privileged position in the formation of meaning. The relationship between text and performance has been passed over in silence—hence the ''surprise discoveries'' when the results of the two semiological approaches are compared—or else grossly over-simplified. This explains why work on signs that overlap text and staging—icons, indexes and symbols, for example—has had so much trouble in proposing a typology of signs that would be sufficiently flexible and at the same time exact enough to take into account the specific nature of a performance or style.

Moreover, the recourse to a *spectacle* text, a sort of *score* where all the scenic systems of performance are articulated in space and time seems considerably preferable. It is often possible to show up the contradictions between systems, and one of the most frequent and most basic contradictions is between the *actor* as material body that is visible and iconized, and the *text* as symbolic system that requires the mediation of the mental staging of performance. Veltruský has clearly shown the ''dialectical tension between the dramatic text and the actor, based primarily on the fact that the sound components of the linguistic sign are an integral part of the voice resources drawn upon by the actor.''[15]

Even among semiologists the idea still persists that the *mise en scène* of a text is only a transcodification of one system into another which is a semiological absurdity! Sometimes, the text is even considered as an invariable signified that can be expressed more or less ''faithfully'' in the signifiers of the staging. These conceptions are simply wrong; it is not because the text remains the same whether uttered by the actors of the Roger Planchon, Antoine Vitez or Peter Brook companies that it retains the same meaning. The *mise en scène* is not the putting into practice of what is present in the text. On the contrary, it is the speaking of the text in a given staging, the way in which its presuppositions, its unspoken elements and its enunciations are brought out that will confer on it a particular meaning. Moreover, the possibilities of staging (the interpretations) are not unlimited, since the text imposes certain constraints on the director and vice versa. To read a dramatic text, one must have some idea of its *theatricality*, and the performance cannot make a total abstraction of what the text says. As Keir Elam puts it, in the conclusion to his book:

> there appears to be little dialogue at present between semioticians working on the performance and its codes and those whose principal interest is in the dramatic text and its rules. But it is very difficult, on the other hand, to conceive of an adequate semiotics of theatre which takes no account of dramatic canons, action structure, discourse functions and the rhetoric of the dialogue, just as a poetics of the drama which makes no reference to the conditions and principles of the performance has little chance of being more than an eccentric annex of literary semotics.[16]

III. *New Tendencies and Trends*

A. *The* mise en scène *and semiology*

Following the first theoretical discussions of the semiologists who proposed a "well-oiled" model that was often too general and abstract, we have come round again, as they did in the early period of the Prague Linguistic Circle, to a rather more pragmatic questioning of the theatrical object. All that functions as a signifier has to be able to explain itself in the particular context of the theatrical performance under analysis, and the *mise en scène* is considered "semiology in action," which more or less wipes out the traces of its own labor but reflects all the time on the placing and deciphering of its own signs. The director interested in semiology (such as Richard Demarcy) "thinks" in a parallel series of signs, he is aware of the proportoning of materials, mindful of redundancies, correspondences between systems: "plastic" music, "spatial" diction, gestuality keyed in to the under-rhythms of the text.[17] He may move slowly towards a generalized rhetoric of staging (or at least of a particular staging). The semiologist should mark (and sketch) the rhetorical figures that regulate the production of meaning resulting from sign systems. The opposition metonymy/metaphor and the principles this represents is a good departure point, but the discussion must not stop there.

B. *Structuring of Sign systems*

Semiology investigates the signifying oppositions between signs belonging to different systems, it makes codes binary, suggests a hierarchy between materials at a given point in the performance. The staging stresses certain signs, and fatally distances others, it "punctuates" the performance through the lighting system and halts in the performance and it isolates se-

.

quences. It observes the phase displacements between scenic systems and enjoys the awareness of these differential shifts, such as a text "contradicted" by music or intonation, a setting that refuses to express minimal meaning unless clarified by text and acting, etc. Semiology is concerned with the *discourse of staging*, with the way in which the performance is marked out by the sequence of events, by the dialogue and the visual and musical elements. It investigates the organization of the "performance text,"[18] that is, the way in which it is structured and divided.

It is linked to that intuitive process which, in understanding a performance, is able to divide it along all sorts of lines: narrative, dramaturgical, rhythmical and gestural. Semiology operates sometimes on the level of paradigm (analyses of the whole system at a given moment), sometimes of syntagm (evolution of the system throughout the performance).[19] It lets itself be guided by the search for new thematic isotopies: elements that are redundant or correlated which are put into perspective so as to authorize a coherent reading of the performance.

C. *Latest Developments*

The present tendency is not towards exclusivity and isolation. On the contrary, semiology is gradually recovering everything it formerly excluded from its methodological field. It is, therefore, now concerned with *the problem of discourse*, speech acts, theory of possible worlds,[20] presuppositions,[21] socio-semiotics.[22] These latest developments show a greater flexibility in the purely linguistic method and a clear desire to set up a poetics or rhetoric of theatre forms, without being intimidated any longer by the genre that is specifically theatre but encompassing all types of performance. Rather than a new science or virgin field of study, theatre semiology appears to be most widely accepted as a propadeutic or epistemology of "performance science," a reflection of the link between the dramaturgical plan and the scenic realization.[23]

Translated by Susan Basnett-McGuire

Translator's note:

Readers with a knowledge of French will be aware of the problem of translating terms such as *spectacle*, *representation* and *mise en scène*, which do not have precise English correspondences. Accordingly, I have used the terms, *performance*, *staging* and *show* at various points in the text, interpreting the use made of the French terminology rather than searching in vain for equivalents.

There is, in addition, the fact that the specialized terminology of semiology is perhaps more accessible to French readers than to English ones at the present time. However, as work in this field in English gradually extends, so there should be less need for a terminology "borrowed" through translation. Moreover, the problems outlined by Patrice Pavis that derive from the dominance of Greimasian theory and terminology are far less relevant to Enlish-speaking readers than to French ones.

Footnotes

[1]Michel Foucault, *Les Mots et les Choses*, Paris, Gallimard, 1966.

[2]Charles Sanders Peirce, *Collected Papers*, Cambridge, Mass. Harvard U.P., 1931-58. Ferdinand de Saussure (1915) (transl.) *Course in General Linguistics*, London Fontana, 1974.

[3]For an account of the history of the Prague Linguistic Circle, see Keir Elam, *The Semiotics of Drama & Theatre*, London, Methuen, 1980; Ladislas Matejka & I. Titunik, *Semiotics of Art: Prague School Contributions*, Cambridge, Mass. M.I.T. Press, 1976; Irena Slawinska, "La semiologia del teatro *in statu nascendi*: Praga 1931-1961," in *Biblioteca teatrale*, (1978), pp. 114-35.

[4]See Algirdas Greimas, *Sémantique structurale*, Paris, Larousse, 1966. Greimas, *Du Sens*, Paris, Seuil, 1970.

[5]Greimas, with J. Courtès, *Semiotique, Dictionnaire raisonné de la théorie du langage*, Paris, Hachette, 1979, p. 338.

[6]Greimas & Joseph Courtès, *op. cit.*, p. 375.

[7]Emile Benveniste, (transl.) *Problems of General Linguistics*, Miami, Univ. of Miami Press, 1970.

[8]Umberto Eco, (transl.) *A Theory of Semiotics*, London, Macmillan, 1977.

[9]Roland Barthes, (1964, transl.) *Elements of Semiology*, London, Cape 1967.

[10]Greimas & Courtès, *op. cit.*, p. 392.

[11]See Vladimir Propp, (transl.) *The Morphology of the Folk Tale*, Austin, Univ. of Texas Press, 1968; Etienne Souriau, *Les Deux Cent Mille Situations Dramatiques*, Paris, Flammarion, 1950; Greimas, *Sémantique structurale*, Paris, Larousse, 1966.

[12]Greimas & Courtès, *op. cit.*, 1979, p.3.

[13]Mihai Nadin, "De la condition sémiotique du théâtre," in *Revue romaine d'histoire de l'art XV*, 1978.

[14]See Evelyne Ertel, "Eléments pour une sémiologie du theatre," *Travail théâtral* 28/29, 1977, pp.121-50.

[15]Jiri Veltruský, (1941) "Dramatic Text as a component of theatre," in Matejka & Titunik, 1976, pp. 94-117.

[16]Keir Elam, *The Semiotics of Theatre & Drama*, London, Methuen, 1980, p. 210.

[17]See Patrice Pavis, "Notes toward a semiotic analysis," *The Drama Review 84*, Vol 23, No. 4, December, 1979.

[18]Marco de Marinis, "Lo spettacolo come testo, (I)," *Versus*, No. 21, 1978, pp. 66-104.

[19]See Patrice Pavis, *op. cit.*, 1979.

[20]See Keir Elam, *op. cit.* 1980.

[21]See Oswald Ducrot & Tzelan Todorov, *Dictionnaire encyclopédique des sciences du langage*, Paris, Seuil, 1972.

[22]See John Van Zyl, "Towards a Socio-Semiotics of performance" in *The Semiotic Scene*, III, 2, 1979.

[23]See Patrice Pavis, "Debat sur la sémiologie du théâtre," *Versus* No. 21, 1978.

Discussion on the Semiology of Theatre

This article is reprinted with permission of *Versus* (No. 21, 1978). It was one of a number of papers dealing with five specific questions on the semiotics of theatre formulated by Marco de Marinis.

In your opinion, what is the proper relation between the "semiotics of theatre" and "theatre studies" (history of theatre, theory of theatre, theatrical aesthetics, etc.)?

This question brings to mind the famous debate, instigated by Saussure and continued by Barthes, about the relationship between linguistics and semiology: are linguistics only part of "this general science," semiology, of which the laws "shall be applicable to linguistics" (Saussure), or does semiology, on the other hand, model itself on the general pattern of linguistics (Barthes)? The semiology of theatre is a recent discipline—its theoretical formulation can be placed historically (the linguistic Circle of Prague in the thirties)—and it is to be expected that it should try to take its place in the spectrum of studies of the performance, without invalidating the other approaches, but also not allowing itself to be devalued to the rank of a methodological "gadget" which is content to employ linguistic terminology metaphorically in connection with some mythical "theatrical communication," and shed no new light on the performance.

In spite of the terms "sciences du spectacle" or *Theaterwissenschaft*, it should be clear from the outset that "theatre studies" could by no means claim a scientific status comparable to that of linguistics. The semiology of theatre, therefore, can neither use, by extension, the rigorous conceptual apparatus of linguistic studies nor share their epistemological objective. What follows is that we need to ask whether the semiology of theatre is an autonomous discipline (like, for example, sociology, botany, etc.) or rather a method and an attitude towards the performance. In the latter hypothesis, semiology would not duplicate the existing approaches, but would integrate itself with them by assimilating into its theory the known results of those disciplines. It would be at the same time the propaedeutics and epistemology of the various *theatre studies*, reflecting on their conditions of validity, and the possibility of using the results of one area to interpret the other.

The semiology of theatre could be differentiated from other *theatre studies* as follows:

Interpretative criticism and performance reviewing: at their best, they "select" from the performance and the text certain indications—details of *mise en scène*, of costume, meanings suggested by the text, the actors' performances—to build up a total meaning, discovering in the chosen signs redundancies or contradictions, confirming or refuting the proposed interpretation.

Of course, this procedure should not be disqualified by allegations of subjectivity or impressionism; rather we should recognize it as unconscious, "wild" semiology, concerned with reacting to the performance as a receiver who judges only what is perceived. What is lacking in this approach for it to be considered as semiology? Only (but this is considerable) an explanation of its analytical procedures. The selection of signs is, in fact, done without considering the problems of breaking the performance down into signifying systems (*découpage*), of the relation between signifier and signified, of the hierarchy of signs and their possible permutations, or of the integration of the sign into the total meaning. There is no clear distinction made between the levels of "sense" (*Sinn* or relation between signifier and signified, or between the signs themselves) and "meaning" (*Bedeutung* or relation between sign and referent, between the work of art and the reality represented, so that one proceeds from considerations of structural coherence of the work to remarks on what the performance reveals about our everyday reality, without examining, *a fortiori*, the relationship between the two wholes.

Theatre history and the study of external conditions prevailing at the genesis of the work have contributed largely to the development of semiology, but in a negative way. The reaction against this type of approach has been so great as to make semiology often appear to be an anti-history of theatre, preoccupied with the final and "actual" result of the production (*mise en scène*) and rejecting totally the archaeological dimension of theatrical signs. The advent of structuralism has confirmed the tendency to dismiss research into the origins and historical development of theatrical forms, in order to concentrate on the internal and synchronic functioning of the system of the performance. Biographical anecdotes about authors, "vulgar" sociology which regards the work as a mere reflection of socioeconomic conditions, and the isolated explanation of historical facts yielded by the text have all definitively been excluded from the semiological method. It would, however, be to the detriment of theatrical semiology to deprive it of historical apparatus, even at the level of synchronical analysis of the performance. It is revealing that there is at present a tendency in structural linguistics to return to History in full force, in an attempt to go beyond the Saussurian opposition between *langue* and *parole*, i.e., between "social system, independent of the individual" and "individual act of will and intelligence" (Saussure). We should refuse, therefore, to see in the "parole"—in theatre, the concrete realization of a work and a particular performance—a purely free and individual usage of ideological, aesthetical and theatrical codes by the author or director. For example, in the analysis of characters' dialogue, we can attempt to determine how it is influenced by the discourse formations of a certain ideology or a certain historical period, thus replacing the so-called "free" discourse of the character in the framework of its historical determinants.

The analysis of theatrical discourse could take inspiration from the very precise existing studies on social formations and enunciation (Robin, Pêcheux, Ducrot). One could rightly expect an explanation of the "stage formations" of even the visual signs of the performance: why this setting, this dramatic space, these social and physical distances between characters? Where does this technique or stage object come from? Why the "smoke," the mirrors, the tiles, the quotations in original language, and all the other "tics" in the Paris productions of 1977? The answers to these questions will inevitably also clarify the synchronic arrangement of signs in a performance.

Dramaturgy in its contemporary theoretical meaning asks how and according to which temporality the materials of the plot are disposed in the textual and stage space. It studies both the ideological and formal structures of the work, the dialectical tension between a stage form and its ideological content, and the specific mode of reception of a performance by the spectator. In its wish not to separate dramaturgy from ideology, i.e., the formal means of transmission and the contents to be transmitted, the dramaturgical approach obviously ties up with semiology, which is also concerned with accounting for the articulation of a total signifier and its corresponding signified. But whereas dramaturgy remains at a very general level in this endeavor, by considering primarily the written text and textual and scenic macrostructures, semiology attempts the comparative operation at all levels of the performed work, and more particularly at the level of stage systems. Its methodology is also inverse, since it sets out from stage signs to reconstruct, by comparing, adding-up and checking the redundancies of signifying systems, the double system of form and content. Finally, and most importantly, dramaturgy remains entangled in the Hegelian problem of content and form ("True works of art are those of which the content and form are seen to be rigorously identical . . . content is nothing but the transformation of content into form"—*Logik der Wissenschaft*). If Hegel is concerned with a dialectical relationship between a form which is nothing but the expression of a content, and a content which does not exist unless expressed in a certain form, in practice it is extremely difficult to define form and content dialectically. That is why dramaturgical studies of a work actually proceed, inspite of Hegel's warning, either from a certain "world vision" which finds artistic expression in a certain way, or from the observation of forms to which certain contents are afterwards attributed. In semiological terms, we could say that the dramaturgical approach presupposes knowledge of the aesthetic or ideological code, according to which the engendering of the message is then explained. Instead of explaining everything by means of a ready-made structure, semiology aims to determine which structuration of the performance the spectator can set up, to what extent meaning is the object of an active elaboration by the spectator, and how the recognition of signifieds from signifiers and signifiers from signifieds contained in the work, takes place.

The *aesthetics or poetics of theatre* would aim at formulating the laws determining composition and functioning of text and stage; it always aims at integrating the theatrical system into a larger whole—genre, literary theory, arts system, aesthetics, category. This reduces the theatrical work to a particular case and inevitably ties it to some philosophical system which is often only vaguely defined. This is why aesthetic theories of the theatre are most frequently normative, proceeding from an *a priori* definition of the "essence" of theatre, and judging the work in terms of its conformity to the proposed model: the theatrical genre is, for instance, defined as centering upon conflict—which disqualifies epic theatre—or it is characterized either as "bastardized" (an irregular combination of codes) or as total and specific (the Wagnerian *Gesamtkunstwerk*). Semiology goes to work on a different level, since it is more pragmatically interested in the internal functioning of the performance, without pre-judging its integration into some predetermined aesthetical theory. It is obvious, though, that the breakdown into systems (*découpage*), the search for minimal units, the relative importance accorded to text or stage, etc., are always the consequences of aesthetic choices, and belong, therefore, to pre-aesthetic considerations.

The theory of theatre can be distinguished (only with difficulty) from aesthetics; it is aimed at finding a non-normative theorization of theatrical phenomena. Following the example of the theory of literature or "literarity" (Jakobson), the theory of theatre is concerned with theatricality, i.e., with aesthetically specific properties of the stage and historically established forms. We are, nevertheless, still far from a unified theory of theatre, because the problems to be formulated include the description of textual structure and of performance, as well as the reception of the performance. Semiology and theatrical theory, therefore, unite, if not in method, at least in the purpose of their approaches.

To conclude, semiology, far from conflicting with other "theatre studies," integrates them and integrates with them; this methodological reciprocity should allow us to make better use of the results of older disciplines, while confirming at the same time their scientific status.

Until now the semiological approach to theatre has generally awarded priority to the written text, or textual level, over the mise en scène *of the text, or performance level, by considering the linguistic-literary element as the most important and significant among all the constituent elements of the theatre. It has even been said that the literary text functions as "invariable element" or "deep structure" of the performance. Do you agree with this position, or do you think that a semiotics of the theatre worthy of its name should necessarily be concerned with all the components of theatre (theoretically placed on an equal level), and especially, that it should redirect its attention from the textual level to the performance level?*

Since theatrical semiology has arisen in reaction to textual "imperialism" and the habit of regarding theatre as nothing but a literary genre, it may seem paradoxical to talk about a semiology of the text. When we do, it must be borne in mind that the text has been restored to its place of one system among the systems of the whole of the performance. Then the question is no longer whether "textual semiology (is) opposed to performance semiology," but whether a text can be analyzed semiotically before (without) the performance during which the text is enunciated. Are we not in fact engaged in performance semiology when we reflect on the text's "situation of enunciation," and, in consequence, on the *mise en scène?*

To avoid a fruitless controversy between the defendants of text or stage, I have suggested a model inspired by Peirce's typology of signs, which organizes theatrical signs according to their dominant function (iconic/indexical/symbolic) and the nature of their relationship with the referent.[1]

Instead of an irreconcilable opposition between textuality and iconicity, we should accept a "dialectical tension between dramatic text and actor, a tension based above all on the fact that the acoustic elements of the linguistic sign are an integral part of the vocal resources utilized by the actor."[2]

The key diagram, therefore, is no longer: Text ⟶ Stage, but:

PERFORMANCE

Textuality	Iconicity
creating situation	possibilities of codification
of enunciation	search for units of meaning
(indexization & iconization	process of stage symbolization
of text)	

The inter-relationship between icon and symbol becomes apparent as soon as one can follow, in the performance, the circuit of codification (of the stage, of visual elements which are supposedly "non-symbolizable") and decodification (of the linguistic text, which, in the theatre, cannot be understood except "visually," i.e., in the situation).

According to this conception, the text is not an "invariable element" or "deep structure" of the performance, but has "to be created" just as the production (*mise en scène*). What semiology has to explain, therefore, is the interaction between the two systems, the "construction" they can impose on each other; what can be made of a text, and what the stage situation can make it say. What Pugliatti[3] calls the pre-textual objective (which "precedes" the linguistic transcription and stage transcodification) could, in this case, serve as mediator in the classic opposition. However, we would first have to clarify to what extent this objective is determined jointly by spatial and linguistic considerations, that is to question again theoretically the theatricality of dramatic writing and the writing of the stage.

If all the stage systems (including the textual) are equal "by right"—the stage invoking all of them to create its meaning—that does not mean that they are all always to be found on the same level or in the same relation to each other. The positivist procedure of segmenting the whole into numerous systems, tacitly assuming that they function in parallels, does not allow us to go beyond simple description of the performance or to clarify the spectator's constitutive act of understanding. We have to choose a hierarchy of codes and sub-codes, keeping well in mind that the choice of a hierarchy itself is made according to an aesthethic or ideological code. This is the case, for example, with the traditional concept of action as a "unique current" which "fuses word, actor, costume, decor and music (a current) which goes through these by passing from the one to the other or through several at once."[4] The choice of "action" (or of "narrativity") corresponds to an ideologico-aesthetical code which obliges the spectator to reconstruct a logic of actions, linked to the linearity of the verbal message and to the cultural code of the Western narrative tradition.

Rather than proposing a static hierarchy or randomly according primacy to any signifying system, we can distinguish basic systems or "articulators" and "grafted" systems (those which are "articulated"). Thus, in Tadeusz Kantor's *The Dead Class*, text and music are based on ("articulated on") the class-room desks and the masks/bodies of the characters. The musical and textual systems are superimposed, because if they were eliminated, the total meaning, dead class, could still be constructed. The metalanguage indicating all the relations between articulator/articulated still has to be elaborated, as well as a theory of the linear breakdown (*decoupage*) and the modification of "articulations" during the course of a performance.

The theatre specialist (and, therefore, also the semiologist of theatre) finds himself in a rather paradoxical and unenviable position: he must study an object (the performance) which, as such, is missing. Indeed, none or almost none of the constituent elements of the performance exists beyond the ephemeral duration of the performance itself; nothing remains but the written text, when that exists. The following question arises: how do you think a semiotics of theatre could resolve the problem of reconstructing the sign systems which are used by a performance and which disappear with it (paralinguistic codes, codes of gesture, spatial codes, codes of stagecraft, etc.)? Of what use can audiovisual recordings be in this regard? (A question as yet applicable only to a few contemporary productions.)

What do we mean by "reconstruction of sign systems?" It is obviously impossible, even for a short sequence, to reconstitute all the systems of a performance. A video tape recording reconstitutes nothing—it merely records the signifying "flux" of the stage event, without isolating or structuring the various systems. It is a mere transcription or transcoding which, at best, provides information about the final product's composition of signs, but none about the signs' productivity, i.e., their reception and elaboration by the spectator. A real reconstruction of sign systems, on the contrary, should consist of defining the systems, determining their signifying units, and establishing the relations between units inside the same system, as well as between parallel systems. Rather than trying to identify the signs of a system exhaustively, we must stress the important moments in the signifying sequence and clarify the main stages of the process of semiosis. If we take the example of the code of gestures, it is immediately apparent that it would be both impossible and useless to notate in some system of codification or another, all the gestural positions of actors. In the case of the biomechanic exercises photographed by Meyerhold[5] (representing an actor in various positons, the consecutive logic of which is not immediately recognizable), all that can be determined is a code of rules governing positions:

1. extreme tension of the body concentrating in time and space several incomplete movements (Meyerhold's principle of "Taylorism");
2. body postures suggesting possibilities of movement without actually initiating them;
3. fixed co-ordinations of parts of the body, e.g., trunk bent forward; arms arched in a circle, head inclined forward, etc.

At present semiology must be satisfied with formulating some general laws of the code, attempting afterwards to reconcile this code with other systems. Often the segmentation into systems does not coincide with the level of the smallest possible units. In this case the choice of an articulating system (cf. above) will facilitate the "grafting" of other codes. Although the segmentation into codes is done according to the matter of expression, the signifying systems must be translated into corresponding signifiers before they can be compared, reconciled, or their articulation on an articulating system studied. In this way we can avoid chopping the performance into a mass of heterogeneous signs, which happens when it is segmented into parallel systems.

In this way we reverse the research method used by Greimas, which starts by creating a general model of meaning, proceeds to the narrative level of the actantial model, and finally specifies and refines its description to encompass the actual linguistic and visual manifestation. We would have to use one method to verify the other, but the "gap" between manifested signs and all that precedes them must still be "filled."

Do you think that a semiotic analysis of the performance should re-examine the old aesthetical problem of specificity? In other words, do you think that the various "artistic languages" (among them that of the theatre) constitute "combinations of specific codes," or, on the contrary, "combinations of non-specific and specific codes?

On the whole, do you think that at some stage a "formalization" (mise en forme), even if it were only of some fragments, of the performance-text (or of one of its codes), will be possible; or do you think, on the contrary, that the idea of "a-codification" as expressed by Metz on cinema should be extended to the theatre also?

The "specificity" of theatre, the "language of theatre," "scenic writing," "theatricality"—these are all metaphors, made attractive by the perspective of a discovery rather than by their actual meaning. Yet, nothing prevents us from verifying if semiology, which hopes to discover some rules of the organization and interaction of codes, can circumscribe a minimal group of specifically theatrical properties. But we should not rest content with a semiological reformulation of the innumerable definitions of theatre; the "minimal" specificity could, in fact, be defined as the simultaneous presence—in the case of spoken theatre—of textuality and iconicity (i.e., linguistic arbitrariness and stage iconicity). This opposition is expresseed variously in the antitheses: acting vs. linguistic text, mime vs. logos, visual vs. acoustic, action through thought vs. action through gesture, and symbolic structure vs. uncodifiable event. The theatrical sign has a syntactical-semantic dimension (relation between sign and object, between signs themselves) as well as a pragmatic dimension (relation between stage iconicity and deixis/enunciation).

In other words, the problem is to decide: (a) whether there is a specifically theatrical sign, i.e., a unit in which stage iconization and textual symbolization could blend to form an irresoluble union which would be specifically theatrical; (b) whether the theatrical performance is a construction of specifically theatrical signs or, on the contrary, a "collage" or synthetic amalgam of the various stage arts (e.g., the Wagnerian *Gesamtkunstwerk*), or an ensemble of systems alienated from one another, never losing their autonomy (the Brechtian epic production).

(a) The answer to the first question has to be, at present, negative. During a performance no theatrical sign is created in which textuality and iconicity could blend into a specifically theatrical product. The symbolic signs of the text, the visual and musical signs remain autonomous even when their combination, their disposition in the sequence or syntagm, produces a homogenous and univocal meaning (e.g., the actor's face lit in a certain way; a certain musical refrain; mime and gesture will produce by cross-checking the *signified*/physical presence, demonstrative insistence/ etc.), but a new total and specific sign, defined by a specific signifier and the corresponding signified, will not be established. There are no "synthetic" theatrical signs in the theatre ("synthetic" in the same sense as the color green is the "synthesis" of blue and yellow), only continuous interaction between the signifieds produced by the signifying systems. What we should examine, therefore, is the possibility of an interaction, specific to the theatre, between the codes of a performance (cf. below).

(b) When we consider the problem of the relationship, more or less close, between the various stage arts, we are not concerned with a theoretical question involving the semiological status of codes, but with an aesthetic and ideological choice made by the director: in the *Gesamtkunstwerk*, where the goal is a synthesis of the arts, the director strives to produce a total illusion of a self-sufficient and closed stage world. For the Brechtian production "the actors, the set designers, the make-up artists, the costume designers, the musicians and the choreographers place their arts at the disposal of the communal enterprise without giving up, for all that, their independence" (*Short Organum*, para. 70). Brecht's refusal to blend the stage materials into one unique experience (*Erlebnis*) is to be explained by his wish to show the process of production of the performance and to facilitate for the spectator the process of decoding the performance.

The term "code" requires precise definition. When speaking of theatrical codes, we often mean the codes of a semiology of communications, i.e., substitutive systems consisting of two groups of signs translatable into each other (as in the Morse code, where one single graphical sign corresponds to each letter). At other times, "code" is opposed to "message": "the traditional opposition between *langue* and *parole* can also be expressed in terms of "code" and "message," the code being the organization which allows the composition of the message as well as that to which each element of the message is referred in order to construct its meaning."[6] In this meaning of the term (also used by Jakobson), the code is considered the object of a construction starting from the message, the discovery of the code and the reading of the message it allows being determined by the know-how of the decoder. Semiology quite frequently switches from one usage of the word to the other, considering (1) that the codes are given, and that they need only be enumerated by tracing them onto the different channels of transmission, or (2) that reading the performance is the same as deciding to use a certain code instead of another, the spectator thus creating the performance by using a chosen decoding grid (Barthes, *S/Z*).

Mounin has already warned against the abusive usage of "code" for "natural language," showing that a code is the result of an explicit and pre-established convention, whereas "the conventions of language are implicit, [they] are established spontaneously during the course of the communication itself."[7]

When, therefore, we speak of the "artistic languages" (which in itself requires some theoretical justification), the existence of fixed and specific theatrical codes should not be taken for granted, or they should at least be limited to explicitly formulated theatrical conventions and rules of dramatic art, in short, to a code in the technical sense of the term.

1. Among the "lexicalized" *specific codes* we could group:

(a) general conventions of performance: the fiction of the character embodied by the actor, the stage which signifies the world, the "fourth wall" of dramatic theatre, two-dimensional space and time (in the fiction and the theatre event), etc.

(b) conventions linked to genres, historical periods, character types (e.g., farce, classical drama, Harlequin).

2. The *non-specific codes* are, by definition, more difficult to enumerate. Here we are concerned with codes which could also be used in everyday life or in other arts:

(a) linguistic codes: for instance, French as a language used both by Molière and by the seventeenth century, and partly as well by the twentieth century;

(b) ideological or cultural codes: everything which allows the spectator to identify the system of values conveyed by the content of the play. This is the perfect type of the "hold-all" code, unstructured and unconnected with a precise linguistic or aesthetic form. It is at this level that a study of the mechanics of response (psychological, sociological, imaginative) to the performance would occur;

(c) code of perception: perspective, perception thresholds, etc.

3. *Mixed codes (specific and non-specific)*: these codes do not form a distinct third category, but would result from the use of an external code (i.e., non-specific) in the theatrical situation, causing the code to be adapted to the means of expression peculiar to the stage. This brings into question again the earlier distinction, which is revealed as a pedagogical means of separating what appears as particular, individual usage (*parole*) in the performance from a group of materials (*langue*) derived from various fields, and of which only the combination or global structure has meaning.

For instance, in the code of gestures, it is practically impossible to disentangle signs belonging to the actor's individual and social reality from those belonging to the gestuality of the represented character. The smallest natural gesture of the actor is transformed into an element of a codified system, since it has to be sufficiently clear and distinct from those of the other characters to be understood correctly by the public. Even the linguistic text, as soon as it is uttered on the stage, becomes distinct from the same text as it could exist in everyday life or another artistic system (novel, painting, etc.). As a matter of fact, the theatrical text takes on a performance value, since it is always related pragmatically to the stage and produces the action in the very act of its enunciation.

"Formalizing the fragments of the performance text" means conceptually reconstructing an object which never exists in the form in which it is perceived during the performance; it also means locating the performance (and the ensemble of semiological systems) in a relationship of interpretation with the interpreting linguistic system. Indeed, as Benveniste has shown,[8] we must distinguish between articulating systems ("because they reveal their own semiotics") and the systems which are articulated (those "of which the semiotics only become apparent through the grid of another mode of expression"). To "formalize" the performance, which is composed of heterogeneous semiological systems (language, gestuality, music, etc.), any interpretation must interpret and categorize the stage systems by means of language, which leads to a "flattening" of the performance, by eliminating the differences in the materials.

Can we envisage a "formalization" which allows the differences to be retained? In that case, we would have to think of a system of notation codifying gesture, melody, voice, etc., and this is far from being technically easy. Also, one would not always be able to compare these codes, because their modes of codification would have nothing in common.

The only "formalizations" that have been achieved until now are the following:

(i) formalization of the circuit of signifiers: how one system is used in relation to another, producing a certain meaning, etc.

(ii) clarifying the relations between textuality and visuality: visualization of the referent; iconic and indexical signs allowing us to move from one field to the other;[10]

(iii) the dialectics of sign types: icon/index vs. symbol, relationship between the pragmatic and the symbolic;

(iv) reconstruction of a code of priority among the codes of the performance; distinction between articulating and articulated systems.[11]

But the only possible verification of such a formalization remains—and this is the specific character of theatrical art—the *mise-en-scène* of the text, with its pragmatic choice of codes and the relative importance assigned to them and their mutual relations. This is an extreme solution, which merely resolves through praxis what the theory can only partially formulate, and without intervening in a concrete way in the development of the performance codes.[12]

Translated by Tjaart Potgieter

Footnotes

[1]Cf. Patrice Pavis, *Problèmes de semiologie théâtrale*, Montréal, Presses Universitaires du Québec, 1976, pp. 29, 96.

[2]Jiri Veltruský, "Dramatic Text as a Component of Theatre," in L. Matejka & I. Titunik, eds., *Semiotics of Art: Prague School Contributions*, Cambridge, MIT Press, 1976, p. 114.

[3]Paola Gulli-Pugliatti, *I segni latenti*, Firenze, D'Anna, 1976, p. 272.

[4]Jiri Honzl, "La mobilité du signe théâtral," 4, 1971, p. 19.

[5]Photographs reproduced in "Meyerhold's Bio-Mechanic Exercises (a photographic series)" *The Drama Review*, 57, 1973, p.113.

[6]A. Martinet, *Eléments de linguistique*, Paris, A. Colin, 1967, p. 25.

[7]G. Mounin, *Introduction à la sémiologie*, Paris, Ed. de Minuit, 1970.

[8]Emile Benveniste, *Problèmes de linguistique générale*, II, Paris, Gallimard, 1974, p.61.

[9]Pavis, op. cit., pp. 52-61.

[10]op. cit., pp. 34-45.

[11]op. cit., pp. 18-23.

[12]Cf. also Pavis, *Dictionnaire du Théâtre, termes et concepts de l'analyse théâtrale*, Paris, Editions Sociales, 1980.

II. GESTURE AND BODY LANGUAGE

On Brecht's Notion of *Gestus*

This article was first published in *Silex*, no. 7, 1978.

It would be a great imp(r)udence to turn to Brecht's theoretical writings in order to extract from them certain concepts, to comment on them and to link them with other commentaries or to propose new definitions in the meta-language of semiology. Brecht's way of posing problems is extremely clear. He carefully illustrates them by reference to his theatre practice. He never hesitates—in the *Short Organum for the Theatre*, for example—to make those corrections necessitated by the evolution of his thinking, and the new demands of his aesthetic and political battles.

It would be highly dangerous, moreover, to isolate a concept for the sole purpose of clarifying it only in the context of written works of theory, without verifying what use Brecht makes of it in his writings or productions, and without comparing it dialectically with other notions of his system. This is precisely what has happened frequently with the concept of epic drama ("epische Spielweise"). "The contradiction betweeen acting (demonstration) and experience (empathy) often leads the uninstructed to suppose that only one or the other can be manifest in the work of the actor, as if the *Short Organum* concentrated only entirely on acting and the old tradition entirely on experience" (Addition to § 53, B.T. 277). So we stand forewarned; and if we insist on making an excursion (incursion) into the unknown land of the *Gestus*, we do so at our own risk, justified solely by the fact that the term itself, although in abundant use in Brecht's "theoretical writings," remains very vaguely and contradictorily defined.

In the vast mass of his writing on the theatre[1] which has appeared since "Non-Aristotelian Drama" (1932-1941) from *The Messingkauf Dialogues* up through the "Short Organum for the Theatre," (1948-1954), the center of gravity is constantly shifting: Brecht formulates his critique of the

"Aristotelian" dramatic form in reaction to the notion of identification and catharsis; then he shows his interest in the possibility of imitation and of critical realism; finally, "theatre dialectics" gives him the chance to propose a method of analysis of reality, and to go beyond the overly stressed oppositions between epic/dramatic, formalism/realism, showing/incarnating, etc.

However, in this journey towards a theory of dialectical theatre two key notions are particularly resistant to thematic and terminological variations: that of the *Gestus*, and that of the Story (*die Fabel*). They are veritable pillars of the theoretical structure, which is massive and solid, but whose foundations need to be examined. Brecht himself comes ever closer to a definition of *Gestus* and Story, without reducing them to an unequivocal meaning, as though he wanted to preserve their richness and their productive contradictions. But it is only at the end of his "demonstration" that he introduces them into the *Short Organum* (§ 61-76); following the thread of Aristotelian demonstration he sets out from the concept of imitation and the spectator's pleasure at that imitation, ending up at the "*Gestus* of delivery" of the performance (§ 76).

The itinerary to be followed by the author, the theoretician and the spectator is perfectly described in two sentences: "Splitting such material into one gest after the other, the actor masters his character by first mastering the 'story' "(64). "The exposition of the story and its communication by suitable means of alienation consititute the main business of the theatre" (70). According to these definitions it seems rather difficult to tell which element, *Gestus* or Story, is logically and temporally anterior to the other; it appears at any rate that Story and *Gestus* are closely linked, and constitute the play and its *mise en scène*. Theatre, in fact, always does tell a story (even if it is illogical) by means of *gesture* (in the widest meaning of the term): the actors' bodies, stage configurations, "illustrations" of the social body. The circle which illustrates the relationship between *Gestus*, Story and Character could be schematically represented as follows:

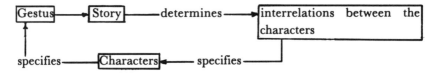

However, instead of accounting for each of the elements of the circle, which would entail a lot of repetition, I shall organize my remarks around the notion of *Gestus*, indicating the possible links with Story.

Definitions

The term *Gestus* first appeared in 1932 in "On Gestic Music"; it reappears several times in "The Actor's Craft" (1935-1941), "On Stage Architecture and the Music of Epic Theatre" (1935-1943), "New Technique of Acting" (1949-1955), "On Rhymeless Verse with Irregular Rhythms" (1939) from the collection "Remarks on Literary Work" (1935-1941), in the *"Modellbuch Theaterarbeit"* (1961) and finally in a systematic manner in the *Short Organum* (1948-1954), in articles 61-63-64-65-66-70-73-76. In this last work, *"Gestus"* (or *"gestisch"*) is often associated with an adjective or a noun making its materiality clear ("the gestural domain," the "gestural content," "the gestural matter") its social character ("a social *Gestus,"* "the basic *Gestus"*) or its faculty for demonstration ("the general *Gestus* of social dimensions").

All these definitons have a common social dimension: "A *Gestus* characterizes the relations among people" (G.W. 16, 753). "The realm of attitudes adopted by the characters towards one another is what we call the realm of gest. Physical attitude, tone of voice and facial expression are all determined by a social gest: the characters are cursing, flattering, instructing one another, and so on" (S.O. § 61). When Mother Courage bites on the coin that a purchaser has just given her, she too carries out a social *Gestus* which is quite precise: that of the suspicious saleswoman motivated by the prospect of gain. That act of biting on the coin establishes a whole fund of social dependencies (future clients, the producers of money and goods, authors and victims of fraudulent practices, etc.). *Gestus* has nothing to do with pantomime which is "a separate branch of the expressive arts, like theatre, opera, and dance." It is distinguished from gestuality (*Gestik*) which "exists in everyday life and takes a specific form in the theatre" (G.W. 16, 752). It has nothing to do with conventional gestures either (the hand raised to indicate the need to stop, for example), or illustrative gesture (declamation), or expressive and aesthetic gesture (dance).

The question of its extent is as complex as that of its specificity. *Gestus* may be a simple bodily movement of the actor (facial expression), or a particular way of behaving (gestuality), or a physical relationship between two characters, or a stage arrangement (a figure formed by a group of characters), or the common behavior of a group, the collective attitude of characters in a play, or the gesture of global delivery from the stage to the public via the *mise en scène*. This range of different kinds of *Gestus* reveals the constant enlargement of the notion of social *Gestus*. What would appear, in its slightest manifestation, as the index of an attitude, becomes an intentional signal emitted by the actor. The actor constantly controls his gestuality, in order to indicate the character's social attitude and way of behaving.

It goes without saying that is not enough for that effort by the actor to end at reproducing stereotypes of social relationships; the actor must seek out the most subtle and hidden signals of normal perception. So he is, therefore, coming directly to grips with social reality, its evolution and the newly invented forms ideology always adopts in order to encode attitudes between members of one class or different socio-professional groups. The *Modellbuch*,[2] through the juxtaposition of stills of one particular actor in his different situations, gives us many examples of these variations of the *Gestus* (cf. Lenz's *Der Hofmeister* where we can see "the rebellious vitality and brutality of Lauffer, born into the lower classes and strapped into the strait-jacket of court etiquette." ["*Theaterarbeit,*" p. 107]).

Social Gestus *and basic gestures*

Faced with the multiple forms of *Gestus*, Brecht is led to distinguish between the simple incidental social *Gestus*, characteristic of an actor or a particular stage business—and the *basic gestus* ("*Grundgestus*"), which is characteristic of the play or of a particular action. "Each single incident has its basic gest: Richard courts his victim's widow; the child's true mother is found by means of a chalk circle; God has a bet with the Devil for Dr. Faustus's soul; Woyzeck buys a cheap knife in order to do his wife in, etc." (S.O. § 66).

The basic *Gestus* describes a condensed version of the story; it constitutes the inalienable substratum of the gestural relationship between at least two people, a relationship which must always be readable whatever the options of the *mise en scène*. This *Gestus* (close to enunciation, a linguistic term which describes the attitude of the speaker to his utterance) gives us the key to the relationship between the play being performed and the public. The author's attitude to the public, that of the era represented and of the time in which the play is performed, the collective style of acting of the characters, etc., are a few of the parameters of the basic *Gestus*. Today we would also call it the "discourse of the *mise en scène* or of the "performance structure" without, however, insisting as Brecht does on the physical character (gesture and attitude) of this relationship with the public.

Once this general context of the *Gestus* is outlined, it becomes possible, through a series of approximations, to indicate its properties and its importance for the theory of theatre. *Gestus* appears to be a remarkable instrument for unlocking the contradictions of action and character, of the individual and the social body, of logos and gesture, of distance and identification.

Between action and character

The discussion about the link between action and characters, and the way in which one is determined by the other, is one of the oldest in theatrical aesthetics. Like Aristotle in his *Poetics*, Brecht conceives of theatre as a succession of actions from which the characterization flows. In the early Brecht, in *Man is Man* for example, the conception of man is quasi-behavioristic and mechanistic. (It is well known how the clownish characters of Valentin and Chaplin fascinated Brecht.) For the mature Brecht, man is no longer pure gesticulation; he cannot be reduced to a single exterior behavior-pattern; he is no longer an "activist" but a dialectical strategist. His way of acting influences and modifies the deepest elements of his nature.

Gestus can therefore assure the mediation between bodily action and character behavior; it is situated midway between the character and the determination of his possible actions (of his "spheres of action" in the functionalist terminology of Propp).[3] As an object of the actor's research, it becomes more and more specific in defining what the character does, and, consequently, what he is: way of being and way of behaving become complementary. The importance to the actor of this way of approaching the *Gestus* and the character is not difficult to imagine. Running through the opening scenes of his *Galileo*, Brecht analyzes Galileo's "stage business": his pleasure in drinking his milk, in washing himself, and in thinking form a *Gestus* which informs us as much about the person of the character (that is, about his possible weaknesses, which are confirmed in what follows) as about his activities as milk-drinker and thinker.

In practice, it is often very difficult to observe the dialectical mobility of *Gestus*, between a way of behaving and a gestuality which are fixed, on the one hand, and a spontaneous and creative activity on the other. It is, however, only at this price that the Brechtian notion retains its efficacy in going beyond the alternatives of action/character. The assembling of different *Gestus* by the actor will then allow him to reconstitute the Story. In the Brechtian concept the Story is not simply (as it is in *Poetics*), the "principle and the soul of the tragedy, with the characters in second place only" (1450a); it is principally the sum total of the *Gestus* and the relationships between the characters, "the realm of attitudes adopted by the characters towards one another" (S.O. § 61), "the groupings and the movements of the characters" (G.W. 17, 1218).

This integration of particular *Gestus* in the story explains its fragmented and non-continuous nature: "He [the actor] must be able to space his gestures as the compositor produces spaced type."[4] The "story-maker" spaces the narrative episodes. The development of the story occurs by leaps and not by a sliding of scenes one into the other. The fragmentation of the story corresponds to the "shifting" gesture (which always implies more than it actually shows). This shifting movement and the fragmentation are, in fact, iconically, musically, reproducing the contradictions of social processes. The Story does not mask (as does the traditional dramatic form) the illogical nature of the linking of the scenes but lets us become aware of it. Thus, for example, the dual attitude of Mother Courage: living off the war *and* sacrificing nothing to it; loving her children *and* making use of them in her business, etc.

If the *Gestus* refers directly to a position in the social reality represented, the story does not have to mold itself to the undulatory and contradictory movement of history, to follow faithfully the same logico-temporal presentation. There is never a perfect parallelism between social processes and the arrangement of the *Gestus* within the plot. The spectator's pleasure lies in rectifying the proportions between Story and history, in perceiving the disconnections between these two levels: thus in *Galileo* we wait in vain for a dramatic scene of retraction. In *The Resistible Rise of Arturo Ui*, the life of the gangster does not follow that of his historical model.

Individual and social

The distinction between an *individual* gesture and a *socially* encoded one is also quite irrelevant to *Gestus*. For Brecht, gesture is not the free and individual part of man in opposition to the collective domination of language and ideology (and for the actor, of the "text to be said"). He does not own it personally; it belongs and refers to a group, a class, a milieu. He always quotes a particular gestuality of these groups, even one of his own previous gestures, as "the rough sketching which indicates traces of other movements and features all around the fully-worked-out figure" (S.O. §39). Man's gesture, as Brecht tries to reflect it in the *Gestus*, is neither conventional (of the type "capitalists walk like this"), nor entirely invented (spontaneous, expressive or aestheticizing gesture). He uses materials from the code of gestural conventions for his own purposes, and to express one or another individual variant corresponding to the specific situation of man, which is never twice repeated in identical form. The *Gestus* does not lead to a puppet-like use of gesture, where the slightest indication of behavior immediately takes on the function of a signal: the spectator (and the actor) is constantly invited to select a few details from the gesture in order to have them reveal a social conduct which is not delivered in its definitive form but remains the object of critical appraisal. So the *Gestus* is in no sense the "cheap imitation" of a fixed sociological vision of human behavior. The creators of *mises en scène* where socially marked figures appear (workers, exploiters, soldiers) have sometimes forgotten this aspect of *Gestus*.

Logos and gestuality

The role of *Gestus* is also very important when it comes to understanding the relationship between logos and gestuality in epic theatre. In a dramatic form where the text is staged, the actors' gestures often only illustrate or punctuate the spoken word by creating the illusion that it is a perfectly integrated part of the enunciator, thus of his gestural universe. *Gestus*, on the contrary, approaches the text/gesture ensemble so as not to eliminate either of the two terms of the dichotomy. It reveals how gestural a discourse may be (see below on the "gestuality" of discourse) by stressing the rhythm of the diction, and the actor's effort in the production and ostension of the text. The stage and the speaking body (the actor) are made "readable" for the audience (if necessary by means of printed banners).

So instead of fusing logos and gestuality in an illusion of reality, the *Gestus* radically cleaves the performance into two blocks: the shown (the said) and the showing (the saying). Discourse no longer has the form of a homogenous block; it threatens at any moment to break away from its enunciator. Far from assuring the construction and the continuity of the action, it intervenes to stop the movement and to comment on what might have been acted on stage. *Gestus* thus displaces the dialectic between ideas and actions; the dialectic no longer operates within the system of these ideas and actions, but at the point of intersection of the enunciating gesture and the enunciated discourse: ". . . in epic theatre, the dialectic is not born of the contradiction between successive statements or ways of behaving, but of the gesture itself."[5]

Alienation

This phenomenon of the "cleaving" of the performance by *Gestus* is, in fact, the principle of the alienation effect. By making visible the class behind the individual, the critique behind the naive object, the commentary behind the affirmation, the attitude of demonstration behind the demonstrated thing, the *Gestus* lies at the core of the alienation effect where the thing is simultaneously recognized and made strange, where gesture invites us to reflect on the text and the text contradicts the gesture. This device, which Brecht did not invent but which he had reinvested with a social (and not simply aesthetic) content is as applicable to social gesture as to stage signs or the arrangement of events in the story. The same signifier (gesture, stage sign, narrative episode) takes on a "double appearance," splits itself into two signifieds: a concrete object, naively "delivered" and an abstract object of knowledge, criticized and "alienated."

Gestus, stage sign and Story reveal at the same time materiality and abstraction, historical exactitude and philosophical meaning, the particular and the general.[6] The dose of these two contradictory ingredients runs the risk of being rather "explosive," since, according to Brecht, the art of abstraction must be mastered by realists. The thankless task of gathering together these contradictory demands falls to *Gestus,* since it always allows for the passage from actor to character, from the body to the reading of it, from the reconstituted event to its fiction, from theory to theatrical and social praxis.

Subject-matter and point of view

The way in which the *Gestus* is determined by the actor and the director poses a difficult theoretical problem: the director, Brecht tells us, must gather information about the era in which the gestures originated, as much as about his own social reality. In the same manner, the spectator, if he is to be able to decipher the characters' attitude, needs to have a degree of knowledge of the ideological code of the represented and representing realities. But does this not create a vicious circle, as it is precisely *in* the play and *in* the acting that we are supposed to find information on these realities, and where the spectator should find himself confronted with a "subject-matter for observation" and not—to quote the philosopher of the *Messingkauf Dialogues*—with "I don't know how many Marxist-based theories?"

In fact, *Gestus* and Story are tools which are constantly being elaborated. They are located at the precise point of intersection of the real object to be imitated (to be shown and told) and the subject perceiving and criticizing this reality. *Gestus* concentrates within it a certain gestuality (given by the ideological code of a certain time) *and* the personal and demonstrative gestuality of the actor. In the same way, the story designates for Brecht the logic of the represented reality (the signified of the narrative), the Story (*histoire* for Benveniste) *and* the specific narration of these events from the critical point of view of the story-maker (the signifier of the narrative or *discourse* for Benveniste).

Extracting the Story or conveying the appropriate *Gestus* will never mean discovering a universally decipherable Story once and for all inscribed within the text. In seeking out the Story, the reader and the director express their own views on the reality they want to represent. This work of exposition has always to be complemented by the spectator's own work, the spectator having the last word, i.e., the right to watch/control the playwright's "view." In the same way, in the case of the *Gestus* shown by the actor, we should not be content to receive it as is (i.e., as a "compact signified" wherein the split between the thing and its critique does not appear). We have to seize the *Gestus* on the rebound, to see in it and to inscribe in it its constitutive contradiction, to understand it as a gesture which is internal to the fiction (gestuality) and as the "*Gestus* of handing over a finished article" (S.O. § 76). What could be more efficacious for the manipulations of a dialectical theatre than the *Gestus*?

Semiosis of Gestus

The most fascinating aspect of the Brechtian *Gestus* but also the one on which there has been the least theoretical work, remains to be commented on—the possibility of "translating" the *Gestus* in different materials and its "conductibility" in several different stage materials, and the problems of its semiosis and its intersemiotic translation.[7]

The most extreme formulation of the enormous resources of *Gestus* is to be found in "On Gestic Music" (1932) and "On Rhymeless Verse with Irregular Rhythms'' (1939). In these Brecht expands the notion of *Gestus* to music and to the text: ''A language is gestic when it is grounded in a *Gestus* and conveys particular attitudes adopted by the speaker towards other men. The sentence 'pluck the eye that offends thee out' is less effective from the gestic point of view than 'if thine eye offend thee, pluck it out.' The latter starts by presenting the eye, and the first clause has the definite gest of making an assumption; the main clause then comes as a surprise, a piece of advice, and a relief'' (B.T. 104). With this metaphor, Brecht describes one of the key problems of theatre semiology: the link between *iconic* system (gesture) based on the resemblance between the sign and its object, and the *symbolic* system which is based on the arbitrariness of the sign.

In this context, the Brechtian *Gestus* is not necessarily translatable into a movement or an attitude. It may be entirely constituted by words (as, for instance, in a radio broadcast). In this case, gesturality and mimic expression, which are quite precise and easy to visualize, ''impregnate'' these words (a humble bending of the knee, a hand tapping a shoulder). In the same way, gestures and mimic expression (in the silent film) or simple gestures (in shadow theatre) can contain words. Words and gestures can be replaced by other words and gestures, without the *Gestus* being modified. The *Gestus* here plays the role of the *interpreter* in Peirce's semiotics. The sign meaning (gestural or prosodic) helps us to associate it with certain equivalents, to constitute the paradigms of possible variations, to establish series and networks of correspondances between voice and gesture.

To a certain extent, every *mise en scène* is a search for an adequate *interpreter* which connects the *mise en place* (placement) of the enunciators and the text to be acted. But such a rich theoretical perspective should not remain, as in Brecht's theoretical writing, at the stage of a declaration of principle. This ''gestic music,'' this ''iconic discourse'' specific to the theatre should seek to define its own units, and to explicate the laws of its own functioning. This aspect of *Gestus* exists mostly in the case of motivated or poetic signs and of onomatopoeia, a marginal area where the sign and its referent are reunited under the patronage of *Gestus*. Unfortunately, this type of *Gestus* remains too global a notion and Brecht possibly limits it too much to syntax and to the rhetorics of the sentence; he only examines the ''(shifting, syncopated, gestic) Rhythm'' (B.T. 115), to which the idea of a knocked-about and fractured world must correspond in the meaning of the text.

In his ''On Rhymeless Verse with Irregular Rhythms'' he reports how, at the beginning of his career, despite his ''disgracefully meager'' political knowledge, he was aware of the lack of harmony in social relationships and refused to ''. . . iron out all the discordances and interferences of which (he) was strongly conscious'' (B.T. 116). He then decided ''to show human dealings as contradictory, fiercely fought over, full of violence'' (B.T. 116). This *Gestus* of syncopation characterizes the speaker's attitude towards the world, and what he has to say about it. It serves as a hermeneutic tool which helps constitute the meaning of the text. It is in the form of the text that one can read the *Gestus* and thus the attitude of the speaker towards the enunciation.

Once again, *Gestus* here fills the breach between utterance and enunciation (*énoncé/énonciation*). It recalls for us the basic truth that a theatre text only finds its full volume and its meaning in the choice of the situation of enunciation. Brecht, who carefully chose a tonality for each play according to the nature of the language used, knew this well: for instance, the German spoken in Prague for *Schweik*, the parody of classical verse for *Saint Joan*, the popular style and the poetic prose for *Puntila*, etc.

Gestus *and the body*

One cannot help regretting that Brecht was not more explicit on "gestic music" and that he did not give any formulas on how to find the *Gestus*, which is best understood intuitively, and by the methodological application of different readings of the text on the basis of different subjective attitudes. It has nothing to do with the "writing of the body" as it has sometimes been referred to in the context of Artaud, Céline, or Bataille. *Gestus* never deals exclusively with the problem of the materiality of the textual signifier; it exists at the level of prosodic and textual signifieds. It is a tool which remains exterior to the text, just as a seismograph is capable of recording the shakings of the earth without being a part of that shaking. The *Gestus* at best is only—but this is not negligible—a meaning "detector," a way of "accompanying the reading with certain appropriate body movements, signifying politeness, anger, the desire to persuade, goading, the effort to fix in one's memory, the effort to surprise an adversary; the fear that one feels or fear that one wants to inspire . . .'' (cf. Brecht's comments on the Chinese poet Kin-Yem).

Is it legitimate, though, to understand *Gestus* as a "simple mimed expression" excluding everything that the signifying work of the body can produce outside of the representation/performance?[8]

It seems quite contrary to the spirit of *Gestus* to conceive of it as the mimetic production of eternally fixed social gestuality. There still remains in it the material "traces of other movements and features all around the fully-worked-out figure" (B.T. 191), and if it is obviously never like the ideograms of Grotowskian gestures, "a living form possessing its own logic," neither is it the reified image of a social relationship.

These brief remarks on *Gestus* are far from exhausting the substance of the notion, and only sketch out a few possible developments. At least, it should be clear how central the concept of *Gestus* is to all of the different theoretical Brechtian paths. And is it not in the nature of the *Gestus*, after all, that it can only be grasped by the actor and the critic in *approximate* form?

Translated by Susan Melrose

Footnotes

[1]My quotations of Brecht come from the English translation of John Willet: *Brecht on Theatre*, New York, Hill and Wang, 1964 (B.T.) For the German texts, not included in Willet's anthology, I have used "Gesammelte Werke in 20 Bänden (G.W.), Suhrkamp Verlag, Frankfurt am Main, 1967. I chose to keep *Gestus* in English, although Willet used *gest*. I had to introduce the terms of *gestuality* (*gestualité*) and *gestural* (*gestuel*).

[2]*Theaterarbeit*, Henschelverlag Kunst und Gesellschaft, Berlin, 1961.

[3]Wladimir Propp, *Morphology of the Folktale*, Indiana Research Centre in Anthropology, Bloomington, 1958.

[4]Walter Benjamin, *Understanding Brecht*, London, NLB, 1973, p. 11.

[5]Benjamin, *op. cit.*, p. 12.

[6]Cf. Bernard Dort, "Le général et le particulier," in *L'Arc*, no. 55, pp. 3-8 et le *Modellbuch:* "Unearth the truth from the debris of the evidence, tie together in a visible manner the individual and the general, retain the particular in the overall process, this is the art of the realist" (*Theaterarbeit, op. cit.*, p. 264).

[7]On the problems of the semiosis of sign systems, cf. Roman Jakobson, "Le langage commun des linguistes et des anthropologues," in *Essais de linguistique générale*, 1963, Editions de Minuit (in particular, pp. 40-42). In English, in *Style in Language*, ed. T. Sebeok, MIT Press, Cambridge, 1960, pp. 350-377.

[8]Guy Scarpetta, "Brecht et la Chine" in *La Nouvelle Critique*, no. 39 bis, 1971.

[9]Jerzy Grotowski, *Towards a Poor Theatre*, Simon and Schuster, New York, 1968.

The Discourse of (the) Mime[1]

This article first appeared in Italian in a book edited by Marco de Marinis, *Mimo e Mimi,* La Casa Usher, Firenze, 1980.

The Inaction of the Earth

What does the mime's body say? It says nothing other than what it does. For the mime, for Amiel, in *One Day, the Earth*,[2] in the beginning was inaction. The body is folded up around itself; its segments are coiled around invisible axes. Arm, hand and finger only obey the force of attraction of the curved line; the head is masked by the body, integrated into a womb-like form from which everything is ready to spring forth. This ball of flesh, from which life and movement will surge, is about to mime the birth of the world. Gradually the body tears itself from its inertia; it opens up and traces a figure of vague contours, passing again and again through the same phases. But how are we to seize the evolutions of this "theatre of the body," an art par excellence of the fleeting movement that no scribe, however quick, can capture? To speak of mime—or, worse still, to write on mime—is to dwell awkwardly on a few moments of gesture. All that remains of what Amiel does, are a few shots that allow us, after the event, to spin out what he says.

Fortunately, mime lends itself to being captured by the photographic lens, for it is made up more of attitudes and poses than of movements; like the eye of the camera, the human eye chooses privileged moments when the body, even in the midst of agitation and transformation, discovers flashes of eternity. People in the theatre call it the *presence* of the body; they point to this paradox of the art of gesture, namely that: "in the discourse of mime, the poetic attitude-image has first priority, overshadowing the movement-translation."[3] But this silence of the body is deceptive. It precedes and prepares for the imperceptible unfolding of the hand, the arm, the torso:

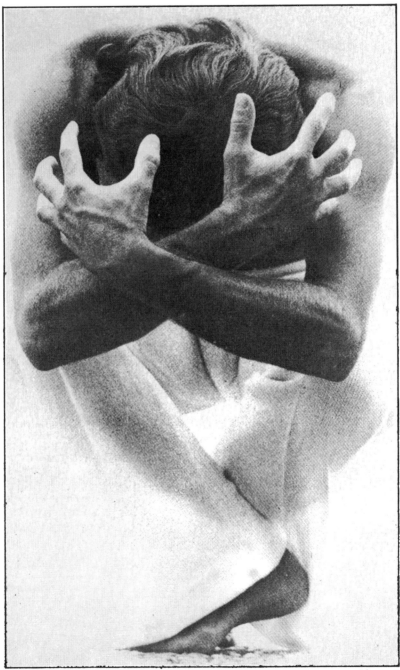

Photo 1

the hands seem to seize hold of a sphere, they know no rest, they concentrate and encompass the world of the story to be created. All that can be read for the moment is the crossing of the forearms and feet, the curve of the back that precludes the temptation to identify the body with something. The mime often begins his evolution with the image of an unusual position, of an artifically produced form, controlled by a rigid body whose center seems masked and displaced.

But before the evolution can actually begin, the key to the reading of the whole sequence must be provided. This key indicates the modality of the body in action, the distance separating normal gesture (ours, the one we normally experience) from the gestural mode in which what follows must be "read." A gap almost makes itself felt, strangely preparing a new vision of gesture. At the beginning of his mimodrama, Amiel embodies an astronaut moving through weightlessness according to laws that have nothing to do with those of our everyday world and to which we have become accustomed through the NASA films. Walking by slow hops on the moon—or on any other planet discovered by our astronaut—the mime elaborates a new system of gesture which. once mapped out, must retain its coherence. Any system or gestural modality is possible, provided it is sustained. The spectator's pleasure comes from his understanding, accepting and finally becoming accustomed to this new convention. The difficulty for Amiel is to play this ease of movement, to produce through a slight bending of the knees the illusion that he will fly away if he steps a little too heavily on the ground. The slightest muscular error and the modal key to the gesture would be accidentally destroyed and, with it, the sense of sequence and the logic of the gestural narrative.

Even more than for verbal discourse, modality indicates the actor's attitude toward his text: persuasion, doubt, irony, play. This is not merely a psychological pointer to the action, but a piece of information on the very nature of the gesture: in the case of mime, gestural enunciation is immediately poured back into its text, it becomes one with it and constitutes it in a narrative of a mode other than the one of "everyday" gestures.

Hence we can feel the paradox of gesture in the theatre of the body. In "real life" our gestures are often superimposed on our verbal discourse to complement it, contradict it, or add nuances to it. In the case of silent mime, it is very difficult to produce gestures that comment on a gestural sequence: any metagestural commentary is in fact reduced to the same level as the other gestures. It is difficult to separate the one from the other, for we grant the same importance to all gestures without seeking to distinguish a substratum of gestures that will be submitted to a metagestural commentary.

The coherence of a mime sequence, which occurs when the same modality is maintained, also seriously limits the possibilities of mime. Thus the spectator is troubled by the intervention of the spoken word in gesture, for the universe of gesture is then contaminated by meaning of a different sort. No exchange, other than a distancing one, can be established between the body and the shock of the sound it utters. Similarly, a mute gestural dialogue between two mimes is very difficult for they would have to find the gestural equivalent in terms of the gestures of the other person. At this point, the mime dialogue quickly results in a cross-coding of two discourses, as when two mutes "discuss" something by means of a common code of equivalences between words and gestures.

That is why the gestural dialogues in the sketches where two characters are playing together are always a little disappointing: thus, in the orchestra-conductor sketch Amiel plays a conductor constantly interrupted by a facetious violinist. If there is a dialogue, it only takes place at the level of psychological reactions and anecdote; we have no problem imagining the words that could be exchanged between the two men. Immediately, the "musician clown gag" ruins the work of the body; it is at once too recognizably anecdotal and banal. When the body tries to say too much, and with too much wit, the body is "talkative," overstated by an overly precise story and discourse.

The mime should therefore be left alone, and his only dialogue should be the one established between what he does and what he does not do, between normative gestures and their poetic deviation: the comparison between two universes of differing coherence and modality, between our immobility and the limits of our body, and his movements and original mode of existence creates the dialogue in the spectator.

But this dialogue is only initiated—with Amiel as with all mimes—when the body begins to unfold, tears itself from inert matter and sketches in a narrative.

The Unfolding of the Human Narrative

The narrative takes place in time and in the unfolding of the whole body. The body is in a vertical position, available for movement, ready to evolve and to adjust to all the shifts of weight. The face looking towards the camera seems the only fixed relationship. The arms are undecided between support and rejection. The angle of perspective deforms the body's symmetry and elongates the mime's stature. As soon as it is freed from weight and inert matter, the body is open to all metamorphoses. Amiel takes as a theme for his variations on creation the genesis of various species of animals: the frog, the spider, the eagle, the gorilla . . . and man. (The last two are difficult to distinguish.) Each gestural narrative takes shape before our eyes, starting from that flash which indicates to us what animal and what action is being presented to us. Some reality effect, no matter how tenuous, is therefore essential to the identification of the sequence being mimed. Even the most abstract mimodrama does not escape this mimetic recognition; indeed, it relies on it to construct the phases of its story.

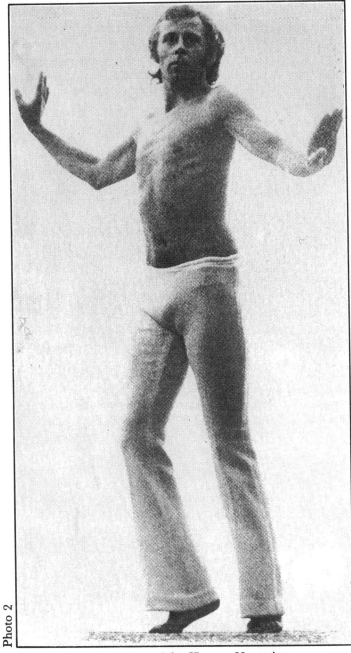

Photo 2

The Unfolding of the Human Narrative

But it is not by mere imitation of an object that mime recreates the reality it seeks to symbolize. Gestural narrativity proceeds musically: the mime produces first an easily identifiable sequence, a basic theme that will then be varied and clarified until the gestural action of this basic theme appears sufficiently autonomous and clear. The body secretes an impression of recognition and strangeness, then sculpts it and pushes it to the work boundaries of cliché. The important thing is that the minimal sequence be clearly understood and that the spectator be able to graft onto it all the different improvisations: it will be quickly understood that the astronaut is absentmindedly manipulating various levers and that the frog is croaking and puffing itself up through the periodic movement of arms and curved back.

The minimal narrative includes only a few characteristic phases of the evolution of the mime: for example, it may be created by the association of certain movements which, taken in the same sequential order, refer unmistakably to the same story.

In fact, the gesture does not have to be recognizable as a theme or have a precise meaning: gestural narrativity is organized syntactically rather than semantically—for example, by systems of thematic or meaningful oppositions (movement/attitude; speed/slowness; jerky movements/smooth movements; life/death; animate/inanimate, etc.). Mimes have often, in their theoretical writings, tried to pinpoint this quality of gesture that distinguishes their gestures from mere "mechanical and geometrical movement in space."[4] For Marcel Marceau, "the mime-actor vibrates like the strings of a harp. He is *lyrical*: his gesture seems crowned with a poetic halo."[5] Beyond these metaphors, we must know how to interpret these intuitions as the metalanguage proper to the gesture of mime: not, as Marceau states, a happy marriage of form (gestural architecture) and content (the social meaning of gesture), but knowledge by the mime of a codification proper to the "normal" gesture, and the art of transposing gesture by extracting from it certain pertinent signs, knowing how to combine them in a contrived sequence that, nevertheless, appears natural.

The gesture of such a sequence can be spaced out and broken down into a precise program. It is always clearly "framed" by a mark indicating the beginning and end of one action so that it appears quoted like a word in quotation marks emerging clearly from the surrounding text. This "framing" of gestural moments clearly structures the spatio-temporal continuum and isolates several phases from everyday gesture and real movement. That is why we often have the impression, when we see the mime, of watching several clearly separated "gestural jerks." Within each phase, the gestural space is modeled, compressed, stretched out, broken down, according to the mime's attitude to his narrative.

The attitudes which many mimes consider to be the result and quintessence of the mimodrama crystallize the whole sequence and form the armature of the story: "what the mime must do is to juxtapose the numerous attitudes that he has constructed."[6]

These privileged moments of mime—the moments of a certain attitude—suggest by contrast all that is left unsaid or rather "undone" by the body, conspicuous by its absence but actively participating in the construction of meaning. We know that the dramatic text (also the poetic text and that of everyday conversations) deliberately says only a tiny part of what we understand through extratextual elaboration, the play of presuppositions and cultural references. In the same way, the "gestural text" very often gives evidence of a very great economy of means: to signify the vanity of the pig sunbathing on the beach, for example, it is enough to have him delicately rub his skin with cream. What is left "undone" in gesture is everything the mime boasts of being able to do without establishing his character or sketching in an action; this makes him all the better perceived. It is this "undone," just as much as the perceivable gesture, which produce the illusion of a new being and a new world, of an endless metamorphosis of mime.

The Metamorphosis of the Eagle

The eagle flies to a background of music—the flute of the Andes—that we immediately associate with the mountains, an empty and blue sky, and a lost civilization of South America. The metamorphosis is immediate: the mask and the movements of the arms recall the image of the eagle, and the miracle occurs—without leaving the ground, with a mere waving of the arms and a slight modification of the level of the shoulders, this eagle flies through the heavens, circles several times, glides and hovers, flapping its wings. The movements of shoulders and head (masked by a vaguely Aztec sculpture) communicate this waving to the elbows, wrists and fingertips: the concave curve of the thumbs seems the final proof of the suppleness of the wings and feathers.

Why is the mask so important in the theatrical event? The mask fixes an essential part of the body, forbidding it to speculate on physical and psychological modifications. In contrast, however, other parts of the body are freed; at the same time, we are free to shift our eye from the carved face that looks fixedly back at us to the body and our newly aware sense of its slightest vibration. Mask and living matter unceasingly do battle until the spectator can no longer distinguish inanimate from human. The mime does not win the battle until the inexpressive assumes a thousand faces, and the object worn on the face is transformed into a substance as malleable and transparent as flesh. The eagle mimed by Amiel is in constant movement; we no longer see the mime's body and his mask; very quickly the two realities fuse into a single creation—the movement and "incarnate" specificity of the mythical bird. The "pig in leotard" (photo 4) similarly succeeds, despite the stylization and deformation of the facial expression, in becoming the only possible extension of the mime's real body. We thus cor-

The Metamorphosis of the Eagle　　　　　Photo 3

rect the orientation of the snout pointing upward explaining it as the vanity of the "playboy" pig who is "putting on airs."

However, the mask fascinates the spectator accustomed to looking for the phatic communication of a physiognomy; soon he gets used to this grafting of a foreign body on living matter. The use of the mask fragments the body, thus deceiving our expectations for psychological explanations; it establishes new units and constructs a whole discourse on the basis of these new units. This is particularly noticeable when the mask has nothing realistic about it or when it is put on back to front (on the neck, back, buttocks, etc.). Thus, Roy Bosier and Julie Goell of the group *I GESTI*,[7] by sticking two semi-spherical objects and a beak on their nether regions and turning their backs to the audience, manage, with the movement of the arm "wings" and the twitches of their posteriors, to create before our eyes birds that stare at us. The mime telling a story always knows how to segment his body into units that are not normally structured that way and are not usually associated to produce a gestural meaning. The mime divides his body into zones of influence which converse and exclude, attract or repel.

The apparent dialogue of Amiel's eagle occurs between head and arm, but is reinforced by the opposition between the lower limbs, "responsible" for the technical problem of vertical and longitudinal movement, and the bird's head (arm and mask), whose duty it is to create the referential illusion.

Other segmentations of gesture are possible, and all the treatises on gesture multiply the "general" positions and meanings usually ascribed to them. The codification sometimes goes to extreme lengths, but still remains more a description of the body according to a linguistic grid or a system of social references, and does not for all that help very much in understanding a gestural project. Gesture always escapes scientific programming and precise description, and the mime demonstrates the impossibility of an *a priori* segmentation of the body (be it linguistic or spatial), since he takes pleasure in "unwinding" and "winding" his body machine.

The metamorphosis is greatly aided by elements external to gesture: light and music. Lighting, which can be used so subtly today, "carves" the body out of darkness, fashions it in its own way, makes it disappear and appear. The relationship between mime and living sculpture is well known, but here it is given prominence. Different colored lighting can also indicate how to read a scene: real/unreal, on the land/underwater, everyday life/dream, etc. It not only shows the body, but it also indicates immediately at what level of existence it is signifying.

This metamorphosis which is the very basis of body theatre has nothing of a mystic transmutation. It is built up patiently through pertinent signs and quotations. In the case of Amiel, it is the man with the red bath towel and the yellow pig's head who gently reminds us of this.

The Quotations of the Little Pig in Leotards

This little pig is even more lovable for putting on very human airs. He is obviously obsessed with his skin. He performs very delicate little movements with his hands to remove body hair, stretch negligently, pose his elbow on his knee to express idleness and the desire for seduction. But, while indicating to us the importance of quotation in the discourse of mime, he does us a particular epistemological service (not to mention his prowess in anagrams: strangely enough, the anagram of *porcs* [pigs] is *corps* [body]). For it is only by reference to everyday gesture that we find the delicacy of the little pig's gestures comic: he is quoting a cultural code, and in the theatre the recognition of the ideological effect makes us understand and smile. The quoted gesture is always clearly detachable from the continuum; it only needs a few signs to be recognized (the astronaut's gum chewing; the coquette's nose in the air; the cowboy taken from a Sergio Leone spaghetti western; the pose of Rodin's thinker in the blind man sketch; etc.). Quotation also very frequently functions as self-quotation: gesture enlarges and clarifies the basic sequence that provided the key to the object being imitated. The "musical" nature of the story and the gestural narrative explains this taste for thematic repetition, quotation and variation.

That is the charm of mime, but also its worst enemy: there is nothing more tedious than a mime repeating himself over and over again, bringing to our notice an action that we have long ago identified and which is purely and simply replayed in the same version. Thus any gesture is quotation of a gesture, i.e., an "inter-gesture" (a fact partly discerned by the Brechtian theory of the *Gestus*). We would, therefore, be tempted to contradict Etienne Decroux when he states that "mime is a succession of present actions" and that "the word alone can evoke absent things."[8]

Moreover, this is also a quotation, by contrast or absence, of a gestural norm systematically violated by the mime: that of our own body and our own way of moving. The mime challenges this norm and only seems to obey his own laws and conventions: he frequently makes us forget the law

Photo 4

The Quotations of the Little Pig in Leotards

of gravity, leans forward dangerously without falling, simulates movements while walking on the spot. The spectator's pleasure is to contemplate himself in this body which always seems to have its own way, free from physical laws, malleable, and capable of shaping and being shaped at will. This explains why we so frequently see a mimodrama whose hero is struggling with an insurmountable physical obstacle (a ball to be picked up, a man to be pushed away, support to be achieved in order to get one out of a sticky situation).

As for poetic language, it is the deviation from a norm, a theoretically neutral set of gestures that enhances the originality of the gestural image, and indicates the artistic procedure being used. Sometimes, without its being essential, the mime (Decroux, Jerry de Giacomi in his "exercises in the style of Decroux") is seeking an ideal plasticity, a body with the proportions and poses of a classical statue. Of course, this ideally harmonious model does not exist, but haunts the sculptor and remains an inaccessible archetype.

The pleasure of quoting with one's body the discourse of others, and, for the spectator, of deciphering these allusive charades, is the whole charm of the theatre of gesture. Gestural discourse is so full of quotations that in the end it becomes an original and autonomous text, making us forget that it is made up of a host of lucky finds, so perfect is the illusion of a body coinciding with the object being imitated. Even, and perhaps especially so, when this imitation has nothing direct and realistic about it, as in the sketch of the hands forming bird shapes.

The Hands of the Magician

Two hands emerging from an invisible body come into play above a screen, pursuing, attacking, stroking and making up to each other. The index finger emerges from the mass of the hand, "stretches its neck," and vibrates, like the head of a bird: nervously, jerkily exploring the world from every viewpoint. It is not far short of creating a strange La Fontaine fable, in which "two pigeons loved each other tenderly" and all human situations and feelings unfold in their strategies.

The mime has a choice between two tactics that correspond to the artistic principles of realism and abstraction: either he embodies a character, and more or less imitates a personality; or, he uses his body in a non-figurative way to sculpt a substance and to reconstruct a reality which is not a slavish copy of the object symbolized.

In the first case, the mime is nothing but a riddle addressed to the spectator, who is invited to do his best to identify the scene. This type of gestures is often simply a superficial and obvious way of deviating from a gestural norm (ours) to return to it very quickly and sustain us in our normal perception. On the other hand, for the body used abstractly, if indeed recognition of a form or social object occurs, this is not achieved through a pure translation from the imitating body to the body being imitated, but through an understanding of artistic conventions and their functioning. Thus, the hands that come out from behind a vertical and horizontal black curtain displace their traditional signified to become the actors in a curious quarrel between two doves. The general form recalls very remotely that of a bird. If we quickly identify the hands as such, it is because the mime has isolated certain traits of his animal's behavior: the knack of nervously moving the head like a periscope, the jerky gait, the persistent aggressiveness of the forager.

Gestural realism, therefore, is not a matter of photographic imitation of

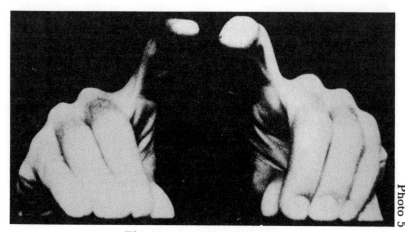

Photo 5

The Hands of the Magician

the object, but of encoding certain relevant traits of behavior and the narrative phases of a story whose steps are always much the same: attack/reconciliation; rivalry/friendship; conflict/pursuit; duel/compromise, etc. The mime expresses with his body how every story is articulated, what oppositions it necessitates and how contradictions punctuate it and form it, and what segmentation he follows to organize the *mise en scène* of his body. It is as if the mime could not escape the meaningful thrall of the story: the spectator is not content to watch action as a static tableau—he wants to see in it a story or drama or, at least, a semantic universe in constant evolution. This accounts for the interest of these innocent gestural sketches for semioticians who, like Greimas, inquire into man's semiotic practices, that is, "somatic or gestural behavior organized into syntagmatic chains, of an algorithmic type, whose directed meaning appears as a global finality, readable after the event, and whose analysis suggests a possible homologation with narrative structures."[9]

According to this conception of gesture as a semiotic practice, any sequence may be analyzed as a narrative, without its being supposed that the gesticulator is telling a story, or that the mime is a pantomime. So the alternative in gestural theatre does not seem to be pure aesthetic gesture, without a social signified, *versus* social gesture, utilitarian and "narrative," without any attempt at aesthetic effect. This dichotomy, too often adhered to in the works of mimes and taken up in theoretical writings, only ends in an impasse, by radically separating pure "danced" gesture from "imitated" "realistic" gesture. One then ends up with two ways which, if taken absolutely and exclusively, offer little interest for the development of the theatre of gesture.

The work of Amiel, at least in the first part of his show devoted to "One day, the earth," tries precisely to escape from this deadly alternative: he discovers gestures which, for the first creatures on earth, are both movements sculpted from a new body, and gestures which are already familiar to us in their details and rhythms. This is the price the spectator has to pay in order to move constantly from an "external" identification, to an internal discovery and to feel that the performance is strangely familiar to him even if he has never "walked on the moon," flown like an eagle or throbbed like a frog.

Translated by Susan Melrose and Barbara Behar

Footnotes

[1]This essay on the subject of Amiel's performance is the critical "pendant" of a theoretical study devoted to the "Problems of a Semiology of Theatrical Gesture," published in "Poetics To-day"(Tel Aviv). It could equally well be completed by the articles on *body, gesture, gestuality, gestus* in my *Dictionnaire du théâtre*, Editions Sociales, Paris, 1980.

[2]A performance seen of the festival "Mime and Mask," *Porte de la Suisse* on January 27, 1979. The only iconographic details I was able to procure are those in the press kit. The photos were taken by Marcel Imsand.

[3]Jean Dorcy, *J'aime la mime*, Paris, Editions Denoel (undated), p. 60.

[4]Marcel Marceau, "Le halo poétique," in Jean Dorcy, *A la recherche de la mime*, Neuilly-sur-Seine, Les Cahiers de danse et culture, 1958, p. 140.

[5]Ibid., p. 138.

[6]Etienne Decroux, *Paroles sur le mime*, Paris, Gallimard, 1963, p. 125.

[7]The performance of "Victoire a la Pyrrhus" also presented at the time of the festival "Mime and Mask."

[8]E. Decroux, op. cit., p. 135.

[9]Algirdas Greimas, "La sémiotique," in *La linguistique*, Encyclopoche Larousse, Paris, Larousse, 1977, p. 226.

III. RECEPTION OF TEXT AND PERFORMANCE

The Aesthetics of Theatrical Reception: Variations on a Few Relationships

If critical thought describes a trajection, so too does a literary work manifest itself as a trajection, i.e., a system of variable relationships established, through the mediation of language, between an individual consciousness and the world. [1]

Jean Starobinski

To hope to grasp "in flight" all the meaningful relationships which can be woven between spectator, theatre object and the world represented on stage would be both a foolish and fruitless desire. The sole ambition in this essay will be to look at the aesthetics of reception and its application to the theatre.

The first step in this analysis will be to distinguish clearly between the theatrical uses of the term "reception." There is, of course, the spectator's reception of the performance and the text performed; this is s situation of concrete communication, and a branch of aesthetics might consist of a description of the psychic processes and the aesthetic and sociological conditions of this transmission. Of course, knowledge of the work thus transmitted and its possible meanings is indispensable to an understanding of this kind of individual reception[2]. In addition to the investigation of individual reception, there also exists the study of a single work as it has been received at different times in history, thus taking into account different expectations and ideological models. The theory of reception in Germany deals with this type of reception: *Rezeptionsgeschichte*, the history of reception—or *Wirkungsästhetik*, the aesthetics of the "produced effect."

The theatrical work has always been subjected to a very detailed analysis of its working parts, an analysis which has described even the most insignificant mechanisms of composition and function. But the question of its reception by the spectator seems to have been totally neglected, except for the famous instance of catharsis or its Brechtian counterpoint, alienation. Such is the paradox of theatre criticism: more than any other art, theatre demands, through the connecting link of the actor, an active mediation on the part of the spectator confronted by the performance; this happens only during the *event* of aesthetic experience. Nonetheless, the modalities of reception and the work of interpreting the performance are very poorly understood. No doubt this fact reveals some suspicion about the theory of reception, which has been accused of idealism because it is too centered on the perceiving subject and too far removed from a structural description of performance. At any rate, current work in the aesthetics of reception (even if it is concerned primarily with the novel and poetry) indicates a willingness to go beyond a narrowly defined structuralism. This new attitude has arisen from the fact that, when the description of literary narrative structures attains a certain refinement (to the point of sometimes being incomprehensible because of its finesse and its fragmentation), it lacks an opening onto the outside world. The hermeneutic dimension, in particular, remains in the shadows. What can be said about it or done with it? What signifying practice can the spectator hope to carry out on the performance? These are some of the questions that the aesthetics of reception will have to answer if the *theatrical relationship* is to be understood.

It is around this intentionally vague term that these reflections will revolve: *reception, reading (lecture), hermeneutics, perspective, critical metalanguage*. They constitute the still rudimentary tools available to explore the nature of this relationship. I shall be deliberately playing with the ambiguity of the *theatrical relationship*, which is, concretely, the position of the spectator facing the stage and, arbitrarily, his effort to constitute meaning by his act of reception. Marivaux's *Jeu de l'amour et du hasard* has been chosen because of its apparent "innocence" (its meaningful clarity) so that I can better demonstrate what a "complicit" reading reveals about our relationship to the text, and in what way the work of reception modifies the "naive" and "initial" interpretation of the play. This interpretation is based on a dramatic text whose potential meanings seem, *a priori*, more numerous than those that could be present in a specific *mise en scène*, even if every *mise-en-scene*, however obvious and simplified it may be, always allows for a wide range of interpretations as well. But, then too, we must consider the mode of production/reception specific to the theatre: the director—and his whole team—enacts an initial interpretation (concretization is the term Ingarden uses) through the *mise en scène* he proposes. This interpretation itself becomes the subject of a second interpretation (concretization) on the part of the spectator, one which has to be taken into account as soon as we try to establish definite limits for the possible variations in the reception of a work at different moments in history and by different audiences.

I. RECEPTION

Despite Brecht's desire for a "spectator's art" and for an attitude at once "artistic, productive, and full of pleasure,"[3] it cannot be said that any unanimity exists about a theory of reception applied to the theatre spectator. As a matter of fact, we are still at the stage of proclamations about the audience's activity and participation, and have in no way arrived at the point of reflection on the cognitive and ideological processes of the spectator. Information theory and the semiology of communication often treat the performance as a message composed of signs intentionally emitted from the stage for a receiver placed in the situation of a cryptologist. These conceptions are too restrictive and even radically false: first of all (and without reintroducing the myth of the "creative genius who does not know what he is doing") the stage is not a source of information encoded like a telegraphic message or a simple utilitarian verbal communication; furthermore, the stage remains a dead letter without the hermeneutic commitment of the reader/spectator. That is why the study of reception cannot be developed on the basis of psychological or socio-economic considerations established via a survey of the theatre public. Knowing what stage or text stimuli the spectator reacts to, and because of what socio-economic criteria he does so, is not without interest, but these data, however quantified and precise they may be, do not cast any light on the spectator's labor to produce meaning; the nature of the aesthetic and ideological relationships which retain his attention, etc.

In fact, we see the reception of a theatrical work as something too frontal and too bound to a unique internal structure of the work and to the theatrical team's production of signs. This object-bound and concrete conception of the theatrical relationship is dangerous. Just because the spectator is always and by his very nature face to face with the performance, we do not have to envisage his relationship as exterior and fixed, and conceive of him as a target of ready-made signals emitted by the stage. On the contrary, we must try to come to grips with this relationship of exchange between stage and audience, one which we all talk about without defining either the interaction or the performance which is "to grow out of it in the eternally incompleted consciousness of the spectator."[4] What is important is no longer the physical location of the spectator facing the performance (in front of, in, separated from, etc.), but rather the work carried out on the object of knowledge (not the thing) which constitutes the performance.

Also to be considered is what T.R. Warning calls the "split in the situation'':

> An internal situation of enunciation is established in opposition to
> an external situation of reception. So the fictional discourse is
> defined pragmatically by the simultaneity of two situations which
> both have at their disposal their own systems of deixis. In order to
> be present in two situations simultaneously, the subject finds
> himself confronted by those contradictory instructions for action
> that communication theory calls the pragmatic paradox of the
> *double-bind* (cf. P. Watzlawick, J.H. Beavin, D. Jackson, *Pragmatics
> of Human Communication,* New York, 1967). It is in the theatre that
> we are able to be present at the typical exemplification and at the
> same time the playful resolution of this *double-bind*, and in fact it is
> the theatrical model which can be considered as the paradigm of
> the situational constitution of the fictional discourse in general. On
> one hand, we have an internal situation of enunciation with
> speaker(s) and receiver(s); on the other hand, an external situation
> of reception which is peculiar inasmuch as, contrary to the usual
> situation of enunciation, the receiver finds himself deprived of a
> relationship with the real speaker. This real speaker, the author,
> has disappeared within the fiction itself, he has been dispersed
> amongst the roles of the fictional characters including, in the nar-
> rative genres, the role of narrator.[5]

It is obvious here how difficult it is to situate the spectator vis-a-vis the
fictional theatrical universe which confronts him. This is all the more so
since the ''group of subjects'' which constitutes an audience is very difficult
to identify. In studies made of an audience or a reading public, they are
either reduced to an undifferentiated, amorphous mass or to a theoretical
abstraction (the average reader or the all-knowing philologist). The
''sociologizing'' survey which establishes the social composition of the
public remains mute on the process of reception and individual acquistion
of the text. Such reception can only be understood if we take into account
two historicities (as Brecht does, for example): that of the work within its
literary and social context, and that of the receiver in his own time and
within a system of ideological and aesthetic expectations[6].

In this light, talking about *communication* between stage and audience is a
pure abuse of language. The quest for certainty about whether the audience
can ''respond'' to the stage message (and in what terms) is futile and contaminated by the information and communication theories upon which it is
constructed. How can there be an exchange between the spectator and the
actor when they operate on different planes: (1) the *fiction* conveyed by
diverse semiological systems which are closed on themselves and (2) the
event, i.e., the disillusioning interruption between the actor and the spec-

tator whose bodies are like *material supports* for the fiction (and not the fiction itself). If there is an exchange between actor and spectator, it can only occur in extreme cases (such as that of The Living Theatre, for example) where the actor does not play a role but *is* himself and where the spectator communicates with him on the level of an exchange of views about the actor's craft.

If the semiology of communication, which is solely preoccupied with a formalization of "signals to be transmitted" in the work, is not able to account for the exchange between stage and audience, that is because it does not conceive of it as a dialectical process between the spectator and a stage object already interpreted by him. This semiological approach breaks the hermeneutic circle. A direct exchange cannot take place (whether a comic or tragic reaction by the public) unless the entire audience feels provoked by a vision (values and aesthetico-ideological procedures) which fails to correspond to its habitual perception and disturbs its habits of perception. Viewing a comic scene, the spectator will not understand and will not laugh unless he can confront the stage *en bloc* with his own norms and feelings of superiority regarding the ridiculous character on stage. At the same time, this reference to one's own position in a context identical with that of the comic character institutes a kind of exchange with the stage: one puts oneself in the place of the character.

It seems clear that the "exchange" everyone talks about will only be comprehensible if we place ourselves resolutely within the frame of reference of the outward and visible reception of the performance by the spectator, and if it can be demonstrated (as did the Russian Formalists in the case of the "strangeness effect" and of literary procedures)[7] that it *is* the spectator/reader who, guided by artistic procedures of the "strangeness effect," decides on the meaning of what he sees on the stage, when this stage gives the appearance of being strange or unusual. It is in these instances of perception of the "strange" that reception can best be observed. Thus P. Voltz, in his study of the unusual in the theatre, was preoccupied with the spectator's activity and his creation of a perceptual rapport with the performance. Attempting a typology of the "strange" ("*l'insolite*") in the theatre, he concludes with a distinction between "a study, *internal to the text*, of the modes of representation of the disconcerting, and a study of the spectator's perception, where the reaction to the peculiar takes on the character of an event in his own immediate experience."[8] Strangeness is finally but one example among many others of the fundamental role of *viewpoint/viewing* (*le regard*) and the relationship to the text and the performance; but it makes one conscious of the pragmatic character of the theatre and of its quality of being an actual event.

The activity of reception needs to be categorized, as H.R. Jauss does on the basis of "classical" phenomena of reception (identification with the hero, pleasure in the comic, catharsis)[9]. These ideas develop out of his work on the "horizon of expectation": a useful notion in our thinking about the close relationship, the exchange even, between the literary work and its consumer. The notion of "horizon of expectation" defines the necessary framework within which our understanding of the work intervenes; it also integrates that comprehension into a literary and sociological traditon:

> Even at that instant when it first appears, a literary work does not surface as a complete novelty flowering forth in an informational desert; its public is predisposed to a certain mode of reception by an interplay of messages, signals—manifest or latent—of implicit references and of characteristics which are already familiar. It evokes what has already been read, gets the reader into one or another emotional disposition and, from the outset, creates a certain expectation of what "will follow" and of "the ending," an expectation which can, as one's reading advances, be maintained, modulated, reorientated, or broken by irony. On the first horizon of the aesthetic experience the psychic process of the reception of the text cannot be reduced to the contingent succession of simple subjective impressions. It is a guided perception, unfolding in a way that conforms to a well-determined indicative schema. It is a process which corresponds to intentions and which is guided by signals that can be discovered and even described in terms of textual linguistics. . . . The relationship of a particular text to the series of antecedent texts constituting the genre depends on a continuing process of establishing and modifying the horizon. The new text evokes for the reader (or listener) the expectation horizon and the rules of the game with which preceding texts have made him familiar; this horizon in the course of reading is then varied, corrected, modified or simply reproduced. Variation and correction determine the field open to the structure of a genre; modification and reproduction determine its boundaries. Questions of subjectivity or interpretation of the tastes of different readers or of readers from different social levels can only be formulated in a pertinent manner if one has first been able to identify the transsubjective horizon of comprehension which conditions the text's effect.[10]

The discovery—even if it is approximate—of the expectation horizon places the work in a relationship with literary and ideological norms. It is the gap between expectation and the new work which explains the work's originality: "The distance between the expectation horizon and the work, between what has up till now been familiar to the aesthetic experience and the change in horizon that reception of the new work demands, determines the artistic character of a work of art according to an aesthetics of reception. . . . The smaller the distance and the less the receptive intelligence is obliged to focus on the horizon of a still unknown experience, the closer that work gets to the level of culinary or entertainment art."[11]

This view of the expectation horizon, from which a work develops and extends beyond previously existing works, is of course only of value on the global level of literary structures; room must be left for examining expectations within the individual work, expectations which the construction and the particular operation ideolects announce and more or less explicitly enunciate. It may also be necessary to clarify to a certain extent the *expectation* generated by the work. General expectation would, for instance, situate Marivaux's theatre in a historical perspective, and would examine how it breaks with the comedy-of-manners tradition of the seventeenth century and announces a problematic of bourgeois drama in which the psychological conflict tends to be absorbed by the perspective of a bourgeois value system, and aristocratic individualism gives way to an economic and social hierarchy of values. The system of expectations in the particular work forms a fixed code, clearly marked and "verbalized" in the text in question. In Marivaux's *Le Jeu,* for example, the expectation consists of the problem of reconciling individual desires and social mores. Once the different camps and alternatives have been defined, the whole play can be seen as variations on how to violate the social norm and, finally, as the solution to that contradiction. In the context of this internal expectation horizon, one should try to specify several mechanisms which open the text to its interpretations: the response to a question posed by the work, the pursuit of a desire, the opening and closing of the discourse, framing mechanisms.

It should be evident now that the aesthetics of reception is concerned with the fact (or rather hypothesis) that every work is the answer to a question it implicitly asks, a response to an interrogation on its place in literary tradition and in the reality of its era. This question/answer is obviously more or less explicit: an era can be imagined in which the question posed is entirely absorbed and eliminated by the clarity of the answer; another (in postmodern texts, for instance) in which the question is the only message and the text is constituted by dint of reflection on its possibility.

But on what level should the question be asked, and how can it be both literary and ideological; how can it be sufficiently general (and thus pertinent from the theoretical viewpoint) and sufficiently specific (to take into account problems raised by the specific play)? All too often the question seems too vast and may give rise to answers other than those contained in the work. So, for *Le Jeu,* the most pertinent question might be summed up in this way: given the class differences and the amorous desire which is directed at a person and not at a social role, how can these two exigencies be reconciled, and what does one do when an individual falls in love "outside his class"? We know that the answer does not really exhaust the question and that the text only responds by a sleight of hand, a lucky chance: it turns out that despite the masks each loves within his own social territory. In other words, the only possible response is to say that the question was false all along, that one can only be attracted by those of one's own social rank, whatever the disguises. Not only was the question very general but also falsified out of necessity: to answer Marivaux's inquiry about the dynamics of a society in which the individual begins to demand his rights (to love, at the very least), it was not really necessary to write *Le Jeu:* Other plays, treating the same themes, could have done so just as well (or less well).

Thus the notion of expectation horizon, however justified and central it might be within the framework of a study of the mechanics of reception, remains in its current form inadequate and too general. As a matter of fact, in analyses of particular works, this horizon is insufficiently outlined and not well formalized in a system or aesthetic-ideological code of the public's expectations. What is lacking, therefore, in this theory of expectation horizon is the formal description of those models which maintain a "dialogue" with the text, a semiological system sufficiently precise and structured to supply a code of the expectations as announced in the text under examination. So, rather than mutually excluding each other, the *semiology* of ideological codes and the *reception* of texts are complementary. However, it would be wrong to make the expectation horizon coded in a text a constant, a fixed element which exists within the system of the work complete in itself. At the very most, by reinserting the work in its historical context, we might be able to approach this horizon at the approximate moment of its creation and entry into literary tradition and the ideological ambiance of its time.

This replacing of the work in its context is known as *historicization*. But what we have to remember is that in order to determine the expectation horizon within the work at the time of its creation, we cannot abstract on the basis of our own *current* attitude and point of view. We must, in other words, keep in mind the fact that the horizon, previously fixed and proper to the work, is also dependent on the more general horizon of the time and place in which the critical discourse is undertaken. This is precisely what has lead Jauss, in more recent texts, to re-examine the clean separation between the two horizons, and to read the horizon within the work in relation to the more general horizon of our current structures of interpretation. This act at once casts doubts on the very theory of an expectation horizon inscribed within the work and brings us back to a much more *pragmatic* attitude with regard to the work analyzed. It also introduces with some force the notion of the situation of enunciation, what Austin called the conditions of success of both the speech act and the presuppositions of the fictional world depicted in the work and described by the reader. With this postulate of a pragmatics of literature, we return to the notion of a relationship between the reader, via the text received, and models of reality: ". . . every reception is defined initially as a confrontation between the receiver and a model of reality which, however mediate it may be, constitutes for him a model of his historical situation. The specificity of this model resides in the fact that it represents this historical situation in the form of a theme, and thus in the form of a factual disorder."[12]

My criticism of the expectation horizon in its present form does not, however, invalidate the pertinence of the concept of the *question* within the work itself. As a hermeneutic tool, this question permits us to cast some light on numerous tensions within the play. In *Le Jeu* the question for the characters is this: how, when between lovers there is no obstacle, is it possible to create an artificial obstacle which will make a character avow his love and make the other understand, through embarrassment and rejection of his avowal, that, were it not for social convention, one would make an avowal of love in return. On the working level of the writer Marivaux (or, if you prefer, on the level of the *global enunciation of the discourse* of the play), the general questions to ask might be: how can an intrigue (a plot), be constructed with characters who are quite able to love each other without undergoing the test of an intrigue? How can situations be created which depend on nothing but a language game? Or on the level of the character's motivation, how might one watch the other without being himself observed? A question which finally can only have one, logically obvious answer: by agreeing to be observed.

It has often been noted that in Marivaux's comedies no obstacle really exists; that one is created, as though capriciously, by the characters in a way which will facilitate their love and its avowal. It permits them to say the opposite of what they think (to say that they do *not* love each other) and to betray themselves by revealing, beneath their refusal, their real feelings. In this sense, the tactic is that of *denial (Verneinung)*: to say that one is not in love, in order in fact to reveal one's desire. So the play is the story of this denial: it permits the lovers indirectly (by devious means) to arrive at an avowal and an enjoyment of the language and the love game. This denial by the character corresponds, at the level of the theatrical enunciation, to a fundamental denial of every referential illusion: the theatre always says in the same breath—"I am a fiction" and "You must believe in it."

But the question is not always readily identifiable in the answer contained in the work. Often the answer is only approximate, an imperfect image of a search for identity, a desire for expression which, through the intermediary of the author and the director, seeks attainment: "*Within the work*, one must look for the specific nature of a desire, of a power (a genius), which has tried to achieve itself and to attest to itself by giving birth to the work."[13] This desire of the work and of genius within the work goes far beyond the individual and conscious will of the author; it corresponds to a whole network of communication and signification which is the reception and interpretation apparatus of the work itself. This network constitutes the critical metalanguage which permits the play to be read as a fiction about its own mode of enunciation and functioning.

Another form of desire seeking to achieve itself is the opening and closing of discourse. The work of art can only take form via the hypothesis and the wager that the work and its interpretation will finally end up letting themselves be read, thus revealing the key to its functioning. The dramatic text frequently begins with an enigma or a contradiction to be resolved. In *Le Jeu*, social and individual enigmas resolve themselves at the end of the play, when the protagonists reveal their true identity. But the opening/closing device does not only occur on the level of content in Marivaux. It is equally present in the theatrical enunciation and in the characters' discourse. In fact one could claim that all his plays begin with a verbal inauguration by a character who claims to have something to say, an answer to give; they end with the acknowledgement that the response is complete. So, *Le Jeu* oscillates between a "why answer?" (I, 1) and a "I have nothing more to tell you" (III, 9).

Opening/closure is often accompanied by a process of situating fiction through the announcement of a "protocol for reading" at the beginning of the text. This protocol assures the difficult junction between the outside world (the event) and the fictional system, by making the starting point of the fiction plausible. In *Le Jeu* the letter that Orgon presents to Mario (a letter which gives the key to the cases of mistaken identity that are to follow) serves as proof external to the plot, it authenticates the situation. Its presentation, while unmaskings occur one after the other, authenticates the confusion, presents the adventures as true. So the motif of the letter serves as a frame for the macro-enunciation and its truthfulness. It establishes the illusion of a connivance between the characters, the author (Marivaux) and the spectator. An answer to an anecdotal and ideological problem needs to be found: the letter (i.e., writing) will supply it.

II. READING (LECTURE)

A second way to approach the *theatrical relationship* (or rather to circle about it at closer range) is to apply the theory of textual and performance *reading*. Obviously *reading* does not mean here the naive deciphering, the hesitant reading of a written text, but the collection of interpretative procedures which lead to the reception of performance. In writing/reading "communication," reading can no longer be considered secondary, but appears as the indispensable counterface of writing (*écriture*). Naive reading (one which takes place without consciousness of the mechanics involved) is condemned as falsifying, because it "systematically effaces the instruments of the production of the work and of its reading, just as the illusionist work of classical aesthetics effaces the procedures of legitimate construction."[14]

The text to be read or the stage to be deciphered are the areas where the reader stakes out his choices of signification: in these open texts which are submitted to his understanding, he is called upon to recognize an order, to make a choice between interpretations, to write a "text within the text,"[15] to play off the latent meanings. As M.C. Ropars-Wuillemier notes, it is a matter of "recognizing in the reading process an act of production and not a pact of fascination, of making something already there emerge through reading, whether it remains at the informal level or whether it needs to be formalized. This implies the rejection of the idea that the text has a mysterious essence. The text should be regarded as a meeting point of established currents and possibilities of meaning still to be constituted in signifying systems."[16]

The mechanisms that influence this reading and the limits of common sense within which one can juggle with interpretation, remain to be defined. The most plausible hypothesis is that the reading is more or less delivered up by the work itself, that it cannot be totally invented by the reader. By admitting in this way that it is suggested by the text—even that "it is a part of the text in which it is inscribed"[17]—we possess the means of getting to that reading by an attentive examination. But at the same time we are caught up in a spin, we produce the vicious circle of reading/interpretation (which is not in fact without resemblance to the hermeneutic circle). So what we have to do is to decide what key to reading we should adopt. The reading which will result from it will no longer have the power to cast off this means of penetrating the work. One must slip furtively into the book (or performance), but one has to make sure that the key used is not a master key which reduces every text to banality.

Numerous approaches to reception have attempted to actualize the possibilities of the work through specific readings. The text has been dealt with as a series of conceptual switching stations en route between production and reception. This can cause the meaning to deviate in several different directions. In *Le Jeu* the presence of such "switching stations" is evident in those scenes where Sylvia's father and brother appear: we always wonder whether it is these two who really control the situation, manipulating and guiding the protagonists by remote control or whether they risk, on the contrary, being overtaken by the very machines that they have so complacently set in motion.

This reading, inscribed within the text to be read, can be considered a descriptive and interpretative metalanguage which may be one or several of the following elements: 1) a system constructed via criticism; 2) a self-reflexive image of the work in the work itself; 3) a literary manner of marking the work with one's own "signature" within the production; 4) an image of the receiver of the work and of his mode of reception, a "guiding" of the reception.

To all these parameters of a textual reading, we must add, for the text that is stage, the numerous transformations of meaning that take place at every level of that enactment. After all, even if certain dramaturgical or stage options are unequivocal, they often mask others, not yet worked out. Furthermore, stage iconicity, despite its apparent obviousness, can never be read *expressis verbis* as a text or a stage direction. Finally, and this is particularly important, theatrical enunciation (rhythm of the acting, gestuality, indications of the actors' positions, "presence," etc.) segments the action, acting and text according to a grid which is proper only to the *mise en scène* in question. What is fundamental to the stage, much more so than the signifieds of the text, is the *iconization* (*mise en vue*) of the word: the text is revealed in all its fragility, constantly menaced as it is by the gestuality which might at any time interrupt its emission, and which always guides the spectator in the rhythm of his reception. The fiction (text plus the different systems, narrative, ideological, etc., which it carries within it) is always at the mercy of interruptions in the enactment: the event, the spectator's material reality, the actor's presence. Only theatre can offer this ambiguous relationship with the stage: language, ideology, and fiction are iconicized, presented to be seen, more than to be understood. This relationship is thus, always inside and outside the fiction, in the *horizontal reading* (obedient to the text, narration, and ideology) *and* in a *vertical reading* (constructed within the event, in the sentiment aroused by the actor's presence and in the hermeneutic act of interpretation).

III. HERMENEUTICS

We might define hermeneutics as "the method of text or performance interpretation which consists of proposing a meaning that takes into account the interpretor's position of enunciation and evaluation."[18] It is impossible here to detail the importance and the diversity of hermeneutic approaches to the text. I can only note briefly the basic oppositions between structure and event, closed system and event, language and speech. These oppositions (which cannot be superimposed one over the other) have been clearly expounded in Benveniste's opposition betwen semiotics and semantics.[19]

There are two different ways of grasping the meaning of a work (dramatic text or performance):

1. By presenting an explanation of its internal structure (the semiotic approach, according to Benveniste).

2. By seeking out its relationship with the referent: "interpreting a text, after all, is not a matter of searching for an intention *hidden behind it,* but of following the meaningful movement towards the referential, i.e., towards that kind of world, or rather being in the world opened up before the text. To interpret means deploying new mediations that the text initiates bet-

ween man and world.''[20]

Structuralism has usually been content to describe a closed system by isolating the rules for the arrangement of signs previously defined and delimited in the work. But this leads to a virtually closed system which can exist only in a theoretical schema, and which takes no account of the unfolding of the work or its concrete enunciation in the event—in performance and reception. It seems necessary, within the perspective of theatrical reception, to bring discourse into play, inasmuch as it is an "event" in its implicit predetermination of reception/comprehension. After all, discourse plays a part in the semantic mode: "the mode of presence of discourse is that of an act, the instance of discourse (Benveniste) which, as such, has the quality of an event.''[21]

In the theatre, this event and the semantic mode, linking the work to the world, are particularly sensitive and even constitute one of the criteria of theatricality. Despite (or even because of) the theatrical illusion which "closes" the work upon itself by hermetically sealing signifying systems (narrativity, gesture, colors, lighting, etc.) the event, that is the uncodifiable element, constantly threatens to "take place," from the moment that the actor unmasks the character in order to "make signs" directly at the spectator, who is thus identified in his role as receiver of the performance. But this instance of "exchange between the actor and the spectator (where) the concrete reality of the theatrical event is played out''[22] is only one of the examples of the theatrical fiction opening out to the world and the receiver. This opening out takes place as soon as the process of reception, in order to function, calls upon personal experience, an ideological code, a pre-history of either text or reader—as soon as the message is staged and is no longer comprehensible without the knowledge conveyed by the situation of enunciation.

Borrowing Wittgenstein's aphorism, "meaning is use," it can be said in the theatre, meaning is *the use made of the stage*. This use of the stage leads to interference between two fundamentally opposed mechanisms: the semiotic mechanism produces systems which are closed on themselves (the written text, the fiction, aesthetic codes, autonomous stage systems, etc.). The semantic rupture dissolves these systems by attaching them to an external interpretative desire and to the event of each reading. Referential illusion and destruction—denial of this effect of reality—are complementary and no doubt located at the source of that indefinable: "theatrical pleasure."

We have just seen that relationships of complementarity can be established between the (semiotic) *structure* and the (semantic) *event*. Everything points to their existence since, in our reception of the work, we continually move from a study of internal relationships to a comparison of the work and the world represented in it. In this way our position is no longer that of an inert observer confronted with an already structured work, but that of a "structure operator," *within the work*. Our manner of approach to the performance and the text is dictated by an effort to prevent the immobilization of our vision and instead allowing it to scan the work.

This scanning process follows the unfolding of the work in such a way that, at certain key moments in the reading/performance, the system of characters, or that of the work's meaning at that precise point in the reading/writing, can be reconstituted. At the moment when such a pause occurs, the work functions partially in the expectation of ensuing events which will then unbalance the system by transforming them. These stopping-off points on the situation (or the actantial model) permit us to carry out a reading which is at the same time systematic and event-bound (the unfolding of different processes). The pleasure to be found in deciphering these pauses is none other than that of the construction of the meaning "in all its meanings, directions" ("*dans tous les sens*") with all the possible openings onto true or false trails. In *Le Jeu,* the quest for meaning is divided up into successive stages in the movement towards mutual understanding between the characters: the unmasking is accompanied by continual steps forward towards the final resolution of the main contradiction (desire/class). This isotropy of the interpreter's progress through "the work" corresponds to the isotropy of "the enunciation of the discourse" which marks the stages in the author's labor of signification.

The character incarnated by the actor is another basic element in a possible rapprochement between the semantic and the semiotic (*sémiotique/sémantique* of Benveniste):

1. *Semantic:* the character has, on the one hand, to be "borne" by the actor and is thus always delivered to us within the here and now of the theatre event: he refers to nothing but himself, being both icon and index (the reality effect of an entity always within a situation). Our relationship with the actor is not within the fiction, but located on the level of a concrete and social situation.

2. *Semiotic:* but on the other hand, the character fits into numerous paradigms according to his own characteristics and to his own pertinent traits vis-a-vis the other characters: he is integrated into a semiotic system and is no longer valid except within a system of differences. Via the character and at the heart of the fiction, the dialectic between semantic and semiotic, between enunciation and utterance (*énoncé*), between the indexical iconic and symbolic, comes into being.[23]

Le Jeu is a perfect example if we want to observe this play between the semantic and the semiotic, event and structure (i.e., between body and ideology as they are opposed in the play). But is not every story, at the metalinguistic level, a conflict between the semiotic and semantic, between the structure and the event? At the beginning of the play, there is a perfect balance between systems: each class speaks its own language; a marriage is to take place between people of the same background. Nothing could disturb these systems except the intervention of chance (history) and bodily desire: the two upper class protagonists have the idea of disguising themselves, and their bodies trick them by making them fall in love with persons they consider below their status. Chance and desire are the disruptive elements which overturn the way they think, making them "sacrifice" themselves in order to overcome their contradictions. This sacrifice is the intervention of the semantic in the semiotic: the event which disturbs the balance of the system and throws into question "the conceived" ideas and bodies.

Dorante is willing to follow his heart's desire and marry the person he believes to be a servant. Sylvia is troubled to the point that she forgets her "language" strategy, her attitude towards class, and almost her "good manners." The servants dream of marrying "above" their station. In short, the whole gamut of ideological and psychological systems is disturbed; things proceed apace and the play could finish (in the 2nd act) with this transforming of values. But Marivaux is careful to reinstate the semiotic at the end of the story, or, rather, to work out an agreement between the semiotic and the semantic. In fact, it seems as though desire and social role are no longer contradictory (at least for the masters) and that the event (the threat to the systems) was after all more or less under remote control by the benevolent patriarchal law—so much so that in the end nothing has been threatened and, quite literally speaking, "nothing has happened" which might disturb order and foretell of an historical consequence to the problems of the play.

The hermeneutic approach undeniably has the capacity to correctly encompass the *theatrical relationship*. By construing both text and performance as basically unstable, hermeneutics brings a great deal of suppleness to the task of interpretation and leaves the way open to the intervention of enunciators, to their capacity to break up the fiction, to open the structure to the unexpected. It is primarily the spectator and reader who can enter such a breach in the interpretation and thus develop their understanding with the greatest possible freedom—provided they are aware from precisely what position they are approaching the text and what expectations they bring to it.

However, this approach—like the research into the expectation horizon—remains too general to produce by itself results which are sufficiently precise and pertinent. The angle of attack offered by *perspective* seems more appropriate for an approach to the theatrical relationship.

IV. PERSPECTIVE

Perspective is another important notion whose ambiguity can be useful for a study of the theatrical relationship, since it designates both the particular point of view of the characters and that of their discourse and ideologies. But it can also be applied to the perspective of the spectator as receiver—the way in which the work appears to him as the result of a multitude of points of view and contradictory instances. Perspective is particularly suited to facilitating the passage between internal structure (the semiotic) and hermeneutical interpretation (the semantic).

Studies of perspective (or point of view) have had far less success in the theatre than they have had for the novel and for narrative technique. However, perspective, originally used in architecture and painting, might well seem to be perfectly applicable to stage arts: the spectator always sees the stage from a particular angle and this point of view determines his perception of the events and his attitude when confronted by the characters: "The Theatre is precisely that practice which calculates the place of things as they are observed: if I set the spectacle here, the spectator will see this; if I put it elsewhere, he will not, and I can avail myself of this masking effect and play on illusion it provides. The stage is the line which stands across the path of the optical pencil, tracing at once the point at which it is brought to a stop and, as it were, the threshold of its ramification. Thus is founded—against music (against the text)—representation."[24]

However, it would be hard to elaborate a theory of reception founded solely on physical perception. Studies of the stage/house relationship give us information about the physical implication of the public, but they can neither explain the internal functioning of the performance, nor the spectator's intellectual and emotive distance when confronting the performance, nor the arrangement of the points of view of individual characters, and the resultant central authorial perspective.

It can, therefore, be worthwhile to transpose optical and geometrical perspective to the level of the fictional universe, and the characters' views about their reality. But the danger then arises that we may totally psychologize the notion by no longer tying it to the specific form, or a discursive instance which determines it. This inherent difficulty in separating the different points of view in the work should not prevent us from isolating the characters' points of view and their interaction. The notion of the play's *internal perspective* (specific to each figure) can be added to that of the spectator's *external* perception. On the basis of an identical theme (conflict, motive, judgment about reality), it is sometimes possible to compare individual perspectives. This reconstitution requires of the critic an aptitude for identification and for "justice" vis-a-vis a character, an aptitude which will afford him the pleasure of seeing the reality represented first through the eyes of one, then another, of the various protagonists without giving preference to one single point of view. Even the contradictions and ideological uncertainties of a figure have to be accepted, and not reduced to an authorial point of view.

However, an objective comparison of points of view would be difficult to realize, since we would have to suppose that the characters' points of view were a realistic imitation of a pre-existing external world (the referent), a discourse copied from reality. But such convincing imitation can only be a decoy, since the text (even the dramatic text that seems to be shared evenly amongst the characters) is not the representation of real discourse. What has to be taken into account here is the work of writing which transforms and recreates reality to be represented according to its own rules. The discourse of the characters is also not necessarily homogenous: within the whole text pronounced by a single character several discursive forms from very different ideological horizons often co-exist. The fact that the dramatic text is divided into roles does not in any way guarantee the unity and the homogeneity of the different subjects who pronounce the dialogue.

Instead of "weighing" points of view, it is just as useful, as in the case of Marivaux's characters, to differentiate the characters more according to their very allusive ideas about the world, than according to the use they make of language, and their relation to the spoken word. In this author's work, such an attitude is at one time instrumental and utilitarian (for the valets), at another time deceptive and playful (for the masters), or finally confiding and self-assured (for the fathers). A comparison of perspectives based on ideas, and the more or less correct statements of the characters, would lead one astray. Stylistics of discourse has to give way to a study of the situation of speech, and, within speech, of different types. It is, moreover, at this level of situation in language, and the play of language, that we first see these imaginary creatures, and their way of using language informs us of their ideological and social status.

This respect for individual views (a very fragile and at best theoretical respect) provides the spectator with the double pleasure of seeing via another consciousness, and of observing the character—pleasures of identification with and of distancing from the Other. This constant changing from a simple *vision* to a *vision of vision,* which Brecht, among others, sees as the very essence of theatrical pleasure, allows us to patiently construct in the course of the performance and our critical reflection upon it, the end product of these perspectives which is then assimilated to the *perspective of reception* "intended" by the author. This perspective of reception—here we return to the theory of reading (*lecture*)—is at the same time: 1) implicitly prescribed by the author (or the subject of the discourse) and 2) left to the spectator's activity of comparison:

1. The mode of reception is clearly legible in the theatre when the manipulation of sympathy is very obvious. This is the case when a character is presented as obviously good or obviously bad. The imbalance is then so great that the spectator immediately adopts the "right choice." The dialectical technique of the "middle road" is arranged to present two equal camps (good or bad) which cancel each other out and produce a resulting force, materialized at times into the *raisonneur* or one of his modern avatars—recitor, narrator, *metteur en scène* arranging the facts. The technique of focalization[25] detaches the central figures from the actantial

model.

In *Le Jeu,* despite the parallel situations between the valets and the masters, the masters definitely play the leading part. And in the couple of masters, Sylvia plays the central role.

2. Yet without creating any contradiction, the play opens two possible perspectives for the spectator. In the "match" between masters and servants, it is impossible to decide who is right. The masters possess language; they play with it brilliantly, inventing stories instead of acting and passing directly to avowal and to deeds as do the servants. So their play seems gratuitous and useless to that section of the public that sees the servants' action as proof of a nature unperverted by self-love and reflective consciousness. The dialectic between play and naturalness, between bourgeois, aristocratic, and popular points of view, is anchored here in the way the play functions, and in its reception.

It is this lack of certainty about a real and just perspective which is the mark of the ideological. Ideology, of necessity, presents itself as "natural" and "impartial." It is often to be found in the collision between points of view and discourses in the third person, in the impersonal "they say that. . . ." Thus in *Le Jeu* the servants have recourse to these neuter forms whenever they have to speak for themselves and confess their feelings. For them, ideological discourse, like declarations of love (which we might expect to count among the most personal expressions) passes through the medium of a language which is not their own.[26]

This raises the suspicion that such a global perspective or receptive position is the hallmark of ideology. Is it not in this neutralization and relativization of discourse and ideas that the dramatic text finds its meaning? There is never a single meaning for what occurs on stage, except in the sense of everything being called into question by the instances of discourse which do not necessarily match the character's words. What is needed here is a study of the discursive formations of the text. This would replace the notion of the characters' perspective (too psychological) with formalized perspectives according to the sources and the configuration of the discourses.[27] Such a study could profitably be rounded off by a comparison of the *possible worlds* of various characters.[28]

The fact remains that the theatre distinguishes itself from literature by the iconization of its enunciation sources, and by the reconstitution (even if it is false, in fact, *necessarily* false) of the situation of enunciation. It is this ability to put ideology into play (in space) which is fascinating about the theatre: the spectator is bombarded with a mixture of discourses that the stage can entirely transform, according to our desires and fantasies: "The stage is that privileged place where our ideology, our ideological condition, is in a spectacular manner checked by the force of desire. This occurs first of all because the ideological is not a fact of presence in the world but of the simple 'wanting to say' (*vouloir dire*): the universe becomes schematic only at that moment when it is observed; and the spectator is nothing other than the presentation, the instituting of a showing, he is an instance of the *making visible*.''[29] Not the least advantage of *perspective* as a tool is that it makes us become conscious of the contradiction between the internal perspective of the play, with its systems of characters, and perspective of reception held by the critic and the spectator, who is placed in a situation of "desiring," when confronted with the actor and the performance. Every performance is of necessity located within this play of views and/or points of view. Marivaux's work offers us a perfect example of this problem of theatrical viewpoint.

V. MARIVAUX AND SEEING

Le Jeu is a play in which the gaze is turned back on itself. Thus it thematizes the problem of the character's internal perspective, of the place of conflict between someone who exists only as a gaze focused on someone else, and one who exists because he is the object of the other's gaze. As J. Rousset remarks so well, with Marivaux

> each play is developed on two levels, that of the heart whose pleasure is the end in itself, and that of the consciousness of the onlooker. Where does the real play lie? It is to be found in the superimposing and the interlacing of these two levels, in the gaps and exchanges which are established between them and which offer us the subtle pleasure of a double view and a double reading. . . . Every play of Marivaux can be defined as a double organism, the two levels of which gradually move towards a state of complete junction. The play is over once the two levels merge, i.e, when the group of characters watched see themselves as they were seen by the watching characters. The real denouement is not the marriage anticipated as the curtain falls, but the meeting of heart and sight.[30]

These lines are perfectly applicable to the play. But it would be wrong to be content with understanding them at the level of the psychological content of the characters and the story narrated (the "properly Marivaudian combination of the spectacle and the spectator, of the person watched and the person watching.")[31] They are equally valid at the metadiscursive level of the play, which is the "story" of a *vouloir-dire* (*need-to-say, mean-to-say*) which ends when everything has been *said* and everything has been *seen*. The isotropy of this "wanting-to-say" (*vouloir-dire*) is easily located within the texture of the plot.[32]

1. Sylvia and Dorante want to be able to say to their fathers that they accept their betrothal. This project of "saying" is to be carried out by ex-

amining each other and by "answering for (their) own feelings" (I. 1). They have faith in their discourse (their ideology) as a means of judging each other, while protecting themselves from the other's advances (from his conquering gaze).

2. Unfortunately, the obstacle of the double disguise which they themselves have set in place means that neither can see the other as he really is; each is suspicious of the other. Sylvia desperately uses her discursive skills to protect herself from Dorante's insistent and mute contemplation; Dorante claims he wants to give up the language of lovers to contemplate Sylvia (II, 9). Far from protecting her, Sylvia's discourse never stops betraying her; she can no longer manage to match what she says and what she does (in II, 9, for example, she is no longer able to leave the stage despite her declared intention). Her *vouloir-dire* is transformed into a *non-vouloir-dire* ("a not-wanting-to-say") which betrays her. What is uniquely meaningful for the young couple and for the spectator is the situation of enunciation, the desire and the pleasure of maintaining contact through words whose immediate significance is beyond them.

3. After Dorante's avowal, Sylvia immediately *sees* with clarity into her heart (II, 12). Discourse regains its equivalency with the social and psychological being. When Dorante agrees to bring his lover's contemplation and his social discourse into accord (in the avowal and the "spoken" desire), Sylvia agrees to remove her mask, to offer herself up to a "personal" contemplation, to *say* ("I no longer have anything to say to you" III, 9) and to *see* ("Do you recognize this letter? . . . I can see clearly into my own heart . . ."). Seeing (desire, body and physical presence) will be legitimized by saying (ideology, rediscovered language, social norms).

As for the two characters, their initiation will have brought them to a way of seeing and a desire which are no longer in conflict. The *vouloir-dire*, the wanting-to-say (to dominate completely by ideology, to be reassured by having one's word accord with the things around one) will coincide with the *vouloir-voir*, the wanting-to-see (the absolute fantasy of seeing which understands everything without any obstacle). The father's letter, at the end of the play, figures as the visualization of the enigma, the recognition of the ideological and paternal order of things. This letter is also a *mise-en-abyme* of theatricality and of the theatrical mechanism since it makes visible (represents) what is said and what is written (the theatrical and paternal word, *la parole*).

The isotopy of wanting-to-say/to do, which we can retrace on the level of the character's perspective (psychological and discursive) corresponds, at the level of Marivaux's own discourse, to the same steps in his writing project. For, the obstacle to *saying* and *seeing* reproduces, within the discourse of global enunciation, the difficulty of allying class ideology and the burgeoning demands of desire and individualism. The author of *Le Jeu* "resolves" this problem by using the happy chance of coinciding desire and class, of seeing and being seen. This is also a way of representing the ideology of an era, its limits and its obstacles, all the while suggesting surreptitious means of transforming it from within. By presenting a counterbalance and a countercommunication for each viewpoint (the masters and the servants), he finally leaves the concluding word to the audience, which is called upon to choose its own point of view and thus take sides from the house in what has been presented on stage as an erroneous assention of harmony between class and desire.

Seeing does not just play a thematic and psychological role. It is obviously the driving force of action and plot (everything happens because the characters always look twice before getting married, confronting their intimate desires and their social position). But it also gives an image of the *theatrical relationship* of the onlooker, an image which becomes thematized in the play and which "theatrically" recounts the fable behind every theatrical game, the consciousness of playing a role and of being only, and eternally, a play-within-the-play. Each gaze leveled on the other person encloses him in a play-within-the-play, and in a relationship from which he can escape only by leveling his own gaze on someone else. This "bracketing of gazes" establishes several degrees of reality and of theatricality within *Le Jeu*. Each character modalizes and modifies the object which he encloses in his contemplation until an unimpeded vision in which we can no longer distinguish those looking from those looked at, and where discourse, too, is annihilated by the "nothing more to say." The spectator dynamics between a perceiving subject and a perceived object no longer exists and discourse dies.

What we rediscover here is the previously sketched connections between hermeneutics and the perspective of reception. This double thematic isotopy of *seeing* and *saying*, in fact, corresponds, as we have seen, to the opposition between a *structuralist* grasp of the work (through the perspective of an exterior reader/spectator) and a *hermeneutic* approach which avoids viewing the internal structure as a "thing" and seeks out the meaning, while not denying the displacement of the critical relationship.

Derrida[33] and Kuentz[34] have quite clearly demonstrated the delusions of narrowly structuralist criticism which tries to display the geometric and architectural organization of a work seen in perspective from a fixed point. Such a work seems ordered and immobilized in front of an observer who forbids himself any movement so that he will not see the work from a different perpective. The work's contradictions (between characters' viewpoints, for example) have to be resolved *within* the text: thus, for *Le Jeu*, criticism attempts by every means at hand to reconcile the contradiction between desire and class, finding justification in Marivaux's own attempts at reconciliation.

But such reasoning, in all these structural descriptions, is based on a fixed object, and does not take into account the global enunciation of the play and the quality speech has of being an event in time, trying to exist within a *vouloir-dire*, only received when the contradictions of content are perceived and resolved by an external public which has the right of response.

It is this subterranean speech which is most important in the play and which alone is worth *listening to*, since it is not the illusory vanishing point of the contents and contradictions finally made explicit and perceptible in the theatricalization, but the voice or voices of ideology and its intermingled discourses.

In this respect, it is noteworthy that the eighteenth century, and more precisely Marivaux's epoch, marks the climax of Italianate theatre founded on perfect illusionism, where everything is theatricalized within a frame which is supposed to contain the stage, action and discourse. This peak of illusion and theatricality crowns two centuries marked, as Michel Bernard[35] has shown, by a theatricalization of the body (seen from the outside, in perspective): a theatricalization which, by visualizing the performance and the architectural structure, represses an internal grasp of the body and depreciates the voice. This paroxysm of perspective and the visual foreshadows an explosion of the closed space, of the unified representation of harmonious discourses whose contradictions are resolved within the text.

We have noticed that in *Le Jeu* it is impossible to determine the resultant of the speeches or the vanishing point of the different perspectives, and further, that only the public chooses its side and thereby decides the way the play functions. The insoluble contradictions of the content draw attention to the autoreflexive functioning of the enunciation which, in the play, serves as a narrative voice, playing with the represented reality by pointing out its contradictions. This is the voice of a "dialogism" which, as Bakhtin has shown, always burst forth in a period when ideology is "moulting," moving from the comfort of monologic certitudes to the uncertainty of dialogic ideologies.

Such is the paradoxical nature of Marivaux's theatre: it seems to be the apotheosis of theatricality, of the illusionist perspective, of language and ideology in clear view and always canceling each other out at a fixed vanishing point. In actual fact, this theatre only finds its meaning in the voice of a discourse which can no longer manage to correctly represent the ideology and its contradictions and which is forced to progress underground, taking shelter in itself and its own production, and obsessively coming back to a consciousness of its enunciation. As with Sylvia, emblem of the conflict between sight and voice, the discourse can no longer say what it *sees*. It can only say that it says.[36]

This Marivaudian conflict between sight and voice is itself nothing more than an illustration of the difficulties found in a science of interpretation and reception. Confronted with the richness of the theatrical message and the infinite scenic mixtures of different *mises en scène*, reception of the performance becomes an act of which all critical trace is lost. From this comes the temptation, close to resignation, to leave description for later or to make do with assertions, otherwise imprecise, that the public "participates" and becomes a legitimate member of the performance. A further result from this is a double threat to theatre semiology:

1) Of falling prey to a formal description of the codes at work, of presenting the performance as though encoded and decodable only in one way.

2) Of falling back into sociologism and dissolving the difference between text and stage in a socio-economic context supposed to mechanically produce the work. The only way of unblocking this alternative consists in the interaction of the structure and the event. The semiological structures of a given performance are only "snapshots" at certain points in the act of interpretation. This interpretation is an act of reading and, therefore, a reconstruction process which can be explained and formalized.

Has the theory of the aesthetics of reception undergone a Copernican type of revolution, concentrating from the outset in the effect produced on the spectator? This seems to be very doubtful! As a matter of fact, from Aristotle to Brecht, the emotional reaction of the spectator has been the center of interest, to the extent of making it the aesthetic and ideological touchstone of the art. But a theorization of the act of reception has not ensued (perhaps quite simply because a theory of the emotions can hardly be adapted to aesthetic perception, as the latter includes psychological, anthropological and ideological phenomena at one and the same time).

The sole and narrow path available to the aesthetics of reception is that of the process of *identification* conceived of as the spectator's *quest for identity*. This identity can be defined *analytically* as the recognition of a previous ego through a process of denial (*Verneinung*), and *ideologically* as the effect of ideological recognition, as "the production of a new consciousness in the spectator."[37]

Analytically: Freud explains the quest for identification by the pleasure the ego finds in reliving in the other's ego representations he had repressed. Denial involves admitting into one's consciousness foreign and disagreeable elements by attributing them to the other's account. It removes guilt and permits the return of what is repressed which, to the subject perceiving, seems to belong to a different ego distinct from his own. Here one needs, on the basis of the scene presented to the spectator, to account for the work of structural reorganization of his conscious self, and the benefit obtained from the present identification. In this way one might produce the beginnings of a description of this frequently mentioned theatrical exchange.

Ideologically: In the same breath one would then have to conceive of identification as the recognition of an ideology experienced as familiar and normative. As Althusser indicates, "it will appear that it is the play itself which *is* the spectator's consciousness, for the essential reason that the spectator has no other consciousness than 1) the content which unites him in advance with the play and 2) what this content becomes in the play itself: the new result which the play *produces* on the basis of this recognition of self of which it is both the image and the presence.''[38]

We can hope that the ideological identity of the spectator will then take shape, and that the work's structure and its accomplishment within the theatrical event will be the *means of this revelation*.

Translated by Susan Melrose

Footnotes

[1]Jean Starobinski, *La relation critique*, Paris, Gallimard, 1970, p. 15.

[2]The beginnings of this aesthetics of reception occurred with the Russian Formalists. The discovery of the strangeness effect (Chklovski's *priem ostranenija*) as the essential characteristic of the artistic effect leads us to seek in reception the source of stylistic deviation and the text's construction. German hermeneutics (Dilthey, Staiger, Gadamer) is concerned with the laws of interpretation which give the work its opening onto the world and its interpretor and produce meaning in the very act of the quest for it. In France, Paul Ricoeur and Emile Benveniste showed the dual nature of every meaning process (semiotic: explaining the text from its immanent aspect; semantic: referring text back to its world meaning). On these methodological bases, the Constance School (Iser, Jauss, Striedter, Warning, Stierle, *et. al.*) construct a theory of artistic reception and of aesthetic experience. For an introduction to these problems, see Rainer Warning's reader, *Rezeptionsästhetik*, Munchen, Fink-U.T.B., 1975, and the recent issue of *Poétique*, no. 39, September, 1979, "Théorie de la réception en Allemagne."

[3]Bertolt Brecht, *Gesammelte Werke*, Frankfurt, Suhrkamp, 1966, vol. 15, p. 275.

[4]Louis Althusser, quoted in Jean Caune, "L'analyse de la représentation théâtrale apres Brecht," *Silex*, no. 7, Avril 1976, p. 105.

[5]Rainer Warning, "Pour une pragmatique du discours fictionnel," *Poétique*, no. 39, Septembre, p. 327.

[6]Unfortunately for critics, Brecht does not give any more precise details of how to grasp and formalize these two historicities. For an initial orientation, one has to refer to the work of Mukarovsky which, along with the structuralism of the Prague School, deals with structuralist research as much as with the theory of reception. In fact, Mukařovský is one of the first scholars to have clearly defined the two dynamic movements which dominate the structure of the work and that of the public's intelligence (which also evolves with social changes). "Aesthetic value is (thus) a process whose free expression is determined on the one hand by the immanent evolution of the structure itself (cf. the tradition of time according to which each work is judged, and on the other hand by the movement and the modifications of the structure of the social life of man" (Jan Mukařovský, *Kapitel aus der Ästhetik*, Frankfurt, Suhrkamp, p. 81). The critic will have to take into account these two evolutions and propose a model which will introduce a dialogue between, on the one hand, the way in which our own reality gives shape to a whole system of expectations and ideological norms. It is essential that we locate the relationship between a fictional text and the reality it describes. This relationship is not, as has long been believed, that of imitation, but of formalization and of "shaping." On this subject, Wolfgang Iser propounds the hypothesis that "each era possesses its own meaning systems, and the thresholds from one era to the next inscribe meaningful modifications within these systems, whether they are hierarchized or internally concur" ("La fiction en effet," *Poétique*, no. 39, Septembre 1979, p. 284). From this point on, a theory of social systems—in other words a theory of ideology—becomes indispensable. A "filtering" of these innumerable meaning systems is possible. This would decrease their number by reducing them to institutionalized structures "lexicalized" into types of experiences and situations previously known and assembled: "If the entourage of the systems can to a certain extent be simplified and immobilized, this is because determined forms of the elaboration of experience (perceptive customs, interpretations of reality, values) have been institutionalized. The systems are multiple but all attached to identical or corresponding modes of understanding: modes of behavior—by rights infinite—are thus reduced by that much and the complementary of expectations is initiated" (Niklas Lukmann, *Zweckbegriff und Systemarationalität*, Frankfurt, 1973, p. 182, quoted in Iser, "La fiction . . ." op. cit.).

[7]V. Chlovski, "L'art comme procédé," in Tzvetan Todorov (ed.), *Théorie de la littérature*, Paris, Seuil, 1966.

[8]Pierre Voltz, "L'insolite est-il une catégorie dramatique?" in *L'onirisme et l'insolite dans le théâtre francais contemporain*, Paris, Klincksieck, 1974, p. 53.

[9]Hans-Robert Jauss, *Ästhetische Erfahrung und literarische Hermeneutik I*, München, Fink, 1977.

[10]Jauss, *Literaturgeschichte als Provokation*, Frankfurt, Suhrkamp, 1970, pp. 175-176.

[11]Ibid., p. 178.

[12]Warning, op. cit., p. 337.

[13]Starobinski, op. cit., p. 24.

[14]Pierre Kuentz, "Le tête à texte," *Esprit*, no. 12, Decembre 1974, p. 958.

[15]Jean Ricardou, "Table ronde sur la lecture," *Esprit*, op. cit.

[16]Marie-Claire Ropars-Wuillemier, "Lire l'écriture," *Esprit*, op. cit., p. 800.

[17]Michel Charles, *Rhétorique de la lecture*, Paris, Seuil, 1977, p. 9.

[18]"Hermeneutique," in Patrice Pavis, *Dictionnaire du théâtre: Termes et concepts de l'analyse theatrale*, Paris, Editions Sociales, 1980.

[19]Emile Benveniste, *Problèmes de linguistique générale*, II, Paris, Gallimard, pp. 43-66.

[20]Paul Ricoeur, "Signe et Sens," *Encyclopedia Universalis*, Paris, p. 1014.

[21]Ricoeur, *Le conflit des interprétations*, Paris, Seuil, 1969, p. 87.

[22]Voltz, op. cit., p. 56.

[23]On the problem of a typology of signs, see Pavis, *Problèmes de sémiologie théâtrale*, Montreal, P.U.Q., 1976.

[24]Roland Barthes, "Diderot, Brecht, Eisenstein," *Image, Music, Text*, New York, Hill and Wang, p. 69.

[25]Manfred Pfister, *Das Drama*, München, Fink, 1977, p. 97.

[26]Examples of neutral language: "Do you consider that he is being ill-treated" (. . .) "Should not one be reasonable?" (. . .) "It must be hoped that this will come about" (II, v). Examples of borrowed language: "I say what I am taught to, that is Madame's doctrine. I study under her" (I, ii) (. . .) "Echo what is said; repeat" (II, v). From *Le Jeu de l'amour et du hasard* in *Théâtre complet*, edité par Fredéric Deloffre, Paris, Garnier, 1968.

[27]See Pavis, "Remarques sur le discours theatral," *Degres*, no. 13, 1978.

[28]Keir Elam, *The Semiotics of Theatre and Drama*, London, Methuen, 1980.

[29]Virgil Tanase, "Le theatre et la dissidence permanente," *Cahiers de l'Est*, no. 12-13, p. 50.

[30]Jean Rousset, "Marivaux ou la structure du double registre," in *Forme et Signification*, Paris, Corti, 1962, p. 38.

[31]Rousset, op. cit. p. 48.

[32]Sylvia begins a number of her lives with: "I tell you," a performative which inserts its effect into the spoken word. The servants and Dorante on the contrary use the verb: "I see . . ." very frequently.

[33]Jacques Derrida, "Forme et Signification," in *L'écriture et la différence*, Paris, Seuil, 1967, pp. 9-49. The article critizes the too rigid structuralist viewpoint in Rousset's work.

[34]Kuentz, in *Esprit*, op. cit.

[35]Michel Bernard, *L'expréssivité du Corps*, Paris, Delarge, 1976.

[36]This particularity of Marivaux's writing can probably also be explained by the role of the metalanguage of the characters which refers to their enunciation and to language. This study was already concluded when I learnt of William Dodd's article "Metalanguage and Character in Drama," in *Lingua e Stile*, Anno XIV, no. 1, March 1979, pp 135-150. The author makes a very interesting distinction in his work between "external metalanguage" and "internal metalanguage." "External metalanguage" ties together the character and the public when the character "thematizes a conventionalized mode in order to transmit information on the nature of the situation" (p. 138). "Internal metalanguage" is that of the character who addresses himself to another character by reifying himself (or his *interlocuteur*) as *emetteur* and his *interlocuteur* (or himself) as *receiver* (and thus each as the possessor of one or several codes) and by reifying the dramatic situation as *circumstances* (p. 143). In the case of *Le Jeu de l'Amour et du Hasard*, metalanguage remains limited to the level of internal use by characters commenting on their speech-situation. Apparently these illusions leave the general fiction of the dramatic universe intact; they do not throw it into question as a Brechtian narrator would. Thus internal metalanguage is reduced to one theme amongst others, a content expressing ideas about the world without this new consciousness threatening any damage to the illusionist dramatic form. In the terms of Szondi, we might say that the thematic content is not yet "precipitated" in an adequate and new form in relation to the tradition of the purely

dramatic form. However we have to note that this destruction of the drama by the irruption of the internal and then the external metalanguage of the characters is to a certain extent introduced and masked by Marivaudian theatre. W. Dodd shows that the two types of metalanguage, although they are "enmeshed almost inextricably in the reality of dramatic texts," can be considered "theoretically distinct." This position seems to me to be just and it would be tempting to describe this "enmeshing." Perhaps it is possible by showing the dialectical exchange between external and internal metalanguage, by using Szondi's theory of the evolution of dramaturgy as the constant modification in the Form/Content rapport.

1. *For the external metalanguage* the *theme* of allusion to the enunciation situation neccessitates the elaboration of a new *form* which can let the theatricality and the epic character of dramaturgy appear. The theme of external metalanguage thus finds itself functionalized in a new form.

2. *For the internal language* the allusion by one character to an other as the source of the message remains within the work of the fiction and thus is above all significant as an original theme and not as a new form. Moreover, this form of dialogue which is conscious of itself does not require, for its expression, the elaboration of a new dramaturgy: it simply produces a theme similar to those concerning the world. Thus internal metalanguage thematizes end "recuperates" the new thematic.

[37]The "movements" of the two metalanguages occur as follows:

1. *External language*: functionalization: new Theme (Content)—new Form.

2. *Internal metalanguage*: thematization: old Form—new Theme.

(On the relationship between Form and Content and thematization/formalization see Szondi: die *Theorie des modernen Dramas,* Frankfurt, Suhrkamp, 1956. French translation by P. Pavis, Age d'Homme, Lausanne. English translation by M. Hays to appear.

[38]Louis Althusser, "Notes pour un théâtre matérialiste," *Pour Marx,* Paris, Maspero, p. 151.

The Discourse of Dramatic Criticism

This text expands parts of my paper presented at the Second International Congress of Semiotics, Vienna, July 1979. An Italian translation appeared in *Quaderni di Teatro*, Anno II, Numero 5, August 1979.

No one can deny that a few words have been said about theatre. But this does not mean *a priori* that all these words can be organized into a critical system or into a coherent discourse. The subject of theatre criticism is so multiple, so rich and, today, so polymorphous that its interpretation "breaks" into a multitude of critical aims and discourses which no longer have anything in common other than a vague desire to choose an aspect of the performance or the text as an impulse or as a "detonator" for liberating one's own critical voice.

It is hardly any easier to define a literary metalanguage or to outline a systematic path for critical intervention for works which are written in the single medium of language. But at least that critical discourse expresses itself by the same system, easily weaving a whole intertextual network between itself and the object to be analyzed. In the theatre, on the contrary—at least for the discourse on performance which is my sole concern here—the critical work must take into account a whole set of signs, a whole world which is visual, auditory, and takes the form of an event, and which by its very nature, aims explicitly at going beyond the narrow confines of articulated language in order to *mean* according to its own specificity. So the discourse of theatre criticism doesn't resemble a metalanguage in the strict sense of the term (a language on a language), but is more like a *writing* (*écriture*) about the bringing together of diverse objects: stage form, lighting, bodies and objects, a text emanating from several sources, etc. It does not always have a system of description at its disposal, nor even a system of graphic transposition of the diverse stage systems. Various "unskilled" techniques have always been used to notate the *mise en scène*, from the production book (with schematic representation of actors' positions, commentary on the psychology of the acting, etc.) to the reflections of diverse semiological approaches; they never really satisfy, on the one hand, because they impoverish the object described, and on the other hand, because they are unable to supply an epistemological reflection on their own system of notation and, even less, on the dialectical relations between all of the systems and the production of the global meaning that results from them.

So we have to give up (and perhaps in the end this is a good thing) the attempt to formalize or even simply to outline an all inclusive metalanguage of theatrical criticism, and to find a descriptive and interpretative grid adequate for the varied components of performance. One can only describe, within the mass of critical discourses, several levels of intervention corresponding to the specific preoccupation of each critical instance. Instead of the traditional classification according to a supposed scientificity or quality (1. "Academic" analysis; 2. Criticism from the creative side and theatre people; 3. Journalistic criticism, etc.), it would be more suitable to make a distinction according to the criterion of the critical aim of the project, i.e., what Jean Starobinski calls a "non-preconceived reading" that is "a simple encounter, unshadowed from the first by any systematic premeditation or doctrinal prerequisite."[1] This "non-preconceived reading" (or at any rate, "as little preconceived as possible") would intervene at the following levels:

I. *Dramatic structures* and *dramaturgy* analyze the text of the *mise en scène* according to the treatment of time and space, the configuration of characters in the dramatic universe, the sequential organization of the episodes of the Story. As soon as the critic takes on the task of supplying information on the Story and the dramatic universe of the play, he deals with dramaturgical questions.

II. The *reception* of the performance is generally analyzed from a psychological point of view: how did I "personally" react to the organization of the *mise en scène*, to the situations and characters? What emotions, from total identification to the coldest critical distance, moved me? In what way has catharsis occurred or awareness been achieved, etc.? The criteria of reception are sometimes purely *moral* (the value of a work of art has for a long time been appreciated in this way); sometimes they are *political* or *philosophical*. Finally, the play is sometimes judged according to its conformity to a literary model, a genre, a type of dramatic construction (for example, the "well-made play"); an ideological-aesthetic norm (for example, the "alienation effect"). What is of interest in this type of critical discourse is its transference of power to the spectator to judge and to appreciate the performance according to what he perceives in it and what "speaks" to him.

III. In the *review* made according to a *critique of "taste,"* insistence is placed as much on elements judged successful (without the key to this success being clearly indicated) as on the obvious defects (without these being "pinned" to the back-drop of an overall structure or a general coherence). This type of criticism is "pointillistic" and impressionistic to the extent that it extracts from the performance, without concern for its internal logic, a few moments—good ones or bad—with which to build a frequently very rapid and superficial judgment.

IV. Following on from the preceding category, remarks on the *actors' performances* are often preoccupied with the success or failure of illusion or verisimilitude; the actors' performances are judged in the absolute, and not within the whole ensemble of the *mise en scène*; frequently, criticism aimed at the character (sympathy/antipathy) are confused with the actor's means of expression in the collective work of staging.

V. Interpretation according to a *theory* or an *aesthetics* puts the play or the *mise en scène* back into a more general framework of a theory of discourses, a model of sign functioning (semiology), a dramaturgy which is characteristic of a certain period or author. This type of discourse has almost nothing to do with *literary criticism*, but according to Barthes' distinction,[2] it is integrated within a *science of literature*, "a general discourse whose object is not such and such a meaning, but the very plurality of meanings within the work."[3] It is hardly important, therefore, whether this science of literature applied to theatre takes the name of *dramaturgy*, or *aesthetics*, or *discursive theories and/or practices*, or *semiology*.

This list of possible perspectives for critical intervention is certainly not closed; it takes into account a few current practices, but nothing will prevent a new viewpoint from describing and formalizing the performance in a heretofore unknown manner.

Instead of approaching criticism from a systematic and logical viewpoint, as I have just done, that is, according to the *things named* (*choses nommées*), one might choose to set out from the existing vocabulary of the critical apparatus, that is, from the *naming signs* (*signes nommant*). In a recent work[4] I proposed a theatrical glossary of about 500 critical terms which I chose according to the criterion of their effective usage as tools to describe, by one means or another, the functioning of a performance. From this corpus, I tried to establish a systematic index grouping of terms, under nine headings, according to a taxonomy that brings together concepts by homogeneous sets chosen on the basis of a classifying principle. I obtained the following systems; in each case a few examples are given:

1. *Dramaturgy*: action, story, fable, catastrophy, rules, unities, etc.
2. *Theatrical categories and aesthetic problems*: absurd, burlesque, pathetic, tragic, etc.
3. *Genres and forms*: comedy, happening, masquerade, psychodrama, etc.
4. *Structural principles*: framework, closure (*clôture*), distance, rupture, coherence, etc.
5. *Stage and mise en scène*: props, decor, space, *mise en scène*, etc.
6. *Actor and character*: actant (acting force), actor, *deus ex machina*, presence, etc.
7. *Reception*: address to the public, identification, pleasure, terror and pity, etc.
8. *Text and discourse*: narrative analysis, context, modality, monologue, etc.
9. *Semiology*: code, enunciation, ostension, sign, minimal unit, etc.

No visible structure seems to underlie and link together these nine subsets, as the point of view of each group varies so much from one to the other: in other words, each group proposes an angle of intervention on theatre without excluding many other approaches. A category such as "structural principles" is almost inexhaustible, depending on the structuring intelligence of the critic. On the other hand, all the technical terms or the words given to parts of the stage are lexicalized and constitute a stabilized metalanguage (thus: *stage [scene] and mise-en-scène*). One of the rare structural principles of this corpus is the frequent mixture of *abstract* and *concrete* terms, because of the "optical" nature of the theatre event or "performance." This mixture can sometimes be sensed within key concepts like *perspective, distance, role, stage, stage form*, etc. The contradiction of meanings is particularly fruitful when this concept is used to account for a concrete arrangement of the stage and a structural principle for its meaning.

The "photography" of a "state of the critical language" is made very difficult by the constant evolution of its vocabulary, the disappearance of certain terms, and the appearance of technical expressions or fashionable ones, or even those which open up new perspectives.

The metalanguage of theatre quickly goes out of fashion, since, as Szondi[5] has shown, in the evolution of dramaturgies there is always a gap between the *message of the form* and the *message of the content*, so that a form used is often no longer adapted to a new dramatic content. The same phenomenon of "time-lag" (or "out of sync") can be observed in the evolution of the critical apparatus which has been developed and adopted for classical dramaturgy (which can be made to span from classical seventeenth-century tragedy to the naturalistic "well-made play"). It corresponds to a dramaturgy founded on segmentation into acts and scenes, on characters representing a certain individuality, and on an illusionist mode of acting. The critical vocabulary describing this genre is extremely precise and readily normative. However, as soon as it is used, through lack of other tools, to account for modern forms, the results are as imprecise as they are misleading. How can we speak, for example, of a "happening" or of a Brechtian "*Lehrstuck*" in terms of action, character, or Story based on illusion?

New critical counter-languages appear in order to do better justice to theatre's evolution; thus, the Brechtian "counter-power" has a coherent set of concepts at its disposal ("A Short Organon for the Theatre"). This new language has become so indispensable, not only to clarify Brecht's plays, but to explain a whole post-Brechtian generation of stage-directors' work, that it has invaded the critical vocabulary and become a new norm. After form and ideology have further progressed, this norm will no longer be adapted to critical understanding, and will thus mask the originality of new practices and falsify the reading grid for future theatre events. The eternal problem of poetics is posed here: if the theatrical form is described by too general and fixed a model, the results are without interest and misinterpret the specific function of dramturgy or stage work. If, on the contrary, the model is too molded to the particular work, it tends to be nothing more than its replica—a scale model—without putting the work back into a more extensive ideological and aesthetic context, and thus without fitting it into a series of different works.

The evolution of critical discourse is explained, aside from these aesthetic-ideological variations, by the theoretical advances of the human sciences and the phenomenon of metaphorization, either "decorative" or productive, that they generate.

The human sciences—psychology, psychoanalysis, sociology, anthropology, etc.—and the structuralist method have left their mark forcefully on the domain of theatre terminology. Each science possesses its own concepts, but these are often not yet well established and tend to overlap into other areas. Thus criticism, even in its day-to-day manifestations (journalistic reviews), often calls upon psychoanalytical notions: the stage becomes, for example, the "unveiling" of the "other stage" where one finds rhetorically expressed an "unconscious figuration" that the spectator, in an act of "denial," recognizes and refuses at the same time, as part of his "inhibited ego" which henceforth is expressed without "censure" in the form of the characters' egos, and as "projections" of one's own "fantasies," etc. Is it always just a matter of the simple transfer of vocabulary, a new means of dressing up old "acquaintances" in fashionable language? Not at all, since a whole trend of *mise en scène*, and even the entire work of sign organization, strives to produce a raw material of images, gestures and behavior which tells us as much about the unconscious mechanisms of creation and the public's capacities for involvement as it does about the proper meaning of the character or text.

More than just a banal transfer of vocabulary or of methodology, the critical use of psychoanalytic terms reveals an approach attempting to produce by means of metaphor a more direct and more conscious relationship with the performance. However, we are still far from an adequate understanding of phenomena evoked by the psychoanalytical metaphor: this explains all the terms used to express *participation, involvement, activity* or structural *reading* by the audience. Here we sense quite clearly that the discourse is delineating a profound reality of the stage *event* and of *theatrical communication* (another obsessive metaphor of semiotics). Very often the discourse remains too metaphoric, referring tautologically to other equivalent terms, and it fails to account for these phenomena by means of a set of objective factors of the theatrical event. So the metaphor, technical jargon, or the "fleeting image" are not always signs of evasiveness or the impossibility of verbalizing; in the best cases, they try to appeal to the imagination and to theoretize an intuition which still needs to be definitively verbalized. Jacques Poulet, the critic of *L'Humanité* and *France Nouvelle* defends himself convincingly against the accusation of "metaphorical writing": "I have reached the conclusion that the imprecision and the (artisitic?) blurring my correspondents reproach me for can be justified as the accepted risk of a way of writing, which *is in fact* the difficult and exalting task of a confrontation of my preconceived ideas with whatever the artists create for me. Journalistic writing, short-lived though it may be, must still refrain from the frivolous, but I refuse to dot every 'i,' to rehash theatre history each time, and I count on the reader to make the metaphor, the litote, and the allusion work. Is this so dangerous ?"[6]

No, in itself, there is nothing dangerous in that! It all depends, so to speak, on the use of the metaphor and the allusion. In order to test that aspect, let us examine the collected press reviews for a single performance: the example chosen is a corpus of 32 texts published in the French and English press on *Measure for Measure*, directed by Peter Brook at the Bouffes du Nord in November 1978.[7] These texts, collected by the International Centre for Theatre Creation, constitute a more or less complete sampling of the press. They will permit us to compare common points and thematic divergences, ideological presuppositions, and a few stylistic "tics."

To start with, one is struck by the convergence of certain remarks, as if the place and type of *mise en scène* automatically attracted attention to a few strong points which distinguish it from more "common" productions. Six journalists comment at length on the nakedness, the "Jansenism," the "leprosy," the "dilapidation" of the theatre building. They frequently ponder the intellectual snobbery that exists in seeking out an abandoned space, "proletarian" and anti-representational, but end up declaring that Brook is above any suspicion of "hexagonal (i.e., French) snobbery" (*La Charente Libre*). The "Bouffes" is definitely worth a visit to admire this studied neglect and example of "poor" theatre (in the Brookean sense of the word). Only one critic (Irving Wardle of the London *Times*), finds a connection between this framework and Brook's radical approach to classical texts.

Another general outcry concerns the numerous foreign accents which make understanding difficult (*France-Soir, Le Figaro, Les Echos, La Nouvelle Republique*, even Guy Dumur in the *Nouvel Observateur*). Only one critic, T. Curtis of the *International Herald Tribune*, going beyond a very French impatience colored by xenophobia, outlines a dramaturgical justification for this mixing of accents. It is understandable that it is predominantly the English critics who question the translation of Shakespeare's play, before delivering their stamp of approval, without, however, defining this very "modernized and argotized" adaptation done in the taste of the day, by the translator Jean-Claude Carrière. The connection between this "reconditioned" text and the interpretation of the play remains without comment.

Another major group of remarks centered on criticism of the acting style. One very rarely finds a global analysis of the "ascetic," "ceremonial" style of acting; compliments and warnings are distributed according to the emotion produced by the actor, or to the experience or lack of certain actors. Moreover, the *mise en scène* is very often at the heart of discussion, even if this is only to state that it is too self-effacing in favor of the text and minimal decor, that the direction of the actors is "boring and unimaginative" and that Brook's technique becomes a "stylistic device" by repeating itself from one production to the next. What is demanded of the *mise en scène* would in fact go against the general meaning: harmonizing the accents, the contradictions, regrouping and banalizing the stylistic gaps and the mixing of genres.

In that respect, the inadequacies of critical discourse are the most startling. Saying that the *mise en scène* is "cold," "dense," "self-effacing," "assured," "adroit," "of a refreshing lack of affectation" does not really help the reader to perceive it. These considerations lack some unifying reflection on the reading of the Story, the rhythm of the acting, the mechanisms of illusion and of criticism, the arrangements of codes and of materials. However, we do have to acknowledge—and this is undoubtedly a new phenomenon in dramatic criticism—the theatricality and the stage event, even if there is a cruel lack of the instruments for their description.

This convergence of remarks should not mask the almost total absence of dramaturgical, ideological, and, *a fortiori*, semiological analysis (with the notable exception of Irving Wardle in the London *Times*). Observations are too fragmented and isolated to be integrated into a global explanation. For example, almost nothing is said about Brook's work on the actor, his physical relationship with the public, and the ephemeral aspect of the acting as an *event*. Finally, the critical discourse—probably because Brook has the status of a public monument—does not take the risk of discouraging or encouraging the public to go and see the play.

The unexpressed judgment seems to be: "obviously it is good because it is Shakespeare, directed by Brook, although it hasn't got that particular twist of the novel and the exceptional."

In spite of the variety of newspapers, of critical styles and talent, I shall attempt a "composite portrait" of these reviews. Titles vary from a simple and classical indication of the play's title, to an interpretive title expressing a general impression: "Ascetics' Rendezvous" (*Nouvel Observateur*), "High Mass à la Brook" (*Canard Enchainé*); to provocative and vulgar titling: "The public is asked to have some talent" (*Le Point*), "On a heap of straw" (*La Montagne*), "The English are furious: Peter Brook back at Barbès" (*France-Soir*). The composition of the reviews alternates a summary description mixed with emotional expressions, occasionally the historical contextualizing of the play, and finally, a commentary on the interpretation of the text and stage techniques used. The articles quite often conclude with a paradox, an expression of regret, a metaphor or witty punch line—"Falstaff wouldn't be laughing now" (Chalais), "She [the actress] gives the impression of a crevice—one with a great deal in it to be discovered" (Godard). Superlatives constitute basic stylistic ingredients: "Peter and William, two giants" (*L'Yonne Républicaine*), "Highly gifted Shakespeare . . . P. Brook, the most talked about English director . . . A high-flying performance . . . admirable acting . . . the young novice stunned by love and terror" (*Télérama*).

One also often finds extraordinary anecdotes about the genial artist, and unusual and paradoxical formulae. The discourse is by nature allusive; it lets us imagine, with a knowing wink at the reader, remarks that are very profound but, unfortunately, too complex and too long to feature in the text. Such allusion very often works by the transfer from the specificity of theatre into other artistic domains: the play is like a horror story, an animated cartoon, a film, etc. In themselves, these remarks could be very interesting if only they referred more explicitly to the techniques and the ways of using procedures borrowed from other arts or intellectual activities.

The ideological presuppositions of the discourse of the critic should by now be very apparent from this brief summary. Without mentioning every newspaper's own political stance—which at any rate in our world of "freedom of expression" need not even be directly indicated in the art pages of the daily press, the drama critic being something of an artist and as such only "half-responsible"—we can note a suppressed ideological discourse—suppressed, but weighing down the aesthetic commentary. It takes the form of the image that every critic quite rightfully has written about what "real theatre" should be. "Real theatre is a great deal more than just theatre," Jamet reveals in *Le Journal du Dimanche*. Tesson confides, in *Le Canard Enchaîné*, that those spectators who do not like Brookian ceremonials and asceticism "like something else, which *might* be called theatre, but is nothing but its bastardized form." Every critic and even every critical text pursues this fleeting image of *real* theatre—this right must be left to the critic as it is to the scholar—and the quest for the phantom is renewed with each new "writing test." But the reader is left with his appetite unappeased, especially if he is hardly familiar with this aesthetic world.

Moreover, his image of theatre is almost always split between a banal theatre for the uncultivated masses, and an experimental form to which only the "happy few" have access. The ideological stance is rarely as clear as in *Le Figaro*: the journalist there would have preferred to see Brook accuse mankind ("his human nature and vices," the "first defect of his natural state, the original sin of mankind") rather than the power which corrupts society. We keep on finding what Barthes called the bourgeois sense of the quantitative and the visible, in the thanks directed to Brook for "a new proof of real work" (*La Croix*) and for the total physical commitment of the actors.

In their accumulated form these ideological presuppositions end up by creating a very solid horizon of expectations.[8] Given that it is Shakespeare produced by an Englishman in an unconventional theatre with the actors of an international research center, we should expect such and such a result, and the performance must be read by means of exactly such a critical grid! Overall, critical discourse knows the tune in advance, being all too familiar with what it is based on. This is what happens when the results are known to the reviewer before the inquiry has even begun.

From one article to another journalistic criticism oscillates between an "objective" description and a self-sufficient (in both senses of the word) exercise in style. But this opposition between description and autonomous writing, between objectivity and subjectivity, is in fact sterile; at any rate it should not separate critics into zealous servants or repressed writers.

Dramatic criticism has not really followed the movement which split literary criticism into old and new criticism, probably because, quite rightly, from the very start there could be few illusions about the "scientificity" ("objectivity," "clarity," "good taste") of any discourse on theatre. Freed from the obsession with the scientific, dramatic criticism has managed to extract the best from both worlds, the reviewer of a performance was never afraid of implicating his personal views in his judgments, and the awareness of his responsibility as a writer has often, in the best of cases, revealed a great deal about the artistic work of theatre people. So today we might almost (obviously, in the most favorable hypotheses) add to the three-fold function of dramatic criticism—"aesthetic police, objective statement and above all publicity"[9]—that of a parallel reflection *in* and *on* scenic and literary writing.

After this detour through journalistic criticism here we are back again—in a well-known example of critical circularity!—at semiology and its place in the concert of voices commenting on theatrical performance. Does semiology absolutely *have to be* opposed to the "bad example" of journalistic criticism as the only scientific and serious approach available? This is what often happens to it, but this "excess of honor" runs the risk of being fatal to it. On the one hand, semiology should not be an abstract discourse on a few signs: in fact it is concerned with the very concrete organization of signs and artistic systems and in that respect should be of prime interest to the "on the spot critic": one "does" semiology as naturally as one "speaks in prose." No critical writing can exist without a metacritical, hermeneutical and epistemological reflection on its own mechanisms, and semiology seems the best equipped to supply it with such a methodology.

It might be utopian to dream of enriching drama criticism by such theoretical demands. In his paper at the Venice Biennale in 1968 Bernard Dort saw as an alternative to the criticism of consumption, a "criticism of the theatre fact as an aesthetic fact and [a] critique of the social and political conditions of theatre activity," that is, a "semiological critique of the theatre performance" and a "sociological critique of theatre activity."[10] But if this separation is frequent in the methodology of theatre, it would be dangerous for this youthful and yet ancient science of semiology to find itself isolated from the conditions of production of the performance. If semiology wants to get out of an academic and pseudo-scientific ghetto, it would be in its best interests to insinuate itself into the cracks of official discourse, into the truncated columns of the dailies, and into the discourses of the producers and consumers of theatre.[11]

Translated by Susan Melrose

Footnotes

[1]Jean Starobinski, *La Relation critique* (Paris: Gallimard, 1970), p. 12.

[2]Roland Barthes, *Critique et vérité* (Paris: Seuil, 1966).

[3]*Op. cit.*, p. 56.

[4]*Dictionnaire du théâtre, Termes et concepts de l'analyse théâtrale* (Paris: Editions Sociales, 1980).

[5]P. Szondi, *Theorie des modernen Dramas* (Frankfurt: Suhrkamp, 1956).

[6]Poulet, Jacques, "De l'objectivité a la subjectivité, et retour?" in *France Nouvelle* of 8/11/76.

[7]Dossier de presse, *Centre International de Créations Théâtrales*, 9, Rue du Cirque, 75008 Paris.

[8]On this notion see H.R. Jauss, *Ästhetische Erfahrung und literarische Hermeneutik I*, München U.T.B., Fink Verlag, 1977.

[9]Bernard Dort, "Les deux critiques," in *Théâtre réel*, (Paris: Seuil, 1971), p. 44. (Paper presented at "Un teatro per une nuova societa," XXVIIe festival internazionale del teatro di prosa, 1968.)

[10]*Op. Cit.*, p. 47.

[11]This text expands parts of my paper presented at the Second International Congress of

Semiotics, Vienna, July 1979.

Reflections on the Notation
of the
Theatrical Performance

This article was first published in Ernest Hess-Lüttich's reader *The Semiotics of Theatre*, Narr Verlag, 1982. A French version was published in *Revue d'Histoire du théâtre*, no. 1, 1982.

Among the lamentations of theatre scholars over their field of study, the old problem of the impossibility of notating and conserving the performance remains high on the list. Whatever the system of notation used, it is readily acknowledged that the notation of the performance simplifies it to the point of impoverishment. Generally, one concludes in advance that this undertaking which consists of talking *about* theatre by making theatre talk is hopeless and doomed from the start. Undoubtedly, every performance loses a great deal—even to the point of its specificity and its very existence—when it is reduced to a system of notation, even one which is highly perfected and thorough. But the reduction is not purely a technical problem, as is frequently imagined; notation is inadequate, not because the necessary technology to make a record of the *mise en scène* is lacking, but because no description can do other than radically modify the object it describes. To "notate" the performance inevitably means to interpret, to make a more or less conscious choice among the multitude of signs of the performance deemed *noteworthy*.

In the course of this overview of some of the methods of theatre notation and of the theatrical problems involved, we shall consider how transcriptions are undertaken, and which systems are responsible for the mediation between the performance/object, and the spectator/reader. As will become apparent, the basic question is not *how to* carry out the notation, but *for what purpose*. The purpose of such work affects the choice of method and the level of approach and formalization of the *mise en scène*: do we want to describe theatre in order to preserve the traces it leaves behind, to give ourselves the means of reproducing it, to become aware of its specificity, or to be able to describe it in a fashion which is already an interpretation? Whatever the case, the question of notation poses a serious semiological problem since we have to specify what operations are necessary for the description of the theatre object: if on the one hand we admit as necessary and indispensable the mediation of a natural language to "denote" the *mise en scène*, our orientation is that of *semiology*: "Semiology postulates, in a more or less explicit manner, the necessary mediation of natural languages in the process of reading the signifieds which belong to non-linguistic semiotic systems (image, painting, architecture, etc.); on the other hand, semiotics discards them" (Greimas, 1979:338).

This opposition between semiology and semiotics opens the way to two different methods of description: the first, semiological, takes into account discourse as the metalanguage of the object described; the other, semiotic, constructs a language whose syntax and rules will suffice to restore to us the object described. Most current systems of notation make use of discourse at one point or another in their descriptions, often in order to avoid the construction of a symbolic system which would be so complex that only the user would have the key to it. Occasionally, on the contrary—and particularly so in the notation of movements within the acting space—notation calls upon a conventional non-linguistic system of graphics. Another semiological problem is posed by the connections between the object to be described and its actual description. This is an argument well-known to philosophers of knowledge: How do we differentiate between a real object and one's knowledge of that object? Does the real object already have a meaning and a structure before the intervention of the perceiving subject? Is there a meaning of the product and a meaning of its reception? An aesthetician like M. Nadin clearly poses the existence of an immanent aesthetic meaning, and of another meaning released by the descriptive meta-language: "Thus, we have to deal with the fundamental question of the relationship between the signs which constitute the aesthetic meaning (and not only aesthetic) of the theatrical work and the signs which participate, at the level of the metalanguage, in the release of that meaning and, resulting from this, of the value judgment which integrates as much the aesthetic criteria (the theatre act designated as of specific value), as all the other criteria concerning the socio-historical realization of theatre" (1978:19). We might want to contest this separation of an independent aesthetic meaning from that meaning released by the meta-language; if the theatre object indeed exists even before the critical intervention, only the metalanguage—whether a concrete notation or a mental notation of some aspects of the work—can really make of theatre an object of knowledge, and manage thus to make it meaningful (in many different ways, obviously). So not only is notation a "necessary evil," but it is precisely notation which gives the theatrical performance its meaning: there exists *no* description and interpretation without some pre-existing form of *notation*. This indicates the extraordinary weight of this notion for the constitution of a semiology of the theatre; our sole ambition here is to outline a few theoretical problems, to name and evaluate a number of currently employed techniques of notation, and to make a number of suggestions for a possible semiology of theatrical notation.

I. NOTATION AND PROBLEMS OF THEORY

The following reflections deal with the notation of the performance, that is, with the notation of the stage realization of the dramatic text.

For the text itself, notation traditionally takes the form of linguistic transcription, with its own methods suitable for indicating change of speaker and the author's or director's stage directions. But as soon as one wishes to describe the unfolding of a concrete production, the system of notation must take into account an unlimited ensemble which can cover visual and acoustic phenomena expressed by means of stage systems. The very term *notation* reveals a logocentric attitude towards theatre: it implies that one transcribes into a visual system signs which are either linguistic (description by means of language) or iconic (mimetic reproduction of scenic objects). In both cases, the *written* character of notation becomes evident. Both symbolic and iconic notation present specific advantages and should be used in combination.

Iconic notation gives a figurative representation of objects on stage: decor, costumes, action set-up. It does not hesitate to exaggerate certain pertinent traits of the represented object, and resembles in this the techniques of close-up and caricature. Its immediacy and obviousness imply a certain imprecision in the mimetic rendering and in the subjective interpretation by whoever does the design or takes the photographs. This direct communication by ostension can sometimes make the reproduction of a performance difficult, for while the general impression is often well rendered, the sense of detail or of proportion may be lost.

Symbolic notation, on the contrary, is not immediately comprehensible, since in this type of digital communication, the reader must possess the key to the sign conventions. The most famous example of such symbolic encoding is the notation made by Polti of the gesture of the Discobolus in the Museum of the Louvre: 115 signs, composed of letters, numbers, and invented signs, are necessary to describe, in nine lines, the pose of the statue. On the other hand, symbolic notation is remarkably well-suited to the outlining of the actors' movements, and to describing the connections between text, music, and gesture, "orchestrated" on one single score (cf. Kowzan, 1979).

But even before deciding on one of these basic modes of notation, one has to determine the function of such a description, adapting the transcription accordingly. Obviously, one might want to notate a performance for a whole range of different purposes: preservation of the *mise en scène* to facilitate the work of the actors during rehearsals; preservation for future genereations as a result of the legal deposition of the *mise en scène* in the library of the "*association des régisseurs de théâtre*" (Paris); notation for an interpretation in the case of semiological analysis and in the elaboration of the "performance-text." The apparent dividing line in these cases of notation runs along the distinction between a *notation for preservation* and a *notation for interpretation*. However, in practice, it is nearly impossible to merely *preserve* (without interpreting), or merely *interpret* (without preserving at least a few elements of the performance). Often, attempts at notation would like to avoid the subjectivity of the analyst by gathering only observable and objective facts: but, it should be clear that there can be no notation without a pre-existing interpretation of the *mise en scène*, even if this interpretation is unconscious or denied. Reciprocally, every attempt to explain the performance presupposes that one chooses a few noteworthy signs.

This necessary confusion between preservation and interpretation suggests that a degree of flexibility must always be maintained between the object described and the method of description. In particular, one should make sure to adapt to each type of theatrical performance a specific mode of description, and to observe thus a constant "to and fro" movement between method and object, in order to discover hidden aspects of the work thanks to the use of the particular method of description, and to make sure that the analysis of the work has a retroactive effect on the constitution of the theory.

The status of the language used in the description of the performance is highly problematic; we might define it as metalanguage, but this metalanguage either employs a linguistic discourse or on the contrary is articulated by means of an independent system of units. There, too, only a *semiotics* (in the sense used by Greimas) would be capable of visually representing the theatre object described, of giving a symbolic notation to it, i.e., a notation which "uses in the form of conventional graphics (geometrical figures, letters, abbreviations, initials, etc.) a set of symbols" and "is used in the visual representation of constitutive units of a metalanguage" (Greimas, 1979: 257). No metalanguage of this type has ever existed for theatre: this can easily be explained by the diversity of meaning systems in performance and the impossibility of homogenizing them into one sole notation. Thus we have to return to a semiology which attempts at best to combine iconic notation and symbolic notation, to assume the presuppositions of its critical discourse and to match its theory to the particular performance. Consequently, one should not detach the metalanguage from the analyzed object, but should seek its traces or suggestions within the performance itself. In fact, the "noteworthy" elements can be indicated not only by the stage directions, but also by the *mise en scène*, which emphasizes (and manifests) the artistic devices, the ideological suggestions, the verbal or visual rhetorical constructs. These "effects of strangeness" ("alienation effects," in the Brechtian sense) only exist if they are picked up by the spectator; their function as commentary and metadiscourse is thus obvious and, therefore, a systematic notation of performance could be elaborated on their bases. A comparison between the *film script* (which precedes the work of the director) and the notation of the *performance-text* will throw particular light on this difference between metalanguage and notation. In the case of the script, the notes for the eventual *mise en scène* are presented as autonomous objects, whose significance will be constituted by the acts of interpretation and notation: an adequate metalanguage is the object of a research which calls as much upon the observation of artisitic and ideological effects as upon the external contribution of a "ready-made" system of notation.

Once the function of the notation has been decided upon, and the best metalanguage chosen, one still has to establish the levels of formalization and the elements of performance one wishes to transcribe. As we shall see later, each method of transcription seizes hold of one particular domain and one particular aspect of the theatre performance. The desire for an exhaustive approach in one system of notation has all too often created the desire to gather *every* element of the performance under the heading of one sole aspect. As E. Hess-Lüttich remarks: "In critically comparing current efforts in different research projects, we can verify that *no system* of notation can take into account all the desiderata: there is no single, *ideal* system" (1979:208). Most of the time, all notation does is record the position of a gesture, an item of the decor, a musical refrain, a pause in the verbal utterance. In these cases, such observations remain fragmentary and unsystematic. As soon as notation regroups several observations of the same type, it begins to organize itself in systems of logical oppositions. This is the case of the dramaturgical choices and of the options of the *mise en scène*. This type of notation—which is the same as an interpretation—is based on the discovery of a logical structure of similarities and oppositions; it regroups according to several general principles a large number of observations of which exhaustive accounting would be an overwhelming task. By permitting, in the recording of the notation system, the systematization of given facts, one places oneself on the level of theoretical abstraction, so that notation is no longer a pure description, but also an interpretation. Thus, for example, we can always read the performance by establishing the actantial model of the characters, by visualizing the schema of relations between those characters. Notation cannot fail to profit from such theoretical schemata, which take into account the whole universe of signification and thereby prevent the "describer" (let us use this term for the person responsible for the notation of performance) from only picking out insignificant details. But at the same time, one runs the risk of betraying the patient and technically exacting work of notation, concentrating only on the "deep reading" of the performance.

All of these theoretical difficulties—which frequently are not even mentioned, as though notation were merely a technical problem which does not involve the performance's meaning—have certainly not prevented the birth of diverse notation procedures. Each procedure has its own particular virtues and limitations, is more or less codified, and always corresponds to a certain conception of theatre and of what one can hope to preserve from the performance.

II. A FEW EXAMPLES OF NOTATION TECHNIQUES

The production book of the *mise en scène* is one of the most valuable instruments available to us for obtaining an idea of the way the text has been staged, especially if it originates from the director's own circle and if it contains in a concentrated form all the indications given in the direction of actors and technicians. At its best, it tends to become a second text, a stage text, which is superimposed over the dramatic text and which becomes the property of the director. As a matter of fact, these records of the *mise en scène* must in theory be deposited in the "library for stage directors" (*Bibliothèque des régisseurs de théâtre*), just as one submits an invention for patenting. In this last instance of notation, the technique used is essentially quantitative: all the details given on every aspect of the performance, from casting down to the names of the companies supplying equipment, are systematically compiled (cf. Vierge, 1956). Of course, the method of presentation varies from one compiler to another; the norm is to write the notes parallel to the text by a system of cross-references. Often the notes describe the attitude and the psychology of the character when he pronounces such and such a word. The commentator is left complete freedom to specify the motivations of the character, deeper meaning of the acting styles, the pauses and the rhythm of the text. Thus the production book of the *mise en scène* becomes a written materialization, the complete score of the work on stage. It reveals to us the intimate vision of its compiler, which is at the same time very valuable and somewhat misleading; indeed, one has the impression that the notation is too authoritarian, that it gives too precise a direction to the reading of the performance. Obviously, an observer from outside the production would have perceived different aspects, and we are troubled by commentaries which may be descriptive, philosophical or moralizing: thus in his *Mise en scène de Phèdre*, Jean Louis Barrault strews his notes with metaphysical, musical and psychological remarks which tell us more about his concept of theatre and of Racine than about the concrete *mise en scène*. Nonetheless, this notation of the *mise en scène* remains a document of considerable importance, a materialization of the optical and acoustic vision of the director at work. A director like Max Reinhardt has left us very precious evidence of his work: his transcription becomes the epitome of stage research. We see each gesture, each step, each piece of furniture, the light; we hear each vocal inflection, each rising tone, the musicality of expressions, the pauses, the different *tempi*. We sense every internal emotion, we know when it must be hidden and when exposed, we hear each catch of breath and each return to normal breathing, we sense the listening of the stage partner, and every sound occurring on stage or off; we feel the influence of the lighting. Then everything is noted down, perfect optical and acoustic visions as if on a score. It is hard to follow, because all the indications are merging, mysteriously, without any reflection or work. We do not know why we hear and see the things we do in just one way rather than another. Hard to note it down (quoted in Passow, 1971:IV). Max Reinhardt sums up in this passage an attempt at seizing hold of the performance, and at rewriting its complete score. His score of *Faust* by Goethe is one of almost unsurpassable precision and intelligibility, thanks principally to the descriptions of movements, to the sketches of decor, and to the psychological and physiognomical directions for the actors (cf. Passow, 1971).

Sometimes production books present a photographic image of the performance, but they still remain a poor substitute for it. In order to remedy this drawback, certain directors work throughout rehearsals with a score, but one which is divided into individual scores entrusted to each actor.

For Schechner, for example, the score functions as a tool: "a throughline is developed for each role which corresponds to the need to locate the exact physical actions, musical tones, and rhythms that embody the themes and moods of the production . . . the performer's score gives him anchor points—moments of contact, an underlying rhythm, secure details: places to go from and get to" (Schechner, 1976:150). Precisely how each actor actually transcribes his course through the performance is unimportant: the notation is likely to be quite unsystematic, an aid to memory rather than a symbolic notation. Such an individual score does open up perspective on the stage seen "from within"; it only acquires meaning when placed in the context of all the individual scores of the actors, a context which is achieved through the director's or spectator's synthesizing and comparative gaze. At the end of such a comparison and cooperation, we are in possession of the global performance-text: "I go to each performance of a play I am directing, not out of duty; and I am not bored. I experience the changes in the score, the variations and modulations, with an excitement. I reflect on the overall pattern of the performance: the development of the story, the leitmotifs. I concern myself with the arrangements and relationships among all theatrical languages: verbal, body, contact, and musical" (Schechner, 1976:151). The score here becomes the passage from an individual text of directions for each actor to a performance text noting the pertinent relationships between stage systems. Notation is not a simple mechanism of transcription, but the outline of the performance and the laboratory wherein its meaning is constructed.

Alongside these compilations of notes for the *mise en scène* intended for the use of the actors, and, sometimes, the researcher, we might direct our interest towards something which, although apparently not conceived for the purpose of conserving the traces of the *mise en scène*, is occasionally very revealing of declared or hidden intentions: theatre programs made available to the audience, press kits, notes relating to the *mise-en-scene*, documents quoted from, and any text that the spectator is invited to read in connection with the play. Such texts supply the "framework" for reception of the play, giving orientation to dramaturgical and stage readings of it, drawing attention to the "artistic discourse" of the theatrical team. However, this type of documentation is difficult to evaluate; it does not necessarily allude to what is to be perceived in the play, but it aims at making the spectator receptive to the play through quotes from other texts or artistic practices (Pavis, 1980, article *cadre*). Work from the raw material of documents is hardly easier. What the English call "documenting the production" must not simply consist of accumulating documents and reconstituting them without any explanation. All too often, theatre archivists are satisfied with amassing facts (photos, audio-visual recordings, drawings of costumes and decor) without explaining how they were used in the *mise en scène*. No isolated stage element acquires its meaning unless its role in the stage enunciation is understood. And that is precisely what is the most difficult to reconstitute: the arrangement, at any given moment, of the performance, of objects and actors, the connections between the stage materials and the rhythm in which they are used.

Indications about the prosodic quality of the text constitute a source of prime importance for the *mise en scène*, and the authors wishing to indicate the correct manner of uttering the text have started out by using them. Current linguistic research into the paralinguistic phenomena of communication, together with methods of transcribing recorded dialogue are of particular benefit in this area. These methods consist of transcribing by a system of conventions the noises of a conversation, the kinesic and proxemic exchanges, the qualilty and expressivity of the voice. However, there are no universally employed prosodic signs, and the system of Gerard de Vire, a playwright from the sixteenth century, appears to be a basic system which gives a general account of the diction of the text. For his plays, de Vire uses seven symbols defined as follows (cf. Ryngaert, 1972:194):

ll or *l/*	: pause
⊢ or *(⊏)*	: two pauses
†	: three pauses
𝓗 or *(l)*	: movement all around the stage area

γ or (α) : low voice
$\mathfrak{D}$: faster speech than the rest
$/$: slower speech than the rest

This system has not been taken up elsewhere, although it does supply a basic "prosodic punctuation." If it seems to be very general and hardly practicable today, that is so in part because we are no longer accustomed to a very rhetorical and codified type of recitation which operates according to extremely repetitive constants far removed from expressive realism. Musical notation remains too tied to the composition of song or music to supply a basis for transcription of rhythm and tonality of voices. One notable exception to this is the notation used by E.F. Burian, who suggests the utilization of the musical system to outline rhythmic order and the "pause-patterns." Rhythmic variations for one sentence ("it was a fine night") are noted within the context of the rhythmic structure of the whole work:

> Each play conceived of in a rhythmic system is called a pause-play. If the value of the note in one measure equals that of a pause, it is then necessary to take this value into account for the measuring of words as well as for the structure of the sentence. Pauses in the stage text are not simply a matter of rhythmic division; nor are they simple interruptions in the tempo of the acting. Pauses function not only on the physical but also on the psychological level; and, it is because they have a physical action that they produce a psychological echo. Only by mastering the rhythmic structure of the play is one able to master the pause-play. Unimaginative directors imagine that a pause is merely an interruption characteristic of the situation and the text. It is not correct to say that a pause is determined simply by the mental state of the dramatic character. It depends just as much on the global rhythmic structure of the dramatic work. One should not arbitrarily disrupt the monologue or dialogue with a pause; even less so if this pause does not correspond to a rhythmical value or to a set of rhythmical values of the whole text or whole play (1939:24).

For the first time here, so it seems, the pause is no longer considered an isolated phenomenon, but an element within an entire rhythmical structure which is dependent equally upon visual systems and the global discourse of the *mise en scène*. This observation suggests a method of codification which does not isolate the prosodic facts, but which takes them into account in the ensemble of all the different signs of the performance. Such a system of notation has yet to be invented, however.

As for the (notation of) movements, on the contrary, there is no lack of systems. We shall leave aside for a moment the notation of the actor's gesture (Pavis, 1980), to concentrate on that of the movements on stage of all the actors in relationship to the recitation of the text. Here again, notation borrows frequently from the musical system. N. Ivanov suggests, for example, a "theatrical semiography" and transcribes the positions of the actors by dividing up the stage space into horizontal lines parallel with the footlights (corresponding to a distance of about fifty centimeters apart). To reconstitute the quality of movement, especially its intensity and duration, Ivanov uses musical notes (white, black, quavers and semi-quavers). To indicate the direction of a movement (from audience to backstage and vice versa), he adds to the note a sharp or a flat. Each actor becomes the object of a musical score, and, just as with the orchestral score, the individual scores are notated one under the other. By inventing other signs to take into account the pauses, the *legato*, the *tempi*, and the intensity, and by combining all this with the "text" of the lighting, we would reach the level of a complete orchestration for stage.

The precision and the usefulness of such a mode of transcription are obvious and if that system or its equivalent has not inspired many other systems, no doubt it is because of poor diffusion and insufficient motivation on the part of directors to systematize their discourse. However, Ivanov's method is, of course, neither universal nor definitive. It is suitable for notating stage figurations in an essentially quantitative manner; one should also have the possibility of adding to it facts on the kinetic interaction of the actors, and particularly the systems of direction of gazes, facial expressions, and gestures, which modalize the speech. This system of notation remains the offshoot of a certain conception of the *mise en scène* which is reduced to the stage movements and the recitation of the text. This is in fact just the tip of the iceberg and what remains of the actors' and the director's work therefore deserves all the more attention.

Alongside these clearly technical systems of performance notation (carried out by the "technicians" of theatre: archivists, theoreticians of gesture and voice, critics, university researchers), we find currently a series of less specialized approaches which usually emanate from the creative side or from those theatres which wish to analyze and preserve a particular *mise en scène* for possible future work. These attempts are characterized by a concern not for the exhaustive and the scientific, but for globality and for a dramaturgical analysis of the performance. The best example is the Brechtian *Modellbuch*, which contains a goldmine of information and documentation on performances directed by Brecht at the Berliner Ensemble (Brecht, 1961). Each *"Regiebuch"* is composed of remarks on rehearsals and textual study accompanied by a complete photographic ensemble. Fifteen hundred photos are taken for each performance, on two different occasions, from the same position: the first balcony, almost in the middle, high up, so that the whole stage *Arrangement* of the actors can be grasped. Two types of scene are of particular interest to the photographer: entrances, exits and changes of positioning; and the specific movements and characteristic gestures. The final selection of the photographs is made on the basis of their ability to illustrate the unfolding of the Story and to reveal its turning points. The director's assistant would already have noted in the text the passages to be photographed. This work is carried out in constant relation to the dramaturgical preparation of the play, particularly when it concerns the search for the play's turning points, its tragic, comic or poetic moments. The photos occasionally help specify, correct, or eliminate an inadequate pose or grouping of actors. After this preparatory phase, photos considered more "aesthetically pleasing" but always just as informative are taken at essential points to reveal connections of meaning and visible contradictions of the protagonists. Finally, a precise documentation is completed with photos for which the actors have posed before or after the performance (costumes, decor, masks, props, etc.).

The dedication and the intelligence of this method are obvious. Its connections with theory and practice of theatre are particularly close. The *Modellbuch* gives an image of the *Grundgestus* of the play; of the interaction of characters and groups in their movements; of the dividing up of general episodes into particular episodes; of the considerations on the characterization of the *dramatis personae* and on the social significance of the events" (1961:296). What may appear surprising and unexpected is the function assigned by Brecht to the *Modellbuch*: "It is obvious that this work is only of value when a performance is worthy of being imitated, or at least imitated in certain details. Its greatest value resides in the fact that something may be conserved for future time, be it the acting style, the decor, or our present taste. Every performance is instructive, and we can learn equally well from the bad ones" (1961:296). If there is nothing to object to here when it comes to notation, we might nonetheless feel slightly perturbed by the aesthetic and ideological presuppositions of this *Modellbuch*. Even if Brecht makes it clear that future *mises en scène* should never be a slavish imitation of the "model," future creators are nonetheless invited to "restore the meaning, the *Gestus*, the content" (1961:315), and thus, to respect the ideological core of the play. This would seem acceptable from any other author than Brecht, who advocated in his own adaptations a totally free use of text considered as mere "construction material." But perhaps we should only see in this contradiction the contradiction of every system of notation which claims to work for other productions and which combines a descriptive commentary with a tightly worked dramaturgical interpretation.

Further examples of this type of global description and mixed notation (commentary and photos) can be found in the *Voies de la création théâtrale*, which are devoted to relatively recent productions of contemporary and classical works. With no unified methodological background, the *Voies*

nonetheless observe a certain number of "golden rules" in response to requirements identical to those of the *Modellbuch* and which are concerned
with giving equal space to highly precise stage description, dramaturgical
text analysis, and an outline of the *mise en scène*. The implicit semiological
presupposition of these studies lies in their affirmation of the *stage* as the
center of theatrical meaning. As for the "ethic" of the notation, it can be
summed up as the desire to gather as much material as possible by integrating descriptions of photos with a global interpretation of the *mise en
scène* and of the dramaturgical choices.

One could have expected that new theatrical practices (improvisation,
théâtre-récit, collective creation) would bring with them a certain reflection
on their own notation, or even a new method for it. The reality is unfortunately rather different: retranscription makes use of the same old graphic
devices (photos with commentary and text of the dialogue). Particularly
disappointing for example, is the very flat notation of *1789* in the Théâtre
Ouvert collection, published by Stock, despite its alluring subtitle:
"Photographie d'un spectacle" (p. 3), the information of the production is
contained in a theoretical (and almost ritual) text on collective creation and
improvisation (Théâtre du Soleil, 1971:81-96). The dramatic text is
retranscribed without any indication of its use in the theatrical space; the
photographs never refer to a specific moment in the text, they seem to aim
at restoring the atmosphere of movement and celebration (*fête*): the
photographic notation is here nothing but an aperitif—to an absent meal.

High hopes have been held for audio-visual recording; probably too
much so, since the results are not necessarily any better than those of the
commentary, of the score, or of the sequence of photos. For it is simply not
enough to improve the quality of the recording, to make the sound less
distorted, the image more faithful to the original: one also has to underline
the pertinent units and characteristics of the performance; otherwise, it is
constantly necessary to refer the potential analyst of the performance back
to the recording itself, relocating the relevant passage, and replaying it as
often as necessary. Any notation implies a theoretization, as simplification
and the choice of a few basic structuring signs. A pure mimetic and
"reproducible" communication of the performance should not prevent the
analyst from interpreting and "deconstructing" the theatre object. If this
work of mediation and description appears here more difficult than the
work based on the performance itself, it is because theatre has thus been
surreptitiously transformed into another medium (sound-tape, video recording, or film). Therefore, in order to recover its initial character of theatre-
fact, one now has to take into account its newly acquired specificity. It
would seem, paradoxically, that theatre has first to be transformed into
something else, in order to be accounted for: to describe is always to
destroy.

The recording of sound (on record or tape) does not serve simply to record voices and the intonations of the actors: it makes us aware of the rhythm of the performance (and all the more so since one is deprived of the image, which "cement" together the different moments of the action, and often masks the phrasing and the prosodic rhetoric of the text as well as the devices and the "vocal tics" of the actors!). Such recording functions as does the counter on a tape recorder, structuring and segmenting the performance in preparation for theatre archives.

Video recording is the modern equivalent of the performance production book, but it is much more precise and allows one to consider all stage materials in their proper relationships. We could say about this technique almost word for word what one usually says about the film adaptation of a literary work. Even if there is no editing after the shooting of the film and if the scenes are shot from one fixed point with no camera change or close-ups, the video film imposes by its own particular framing a limited and *partial* vision. It is not useful for the camera to film the whole stage area from an unchanging distance; it concentrates on that area of the stage space where the characters of the given scene are performing. The main advantage (but also the ambiguity) of video-taping is undoubtedly the possibility it has of stopping at one particular image, of repeating one particular sequence. We are back again at that old day-dream of the theatre analyst who would like to be able to reflect at his leisure upon certain moments of the performance, by violating the dictate of the temporal uniqueness of the theatre event. But this game of play/replay—hardly a game of fair-play for the actors!—is still not a deconstruction of the *mise en scène*; we would still have to begin by making manifest the artistic procedures used, by extracting the codes in the images and in the text. In short, video-taping encourages us to elaborate a semiology of its own specificity, involving the mediation of camera and of video filming in its capturing of meaning produced on the theatre stage.

Thus audio-visual notation, in the best of cases, is nothing more than a faithful replica of the *mise en scène*; it is a first step towards a real written symbolic notation. Quite the opposite of the filming process, the final stage of performance notation is that of the *découpage* and the synopsis of the performance; both procedures interpret the production as much as they record it. The connection between the state of technological development and the dominant system of notation is manifest; what is less obvious is that every technique of notation corresponds less to a way of seeing and emphasizing certain elements of the performance, than a way of failing to see other elements. It is quite simply a question of being aware of what one is able to discover or to discard.

It might be very difficult to notate a theatre piece based mostly on stage images. In her book, which coined the expression "Theatre of Images,"

Bonnie Marranca (1977) undertook to transcribe three avant-garde plays: *Pandering to the Masses: A Misrepresentation* by Richard Foreman; *A Letter to Queen Victoria* by Robert Wilson; *The Red Horse Animation* by Lee Breuer.

Foreman's play is notated in a fairly traditional way, since it contains dialogues, characters and precise stage-directions. Wilson refers to his plays as an opera, although it is mostly a verbal declamation. The scenario as printed in Marranca's book gives a very visual picture of the rhythm, showing clearly the repetitive patterns, the exchanges of lines and the language games between Christopher Knowles and Bob Wilson. The typography gives the impression of a computer-like text, which is to be understood as an accumulation of informations and an exchange of coded messages, of which the spectator never gets the key.

It seemed the most difficult task to write about Lee Breuer's *Red Horse Animation*, because the notation system had to take into account a very unusual delivery style, since "structured as a choral narrative, the piece compels the actors to speak *out* rather than speak to one another" (Marranca, 1977:113). In order to give an image of the specific use of space, the script was transformed into a comic strip using clear forms and bright colors. This seemed a good solution to give a visual feeling of the spatial image and to have the viewer feel the "physicality of the text," which "is duplicated in the actors' rigorous body movements: spinning, acrobatic falls, turning and rolling over" (Marranca, 1977:116).

In these three examples of contemporary theatre, it seemed that a specific notation system had to be invented, and that the notation was more than "a way of remembering"; it became an art object, both the work of art and the commentary on it. It showed that notation did not have to be abstract and scientific to be both precise and imaginative.

Every method of notation cosidered up to this point comes to grief at the same problems of the transcription of the acting style, of the *rhythm* of the *mise en scène*, of the *interaction* between stage and audience, and, globally, of the *interdependence* of the stage arts and techniques. It is precisely in these areas that semiology can help us formulate a few methodological remarks. These will certainly not lead to a "miracle notation," but they will perhaps prepare the ground for a coherent outline of the basic signs of the performance; to the "reading and writing" of the performance-text.

III. TOWARDS A SEMIOLOGY OF NOTATION

Curiously enough, the preoccupation with the notation of the theatrical is not the prerogative of bloodless technocrats and scientists; this "obsession" can be found in numerous "mythical projects" of the greatest theoreticians and artists. These experiments are mythical insofar as they do not envisage a concrete application of their intuitions to any kind of technology, but imagine their notation as a mirage and a limit toward which theatre tends and in which it runs the risk of annihilation. These mythical projects provide a natural starting-point for our "daydreaming" on the "writing" of performance.

In the *Theatre and Its Double*, Artaud is searching for a new language of the stage which is capable of moving beyond the old conception of that stage as the refraction of a pre-existing text. But this new language cannot take shape without some method capable of preserving its force and its specificity: a system of notation which transcribes everything which goes beyond the spoken word:

> Meanwhile new means of recording this language must be found, whether these means belong to musical transcription or to some kind of code.
>
> As for ordinary objects, or even the human body, raised to the dignity of signs, it is evident that one can draw one's inspiration from hieroglyphic characters, not only in order to record these signs in a readable fashion which permits them to be reproduced at will, but in order to compose on the stage precise and immediately readable symbols.
>
> On the other hand, this code language and musical transcription will be valuable as a means of transcribing voices.
>
> Since it is fundamental to this language to make a particular use of intonations, these intonations will constitute a kind of harmonic balance, a secondary deformation of speech which must be reproducible at will.
>
> Similarly the ten thousand and one expressions of the face caught in the form of masks can be labeled and catalogued, so they may eventually participate directly and symbolically in this concrete language of the stage, independently of their particular psychological use" (1958:94).

Even if it is in the tone of programmatic invocation, Artaud postulates the existence of a way of notating body, facial expression, and stage. The "transcription" is characterized precisely by the fact that it cannot be reduced to spoken language, it "oscillates" between *musical transcription*—that is, a symbolic, written system, made up of coded and repeatable signs—and *code language*—which is closer to the myth or the hieroglyph, that is, to motivated signs, capable of a synthesis between the arbitrary and the motivated, the symbolic and the iconic. Artaud never chooses between these two poles of notation, but juxtaposes them like the terms of a contradiction, which is that between his desire to *make* a new theatre and to "express" this theatre to come: "And a means will have to be found of notating, as on musical scores, with a new type of coded language, everything that has been composed" (1964, vol. V: 37). It would be ridiculous to reproach Artaud for his hesitation, indeed for his theoretical incoherence; he never concretely puts the question of the technical means of expression of his new stage language. Not simply because he despises this prosaic task: for him, notation does not follow the theatre act, but coincides with it, in the sense in which Grotowski can say that the actor "writes" by producing with his body hieroglyphs which are at one and the same time the sign and the thing. Artaud seeks a performance and a notation "where gestures, attitudes, signs will be invented immediately on stage, as they are thought" (1964, vol. V: 37).

Artaud and his reflections on the physical and intellectual apprehending of the performance mark a "revolution" where the score is no longer a tool, but an object, no longer a transcription, but a "writing," not a metalanguage but an actual work of art. In the same manner, contemporary music often works on the outer limits of both the acoustic and the visual universe, giving a graphic dimension to acoustic matter. A. Logothetis' score of *Labyrinthos*, reconstitutes, on the basis of signs of action, signs of association, and signs of musical pitch, a maze of labyrinths for the musicians, who are called upon to reconstitute "on sight" the route followed by their instruments within the global execution. The limits between the graphic description and the external object described are fluid: time and space, object and notation are consubstantial. Theatre rarely reaches such extremes; or when it does, it may be in the form of an exercise in reading/writing, as in the case of *Visual Scripts,* elaborated by David Cole (1976: 27-50). Cole is experimenting with visual models which are beyond the opposition between an (iconic) *scale model* and (arbitrary, symbolic) *functional model* between a theoretical study, and a practical activity of the theatre, between doing and thinking. Such a script is "a pattern of imaginative order achieved in some medium other than performance, which offers itself as the basis for a performance event" (Cole, 1976:31). The scripts consist of a series of exercises for actors; the actors are invited to improvise according to geometrical forms, graphs, or diagrams "connecting" several characters. The creation of models and the conception of the theatre as a modeling activity and as a mimetic approach to social relationships are very similar to the concepts of the Brechtian *Modell* and via this author to the secondary modeling systems of Lotman and of semiotics.

The reversal which Artaud introduced and which finds theoretical support in the visual scripts of Cole, leads to productions which "write" and show their score in the very space of the performance. This is the case with the "semiography of a score" by Jacques Polieri: "To project sound in a space not only in the acoustic or auditory sphere, but to situate the instruments as visual signs, to catalogue them into groups and sub-groups connected to each other by basic relationships from the point of view of function and form, such is the ambition of the present essay" (1971:183). The stage situation of the instruments, of the soloist, of the acting areas, delineates a huge spatial score: the performance notates itself in the very act of its creation. Each of the 52 sequences of the musical score is registered on a "bidimensional graph" notating the intervention in space and time of all the elements of the performance (voices, instruments, electro-acoustics, movements, etc.). This type of "semiographic" notation is "naturally linked to the fixed and mobile position of the spectators, and could be the analytical model for any performance place, provided that one expanded the data and increased infinitely the parameters (position of the spectator, angle of vision, movement, reception, etc.)' " (1971:188). In this way notation becomes essentially an electronic program, which mainly controls the lighting effects. What this means is that the theatrical act, its programmed production, and its spatialization become one and the same thing: notation therefore no longer takes place after the event, and according to the perception of a real or ideal spectator, but coincides with the theatrical object itself.

All of these mythical attempts to discover a means of notation of performance end up in the same inversion of notation and notated, as if notation were an end in itself, a way of going beyond the reality to be described and of becoming a kind of ultimate book in the sense in which Mallarme could write that: "The world is made to end in a beautiful book" (quoted in Scherer, 1977:151). In the same spirit, Paul Klee paints, in his *Fugue in Rot* (1921) the plastic, colored movements of music. Such a painting could well serve as the emblem for the current of ideas which seeks visual correspondances—overlapping, repetitive forms, arranged horizontally as on the lines of a score—for a non-figurative musical structure.

But as soon as we study concretely the technical means of achieving all these writing-notation projects, we have to decide to what end they are undertaken and to choose a particular aspect of the performance. Obviously one should not expect from semiology—as impatient and malicious detractors imagine—a "magical" new method of notation. More modestly, semiology reflects upon the *formalization* of systems and codes, on the elaboration of the *performance-text*, on the *presuppositions* of critical discourse, and on the critical stance of the audience.

The formalization of certain systems at work in the performance appears as a pre-condition to any description/notation. This is the price the "describer" must pay to be able to work on an object of knowledge and on the real stage object. As a particularly formalized system, which is also to be detected and translated into a network of relationships, we think immediately of the existing codes; in this we follow the definition of Metz for the filmic codes: "each of the partial fields from which one can hope for a certain formalization, each unit which requires formalization, or even each level of structure in any class of films" (Metz, 1973:138). In order to describe the codes of performances one has first to decide on a level of formalization and on its units: for example, a clear decision must be made whether to place oneself on the level of the narrative system, or that of gestural oppositions, on the level of the system of colors or that of the representation of stage materials. The code has semiological interest, and so is of value for notation only if the oppositions constituting it are pertinent to the meaning of the *mise en scène* and if it is equally possible to understand the reciprocal articulation of the greatest possible number of codes. Thus we are approaching the notion of a *system of codes*, or of a *performance-text*. In practice, it is often difficult to determine what signified(s) one could

The "drawing" of the performance-text would then have to be accompanied by reflections on ideological and aesthetic presuppositions of its critical discourse, which are themselves as lucid as possible. It is at this level that the reflections on the actual aim of notation should intervene. Such an intervention—even if it can never be innocent and must always remain on the plane of the ideological, without reaching the stage of the scientific (cf. Althusser, 1976:67-125) would at least have the merit of not deceiving the reader about the fact that any discourse has automatically an ideological position.

To fully reconstruct a performance-text, every possible piece of information relating to the *situation of enunciation* should be provided: the situation overdetermines the text, which can only acquire its meaning when the conditions in which it is enunciated are made clear. These circumstances of utterance are, of course, essential, since they form the parameters of every new *mise en scène*, conferring upon it its proper color. The different markers of the enunciation include the intonation, the gesture which modalizes the speech; the figuration of stage space, and, in particular, the proxemic relationships between actors; the rapport established between stage and audience; the meaningful connection between the dramaturgical analysis and the concrete appearance of character and action. Notation therefore strives to show the close link between the said and the shown, the utterance and its enunciation, the said and the non-said. The force of meaning in the theatre is obviously to be found here and these elements must absolutely retain the "describer's" attention. For this, the discourse—the commentary—is particularly apt. We might suggest that it is of utmost importance that this commentary inform us at precisely what moments the "directions of enunciation" have an effect on the text and what "counter-code" they produce.

Finally, the performance-text could not be complete without some information about what we might call the *framing device* of the representation/performance. Understanding and "capturing" the stage event always means fragmenting the continuum into meaningful ensembles, creating frameworks within which—by virtue of the principle of semiotization which transforms every theatre act into a sign—a certain number of principles and laws remain uniformly valid. Such a framework indicates, for example, that signs from different codes can be read in their own combination, before the result of that combination—the new framework formed by them—becomes also associated with other frames, so that meaning arises as and at the interaction of those frameworks. In this way the *mise en scène* becomes a complex of frames which are relatively autonomous and composed of hierarchized sub-groups. In this, our conception is very close to Mukařovský's notion of semantic gesture. The semantic gesture is the organizing principle of the semantic intention; this notion aims at replacing authorial intention by a dynamic structure which links the components of the work to the progressive construction of meaning and thus of the aesthetic object (cf. Červenka, 1976). So the "space-outline" has to indicate what signs are present and, above all, how they impose design—design as form and design as intention.

Paradoxically, the notation of the performace-text will only be fully satisfying if it relativizes itself and denies its very existence. For it seems more useful, instead of tending towards *one* neutral and universal notation, to present several different notations, depending not only on the desired aim of the critical discourse, but also on the spectator who watches the performance. By the same token, this relativistic view destroys any hope of a "scientific" notation, at least in the slightly positivist sense of the world. In order to account for the performance, we would have to instruct the "describer" on the physical and intellectual position of the audience confronted with the theatrical event. How, for example, can we notate *1789* (a play by the Théâtre du Soleil), without a knowledge of the scenographic disposition of the Cartoucherie, the moments of simultaneous action in different spaces, the orientation of the public between five elevated acting spaces? (The brief indications in the booklet are, once again, quite insufficient.) The ideal "space-outline" would give details on the major changes in the "audience vision": not only on the concrete space, the perspective from which the play is seen and heard, but also the *distance* (or proximity) of the acting, the manner in which the actors appear to us as close to life (credible) or distant (alienated). We can only dream of a means of estimating and inscribing on the "space-outline" these factors of perception, in the same manner as one indicates in music whether the piece should be played *legato, staccato, allegro* or *sostenuto*.

At the end of this odyssey through the variously real, mythical or programmatic territory of theatrical notation, one cannot help coming to a rather skeptical and disillusioned halt. If no system of description really prevails for the study of theatre, perhaps this is for the very good reason that theatre re-invents itself with every passing age—even with each new performance—and that it always exists *elsewhere*, only ever letting itself be formalized within the Derridian "closure of the representation" (Derrida, 1967)—that is to say, in the repetition of theatre which means its own death.

This is precisely why we always have an uneasy conscience when notating the theatre, as though we were carrying out a forbidden act which makes the very object supposed to be re-presented, disappear.

However, if we can but perceive this descriptive process as the very act of birth of meaning, will it not become evident that every act of notation is already an act of theatre—and sometimes, a theatrical act?

Translated by Susan Melrose

130/Patrice Pavis

Bibliography

Althusser, Louis (1976). *Positions*, Paris, Editions sociales.
Artaud, Antonin (1958). *The Theatre and its double*, New York, Grove Press (Translated by M.C. Richards).
Artaud (1964). *Oeuvres*, Paris, Gallimard.
Barrault, Jean-Louis (1946). *Mise en scène de Phèdre*, Paris, Seuil.
Burian, Émile F. (1939). "Prispevek k problému jeviští mluvy," in: *Slovo a Slovesnost*, vol. 5 Prague.
Brecht, Bertolt (1961). *Theaterarbeit* (B. Brecht et al.), Berlin: Henschelverlag.
Červenka, Miroslav (1976). *Der Bedeutungsaufbau des literarischen Werkes*, Munchen: Fink.
Cole, David (1976). "The Visual Script: Theory and Techniques," in *The Drama Review*, vol. 20 no. 4, (T 72).
Derrida, Jacques (1967). *L'écriture et la différence*, Paris: Seuil.
Greimas, Algirdas, and Jean Courtès (1979). *Sémiotique*, Paris: Hachette.
Hess-Lüttich, Ernest (1979). "Korpus, Kode und Kommunikation,' in *Kodikas/Code*, I.3, Tubingen.
Hess-Lüttich (1978). "Semiotik der multimedialen Kommunikation," in T. Borbe/M. Krampen (eds) *Angewandte Semiotik*, Wien: Eggermann.
Ivanov (1977). "Per una semiographia teatrale," in G. Bartolucci et G. Ursic, teatro-Provocazione, Venezia: Marsilio Editori (article paru en russe dans *Teatral'nyj Oktjabr*, Leningrad, 1926).
Krejča Ottomar (Oct.-Dec. 1970). "L'acteur est-il un singe savant dans un système de signes ferme?" in *Travail théâtral*, no. 1.
Marranca, Bonnie (1977). *The Theatre of Images*, Drama Book Specialists, New York.
Nadin, Mihai (1978). "De la condition sémiotique du théâtre," in *Revue roumaine d'histoire de l'art*, XV.
Passow, Wilfried (1971). *Max Reinhardts Regiebuch zu Faust II*, Band I-2, München: Kitzinger.
Pavis, Patrice (1981). "Problems of a semiotics of the theatrical Gesture," in *Poetics Today*, Vol. 2, no. 3, Spring 1981, Tel-Aviv.
Pavis (1980). *Dictionnaire du théâtre, Termes et Concepts de l'analyse théâtrale*, Paris: Editions Sociales.
Polieri, Jacques (1971). *Scénographie-Sémiographie*, Paris: Denoel-Gonthier.
Ryngaert, Jean-Pierre (Mars-Avril 1972). "Un exemple du jeu de l'acteur au XVIe s.: le theatre de Gerard de Vire," in *Revue d'Histoire littéraire de la France, no. 2, Paris: Colin.
Schechner, Richard (1976). "The Director," in J. Robert Wills (ed.), The Director in a Changing Theatre*. Palo Alto: Mayfield.
Théâtre du Soleil (1971), *1789*, Paris: Stock.
Vierge, Gerard (1956). "Utilité de la conservation des mises en scène écrites," in *La mise en scène des oeuvres du passé*, Paris: C.N.R.S.
(Les) Voies de la création théâtrale (1970-1979). (Ed. Denis Bablet et Jacques Jacquot) Paris: C.N.R.S. 7 vol.

Towards a Semiology
of the
Mise en Scène?

This paper was presented at the Conference on The Theory of Theatre, University of Michigan, April 17-19, 1980. An Italian version appeared in *Quaderni di Teatro,* Anno III, Numero 9, August 1980.

The question mark above is not simply a rhetorical flourish. There is no *a priori* certainty that a semiological theory of theatrical *mise en scène* can be elaborated. The words may pass themselves off as clear and scientific but they remain not much more than a very vague slogan aimed at camouflaging a poorly understood practice: how meaning is produced in the theatre performance from a great many unknown factors. So the notion of *mise en scène* is a very vague and ideological one, which is a *modus operandi* for theatre people or an aesthetic norm for the critic. The term *mise en scène*, universally employed today in theatre work, covers a wide range of stage practice, both in Occidental theatre history and in contemporary stage experimentation; it only vaguely points toward the general idea of the disposition and realization of the dramatic work. From a taxonomological viewpoint it sometimes refers to a precise moment in history (towards the middle of the nineteenth century) when the *metteur en scène*, responsible for organizing the performance, first appeared on the scene. Sometimes it designates an aesthetic practice of expressing and enunciating the text through the stage, and in this way establishes itself at the meeting point of the *interpretation* of a text and its artistic realization. The function of *mise en scène* seems by nature pragmatic, since it has to solve the problem of the scenographic "de-monstration" of a set of signs—including the text—for a specific public. It is very difficult to use it as a conceptual tool for theatre semiology since it appears to be the *result* of a global process of text reading and *interpretation*, in the widest possible sense: indeed, how can we formalize and describe a notion of "staging" that presents itself as a reflection on the alliance of stage systems, on the coordination and the centralizing reading of the dramatic work? So many parameters and unknown factors are involved in the development of meaning that it becomes sheer folly to retrace its genesis. This explains why semiological analysis has up to now been satisfied to examine a single element of text or performance (actantial models, the actor's work, spatial structures), the combination of a few signs, or, at best, the enumeration of some of the options of *mise en scène*. No doubt it is rather premature to want to isolate the workings of a *mise en scène* and, *a fortiori*, of *the mise en scène* of a certain type of text. But if we want to account for the current assimilation of "theatre" to a work of *mise en scène* and reflect on the narrow links between a general semiological model and the "practical semiology" that every *mise-en-scène* is, we must be prepared to risk making hasty generalizations. The appearance of *mise en scène* has for far too long been reduced to a moment in history at which a central intelligence—the *metteur en scène (director)* began to control the ensemble of materials and so confirmed the thesis of the autonomy of theatre art. On the other hand, there has not been much reflection on the production of meaning (before and during the reign of the director) in terms of the dialectic between text and stage, the combination of signifying systems and the establishment of relationships between signs from different stage systems. The production of meaning has often been assimilated into a specific style or the personal taste of a period or an individual, thus eliminating discussion ("tastes and colors . . .") and debasing *mise en scène* to the level of a technique of expression, of a "spiritual" contribution to a text by that "ingenious but tyrannical" creator, the director.

In opposition to such *idées reçues*, I would like in this essay to verify two ideas which are so obvious that they either pass unnoticed or are thought to be trivial:

> 1. *Mise en scène* is semiological analysis in practice: hence the difficulty of talking about it *after* the event in a coherent metalanguage;
> 2. Semiological analysis is a *mise en scène* (in space and in a system) of certain signs received from the performance.

I shall not try to assimilate semiology and *mise en scène* completely, under the pretext that they both organize meaning systems according to meaningful sign networks, but it can be observed that in the case of the *mise en scène*, it is difficult to distinguish the *object* of study (the *mise en scène*) from the (semiological) *study* of the object. So, the primary questions here will be precisely: can *mise en scène* be understood as a semiological concept, and does this tool give us the rhetorical key to the manner in which a *mise en scène* operates on a text and to the universal mechanisms of textual interpretation aimed at scenic enunciation?

In order to narrow down the field of study and to avoid an abstract and haphazard treatment of all the aspects of *mise en scène*, I shall limit myself to a few considerations about the link between *text* and *performance* in the Occidental theatrical tradition that requires a text be interpreted for acting on the stage. One needs only to turn to the *mise en scène* of the classics, where the contemporary director not only has to know how to re-read the text and a whole dramatic universe far removed from his own horizons, but also has to propose a concrete stage realization of it which "speaks" the up-to-date language of a concrete public. The problem of the text/performance link (T/P) is not new and every reflection on text-based theatre has to pass through the orienting grid of the stage and through the director's responses to his reading of the text. But most of the time analyses of the *mise en scène* are preoccupied with whether the stage "correctly illustrates" and extends the text, whether the *mise en scène* fulfills its mission of "*theatrically*" ("expressively," "attractively") saying what the script has already said *textually*. But such responses are completely unsatisfying, since they are based on precisely those theoretical presuppositions which I want to attack here. Furthermore, I am not concerned with presenting the history of the notion of *mise-en-scène*, nor with sketching the most frequently used theories of the current ways of treating the classics, and even less with falling back into the naive—and ideological debate on whether theatre is pre-eminently text *or* performance. It serves no purpose to know whether theatre is gesture or spoken word, literature or performance, to observe that the current tendency of the avant-garde and its theorists is towards the dominance of performance and of the actor's body after "theoretically" getting rid of the ball and chain of textuality and narrativity.

Concentrating on the relationship between text and performance (this is a relationship which can be quite precisely defined as *mise en scène*) I'd like to explain *the work of stage interpretation* as that of *the writing of a performance text* —based on a theory of fiction to which the director, and after him, the spectator, must needs have recourse. This theory of *fictional discourse*, which assures the mediation between textual reading and stage writing, clarifies the manner in which the director, who is both reader and stage writer, structures the universe of possible worlds, develops a metatext which generates the stage enunciation of the dramatic text. Thus *mise en scène* appears as a pragmatic activity involving the reception by a public called upon to perform a semiological undertaking as much as the production of a theatrical team. This kind of reflection, appealing as it does to ideological mechanisms, also has the merit of enticing semiology forth from its gilded ghetto (i.e., science of the internal functioning of performance signs); it relates this artistic activity to other social practices and innoculates semiotic discourse against any desire to close the performance on itself, thus against any temptation towards formalism.

Of course the definition that I have just given of the *mise en scène* of the written text—a dialectical relationship between a textual, linguistic system and a performance (any ensemble of visual and auditory signs provided that they are not linguistic)—is very restrictive. Numerous other cases are possible: performance without a text; a text simply read on stage, etc., these being the most extreme cases. Overall, I subscribe to A. Veinstein's traditional definition of *mise en scène*, retaining here primarily his second meaning:

> The term *mise en scène* has two distinct meanings: it designates, on the one hand, the ensemble of means of stage expression (acting, costume, decor or set, music, lighting, furnishings) and, on the other hand, the function involving the elaboration and the spatial and temporal arrangement of these means of expression in order to interpret a dramatic work or a theme (Veinstein, 1976:35).

If, unrepentant logocentrist that I am, I stress the relationship between text and performance to the extent of making it in this type of theatre the very life source of the concept of *mise en scène*, it is because that relationship remains the most ambiguous *couple* in the *performance* (*performance* in the widest sense: the theatrical event that includes the audience as participant in the performance. Cf. Schechner, 1973:20). This couple is central to classical theatre and its *mise en scène*, since it indeed produces meaning, being the interaction and infinite dialectic of one element with the other and since it is located at the nodal point of the fictional discourse issuing from the text, interpreted and made concrete in its stage expression.[1]

The fact that we distinguish T and P within the *mise en scène* does not prejudge their relationship, and in particular does not necessarily mean that the text is the more important, that it is translated by the director into its ideal meaning, then expressed by the stage. In the *mise en scène* of texts, the director cannot do other than *read* the text he intends to stage. Explaining the later interactions between T and P is quite another matter.

MISE EN SCÈNE AND PERFORMANCE TEXT

Before analyzing the narrow relationship which exists between Text and Performance, it seems useful to enumerate and define the components of the theatrical event and to locate the dramatic text within the *mise en scène* (or in our reading and rewriting of the performance text):

MISE EN SCÈNE (or "PERFORMANCE TEXT")

Text $\longleftrightarrow$ Performance
(T)   (P)

Historical definitions of *mise en scène* (Veinstein supplies a concentrated form of these) vary according to the number and hierarchical importance of stage components.[2] *Mise en scène*, then, is an aesthetico-ideological category founded on an *a priori* idea of what theatre *should be*. Therefore, it is hardly surprising that these conceptions vary considerably from one school to another and that *mise en scène* is often assimilated with an idealized conception of theatre instead of being envisaged as something that functions or that opposes different stage functions. This is the case, for example, of E.G. Craig's conception:

> The Art of the Theatre is neither acting nor the play, it is not scene, nor dance, but consists of all the elements of which these things are composed: action, which is the very spirit of acting; words, which are the body of the play; line and color, which are the heart of the scene; rhythm, which is the very essence of dance (1976:29).

These necessary components of performance—and thus of *mise en scène* since the spoken word is one of them—are simply "articulated" according to the action. This definition is symptomatic of a conception of performance which is more normative than descriptive, a conception based on an aesthetic view which attempts to underline the autonomy of theatre as a means of expression. Besides, it is worth noting that Craig is more concerned here with the central role of the *metteur en scène*, the miracle man of unification, than with the *mise en scène* as signifying activity founded on meaning-making by inter-relating heterogeneous elements. If in this essay I speak of *mise en scène* rather than of *metteur en scène*, it is because I am more interested in the process of meaning than in the person often nominally charged with accomplishing it. Though the director has not always existed, there has always been a *mise en scène* more or less systematic and effective as soon as textual and stage materials are combined in space before an audience. So I understand *mise en scène* as a structuralist notion in the sense of a specific combination of stage materials. However, this structural notion has been actualized at many different times in history in just as many different aesthetic conceptions.

In the majority of aesthetic theories of performance, one has simply sought the means of deciding whether theatre is autonomous and "welded" together by the *mise en scène* or whether it is a composite of the fusion of the arts (e.g., Wagner) or the reciprocal alienation of "sister arts" (e.g., Brecht). Such definitions become clearly impracticable when we try to apply them to different types of performances. As a matter of fact, they are ideological and historical views for which it is preferable—if we want to approach a global and functional theory of *mise en scène*—to substitute a functionalist definition.

Such a definition does not rely on obligatory constitutive elements but rather on a type of relationship between stage systems (such as decor, actor, music, etc.); it appears not as a miraculous fusion of different arts (music, painting, poetry, etc.) but as a combination of *codes*, i.e., reconstituted systems consisting of "units which aspire to formalization" (Metz, 1973:138). For example, one might follow the "thread" of the gestual code and that of the music. Thus the performance would be "dissected" into a series of codes which either "progress" parallel to each other and at the same rhythm, or cut across each other, sometimes coinciding, through common signifieds, opposing each other. Such a performance text consisting of several codes is sometimes explicitly chosen by the director; but it might equally well be established and decoded by the spectator for whom the *mise en scène* is thus available to be "read" and even to be organized, i.e., "written."

From this point on, the *mise en scène* is no longer (or at least no longer entirely) an indication of the intentionality of the director, but a structuring by the spectator of materials presented, certainly, according to certain guide lines, but whose linking together is dependent on the perceiving subject. This notion of *mise en scène* operates a radical transformation, moving from the finalized exterior object to the structuring effort of the perceiving suabject. It has become a structural principle of organization which generates and creates the performance from projects/propositions of the stage and responses/choices of the audience.

The performance text is thus always an open structure, or at least, "half-open," according to the textual genres and the style of the *mise en scène*. Not only is it never fixed, as in the cinema, but there is always "play in the structure" and the writing of this text depends, to a considerable extent, on structures organized by the audience. The spectator's liberty to maneuver, to which directors attach so much importance (cf. Schechner, 1973), depends as much on the potential for open combination of systems as on a knowledge of the ideological codes of the reality reproduced: this is not a simple matter of techniques of manipulation, but has especially to do with recognition of the ideological and transformational character of the text and of artistic activity in general. In this way theatre space might resemble a gigantic score on which the actor and the whole theatre team trace out figures, stops and starts, arrangements of characters, living and moving *tableaux*. Through a system of notation one might then envisage a transcription of the variations and the profile of the performance text considered longitudinally (as a succession of situations and systems) and transversally (as the structured and synchronic aggregate of codes). Writing/reading the performance text consists of structuring the continuum of the performance into meaning-blocks, into chains of episodes or of attitudes, in transitions reflecting the changes of situation or rhythm: thus is drawn an immense and continuous hieroglyph (which can be abstract and figurative). We know what advantage a director like Brecht would extract from the groupings, transitions and attitudes of the actors in order to write on stage the contradictions and the ruptures of characters—setting dramatic art in motion by blending together choreographically inner and outer conflicts. This reveals by the same token that such a performance text is only decipherable in its intertextual relationship with a social discourse, an aesthetic and ideological project close to that metatext of the *mise en scène* of which I shall speak in the pages that follow.

The score of the performance text, once it is established, questions the dramatic text proferred on stage, questions its status, its relationship with the stage enunciation and its specificity.

DRAMATIC TEXT VERSUS THEATRICAL TEXT

A long tradition of criticism, still felt today, sought to characterize the dramatic genre through criteria assumed to be universal, e.g., the sharing of the text among several characters, the use of the first person, conflict, etc. This is the basic attitude of structuralist poetics: it defines the poetic (or dramatic) text by a set of stylistic criteria, obtained most often by comparison and contrast with non-artistic discourse (cf. Doležel, 1979:522). But all of these traits vary considerably from one dramaturgy to another and are contradicted at one moment or another by new characteristics, particularly in the twentieth century with the experiments of epic theatre, the happening, or *théâtre-récit*. The difficulty, in the theatre, is that the renewing of practice does not (or does not *uniquely*) take place through stylistic or textual modifications, but by changes in and the contribution of visual elements, thus by a new pragmatic use of the stage and of the stage/audience relationship. The result is a profound change in the situation of reception and in the very nature of the theatre event. Thus, the pragmatic approach—which examines the conditions of theatre enunciation—seems to be particularly favorable to theatre; but we still need to reflect upon the methodological consequences for the theatre of a textual-pragmatic approach. The current tendency to apply the *speech act* theory indifferently, as does Pratt (1978) to the literary and to "ordinary" texts seems over-hasty, insofar as it erases every difference between the two texts under the pretext of a common illocutionary situation. As Doležel remarks, "pragmatically-based theories of literature are usually motivated by the failure of structural poetics to prove beyond doubt that there exists a set of intrinsic (imminent, text-inherent) properties which distinguish the class of literary texts from all other classes" (1979:526).

One should be very careful in the use one might make of pragmatics and the theory of speech acts. All we can do, given the current state of things, is apply it to general considerations on the use of text in the theatre. Thus, instead of defining the dramatic text dramaturgically or stylistically, i.e., normatively and according to a taste and an aesthetic which are dated, it is certainly easier (if not more satisfying) to define it pragmatically according to illocutionary criteria. Just as there is no textual property that enables us to identify a text as fictional, so there are no properties for the dramatic text other than its illocutionary force and its "non-serious" attitude (i.e., not committing the author to the truth of what is said). It is nonetheless possible to differentiate the fictional text in general from the dramatic fictional text —at least in that specific case of spoken theatre allocated to the speaking characters: "The author of the play is not in general pretending to make assertions; he is giving directions as to how to enact a pretense which the actors then follow" (Searle, 1975:328). We arrive finally at this tautological statement but at least it has the virtue of defining the theatre text by enunciation and its concrete use and not by unalterable and intrinsically textual characteristics: theatre is—and thus the *theatrical text* is—that which is, could have been, or could be presented in the theatre, i.e., a place for viewing, where a watcher and a watched, a hearer and a speaker meet. Such a purely pragmatic definition of the *theatre text* (and no longer of the *dramatic text* to which we can continue to attribute certain specific traits) will of course not obviate the fact that each period and dramaturgy offers a repertory of commonly recognized dramatic characteristics (e.g., the classical comedy and the resolution of conflicts, verbal exchange, etc.). Furthermore, if it now seems impossible to define the dramatic text in terms of what it is, it is at least possible to say what it lacks: precisely the condition of being pronounced in space and the requisite complement of information that every *mise en scène* brings. To borrow a useful image, we might say that the "holes" in the text—"holes," so to speak even larger than those of any other fictional text—are "plugged" by the choices of *mise en scène* and stage figuration. The visualization immediately clarifies a large number of "zones of uncertainty" of the dramatic text. But it likewise masks other zones of uncertainty, so that no *mise en scène* ever really exhausts the text of origin.

The theatre text is only rarely (this is the case in current practice where cinema and theatre converge) a simple *scenario* or *script* which serves to elaborate the global performance text: indeed, the fact that it is pronounced and heard *in extenso* in the course of the performance restores its absolute value, permits it to constitute a symbolic fictional reality which might oppose itself *en bloc* to or play with the visual elements of performance. This is the "play" that every *mise en scène* provokes.

The too simplistic idea has sometimes been advanced that the *mise en scène* of the text is an "execution" (in all senses of the term) of the stage directions. Although one cannot theorize *in toto* about stage directions (which are either spatio-temporal indications, directives on the acting, or a commentary by the author on a character or an action) one might at least say that stage directions, despite their extra-textual and supra-textual status, are neither the truth of the text, nor the author's metatext on the dialogue.[3] To the extent that they are composed by the author, we cannot of course ignore them, but we can hardly consider them as the verities of the *mise en scène*. That would require treating directors like children who had to be led by the hand, and we know that a man of the theatre and theoretician of the *mise en scène* such as Craig used to consider the didascalia an insult to the director (1976:35). Stage directions should instead be regarded as Searle remarks, as similar to the dramatic text inasmuch as "the illocutionary force of the text of a play is like the illocutionary force of a recipe for baking a cake" (1975:329). As with the cake, some will prefer to scrupulously follow the recipe and others will add a "pinch of salt" or will substitute their own culinary technique: the only criterion—to retain the culinary metaphor—is perhaps that "the proof of the pudding is in the eating." Dramatic text and stage directions both set in motion illocutionary forces: the global speech act is then that fiction brought about through the ensemble text-didascalia. Each character produces within this global speech act individual speech acts, fictions within a fiction, which, through doubling up and the effects of "a-play-within-a-play" create a "reality effect."

Finally, it needs to be made clear that in the theatre not *every* text is a text. Can we define the dramatic *text* (to distinguish it from noise, music, assonances or rhythms) as that which lends itself to a fiction, i.e., is translatable into a possible world, into a system of signifieds? The danger of such a definition is that it reduces the notion "text" to that of figurative text, something having a visualizable referent. In so doing one eliminates a whole set of texts which are not figurative, and which do not lend themselves to figuration, to a mental representation. But it is almost impossible to draw a line between figurative and non-figurative: any such attempt would amount to deciding which texts *mean* something and which texts mean nothing at all. One can nonetheless use Sartre's distinction between the language of the prose writer where the words have the value of signs (as the immediate means of passage towards a signified) and poetic language where words have the value of things, thus of signifiers: this difference takes on its full value here in the context of the dramatic text. In the first case, the text as heard is immediately transformed into fictional discourse and a symbolic reality, a theory of fiction is then able to symbolize the whole text as a discourse and to set it "against" the iconicity of the performance; in the second case, the text remains a "brew of signifiers," closer to music or onomatopaeia than to articulated language. In the place of the fiction there is at most the elaboration of an act of enunciation, a "pantomime of writing." This second case is to be found in those theatrical forms which are solely spectacle. In the work of Robert Wilson, for example, the text has value only as a rhythmic or repetitive structure: all figuration is excluded from it—at least in the way an audible text could have a figurative meaning—this sort of "text" is then reduced to a material on the same level as the music, color or gesture. This does not mean that the figurative—a text that lends itself to the development of the fiction—is totally deprived of the non-figurative quality which assonance or versification, like a super-impression, confer on it, but this dimension is generally subordinated to the figurative energy of the fiction being conveyed.

It remains for me to outline the status of the dramatic text in its transformation, through the *mise en scène*, into a concrete enunciation. The dramatic text has its status change in the course of the *mise en scène*, that is, through its interpretation. In fact, it passes from a written to an enunciated text and in this passage the whole enunciatory apparatus is modified. In its *mise en scène* the text is reborn and rediscovers its status as "situational" discourse, a status it held before being "transcribed" by the author and "deposited" on paper. One might well suppose, that in the act of being written (whether by a single or a collective author) the text effaces certain marks of its enunciation: we simply lack access to the author's process of visualization and conception of the situation prior to this "depositing" of the text of the dialogues on paper. In the written text, from which the speech of its author has been withdrawn, the reference—i.e., the relationship of the signs to the world—is no longer visible, it is no longer shown and lived as in the concrete act of its enunciation. Such is, according to P. Ricoeur (1974), the difference between written and spoken language: "In spoken language, what a dialogue ultimataely refers to is the situation common to the interlocutors, that is, aspects of reality which can be shown or pointed at; we say then that the reference is 'ostensive.' In written language reference is no longer ostensive: poems, essays, and fictional works speak of things, events, states of affairs, characters which are evoked, but which are not there" (1974:105). The *mise en scène* of the dramatic text, that is, its stage enunciation by actors or by other stage means, is a return to oral discourse. But it would be naive and incorrect to believe that this return restores to us, as such, the reference and the situation of enunciation of the author's text. The operation of putting into speech (*mise en parole*) is not the inverse process of writing a text. The *mise en scène* of the text is not the rediscovery of the enunciation of the author as he might have experienced it, in composing his text. We cannot rediscover *the* real referential situation of the author.

However, this "staging" ("enacting") of the text is definitely a way of making the text speak; it creates a possible situation of textual enunciation of the text in which several marks of that enunciation are given (the gestuality and mimicry of the actors, the rhythm and phrasing, the reconstitution of a dramatic situation). Thus the *mise en scène* is an attempt at *re*constitution—and even constitution—of a dramatic situation and of a situation of enunciation which might permit the grasping of the text proferred by the characters in this enunciation. Just as the isolated word only finds its meaning within a discourse (in the concrete event of an enunciation), the dramatic text only finds its meaning in that stage enunciation which is the *mise en scène*. The *mise en scène* is thus an appropriation by the stage of texts that it (re)places in a situation and thus (re)constitutes.

There are no rules for recreating the situation of enunciation, from the written text, that is its ideal *mise en scène*. The only requisite—this is one ideological option among many others—would be to make sure that the recourse to reference and to the text's situation of enunciation makes it possible to account for the greatest possible number of aspects of the text, without having these aspects contradict each other constantly; in short, that the interpretation of the text by the stage be at once *productive* and *coherent*. In this I would agree with Ricoeur in demanding of every interpretation of a written text (whether this be by a hermeneutist or by a director) that it be the most probable of possible guesses and that it ally subjectivity and objectivity: "a construction may be said to be more probable than another, but not true. The most probable is that which (1) accounts for the greatest number of facts provided by the text, including potential connotations, and (2) offfers a better qualitative convergence between the traits which it takes into account" (1974:104).

These few notes on dramatic text—somewhat tenuous in view of the lack of specificity in this type of discourse when it is not placed in relation with its stage enunciation in a concrete *mise en scène*—leads us now to the heart of the debate: the specific type of relation between text and performance and the possibility of formulating a coherent theory of the *mise en scène* of a text which takes into account a theory of fictional discourse.

TRADITIONAL VIEWS OF *MISE EN SCÈNE*

One would be quite justified to start off by questioning the validity of the opposition between text and performance through which I have defined the work of the *mise en scène* (or "*mise en exergue*") of the classical text. From a semiological point of view, one can only confirm that the text and the stage operate on different symbolic levels: one is based on a linguistic system of arbitrary signs (and thus must be first of all translated into signifieds before being understood); the other is founded on iconic signs which present a figurative form of that reality of which they are the signs—which does not mean that they do not obey opposition systems too, forming a very structured discourse. Speaking semiologically, linguistic arbitrariness and stage iconicity cannot be reconciled or mutually canceled out by a common system. That is why the attempts to isolate a universal theatrical sign which participates in the two modes of symbolization are doomed to theoretical failure—at least when one aspires to use Saussurian semiology which was founded precisely on the irreducibility of the arbitrary and the iconic. However it would be wrong to see in this effort to fuse signs into a theatrical sign an enterprise which is separate from the practice of *mise en scène*. As a matter of fact all symbolist theories tend towards just such a synthesis (cf. Craig, Honzl, Wagner, etc.) at the point where they claim to unify stage arts in a specifically theatrical harmony. Inversely, attempts at "deconstruction" (in the style of Brecht, etc.) accentuate the breaches between the different codes or sign systems, finding in their collision the guarantee of their functioning.

Curiously enough, today we are once again attempting the impossible reconciliation of text and image under the auspices of *action*, an action at once in the text (seen again as *speech acts*) and on the stage (the place of social practice). Schechner, for example, confirms that the opposition between *script* and *performance* dates from a particular point in history. Before the intervention of writing, design was assimilated into painting, thus into action: "Ultimately, long after writing was invented, drama arose as a specialized form of scripting. The potential manifestation that had previously been encoded in a pattern of doings was now encoded in a pattern of written words. The dramas of the Greeks, as Aristotle points out, continued to be codes for the transmission of action; but action no longer meant a specific, concrete way of moving/singing—it was understood 'abstractly' as a movement in the lives of men. Historically speaking, in the West, drama detached itself from doing. Communication replaced manifestation . . . The avant-garde in the West, and traditional theatres elsewhere, refocuses attention on the doing-aspects of script, and beyond script altogether to 'theatre' and 'performance' (1973:7).

This historical view has the great merit of illuminating the mutation of action, which, at that moment, in classical, "textual" theatre—was removed from the text to stage practice. So a whole theory of action and theatre needs to be constructed so that the pragmatic nature (illocutionary, in Searle's term) of the dramatic text is brought back into focus. One would then see that in theatre *telling* and *doing* are not necessarily antonyms as they are in day-to-day speech (cf. Pavis, 1981).

However, in order to avoid confusion, I shall examine the opposition between text and performance, *dramatic poem* and *drama* (Craig, 1976:30), telling and doing, starting with a review of some prejudices concerning the relationship between text and performance, and moving to an examination of how *mise en scène* can prepare the way for a general theory of real and fictional action.

The conception most people form when they reflect on the role of *mise en scène* (from which every other role flows) is one of a stage rendering of a pre-existing textual message. Stage expression should supply a more or less faithful (another magic word) equivalent to the text. It is sometimes felt that it is the function of the stage directions to transcode information about the dramatic universe into a decor or a stage figuration. Moreover, such observations are unencumbered by explanations concerning the logic of the transcription. It would seem that it is concrete experience which "proves" that we can—and must—rediscover in the performance whatever was previously in the text in the performance (essentially in the form of didascalia). Such a view, one which considers the *mise en scène* to be the "simple degree of refraction of a text onto the stage" (Artaud, 1964:142), is the manifestation of a logocentric philosophy of theatrical art and it is all the more able to resist theoretical criticism since one cannot help finding correspondances between text signifieds and performance signifieds. In this case the *mise en scène* seems to do nothing other than confirm what the text has already suggested or replace what the didascalia communicated to the reader. But it is quite obvious that a *mise en scène* does not just reproduce the text—unless its intention is to be very redundant and, finally, superfluous. *Mises en scène* have better things to do than simply re-express visually elements already announced by the text. Then again, such re-expression can be indispensable to the production of meaning in cases when, for example, the text talks about an attitude or an object which the director *must* make visible. When he *does not* do so, the non-observation of these visual elements described in the text becomes very significant, and all the more so when that non-observation is itself unobserved: in this way verbal decor (Shakespeare's "word scenery") allows the director economy in his sets while still suggesting them to the spectator's imagination. At any rate, a T/P parallel is in no way obligatory for a *mise en scène*.[4]

It is no doubt because of this argument that a diametrically opposed thesis is formulated: performance and text are of a totally different character; here performance is an addition to the text, which is retained as such but somehow reduced and almost drowned under the mass of stage signs that the director alone can decide to use. Furthermore, in this context, the dramatic text is in no sense grasped as a potential text which staging will modify and "constitute" in the act of enunciation; here the director is completely liberated from the figurative suggestions of the text, a position which is, to say the least, rather extreme, if not positively terroristic.

This attitude points toward an equally common position: the director is content to allow the text to be heard—via the actors—but "seasons" this recitation with images which come from his personal and totally independent means of self-expression; hence the implicit equation: text = imposed "trope" belonging to the writer; performance = free trope imagined by a totally independent director.

In one final instance, the notion of the inseparability of text and performance leads to the hypothesis (in itself fairly accurate) that the dramatic text is incomplete without the stage's support; and, in an extreme instance, that there is a satisfactory *mise en scène* only when we are unable to determine what comes from the text and what is added by the stage. This implicitly pre-supposes that the text suggests one *mise en scène*, and only one, if it wishes to have an "ideal" staging. This is the stance of a theoretician like R. Hornby: "a script is realized (or embedded) in a performance via an interpretation, but that interpretation is not something separate from the script but rather itself a function *of* it" (1977:107). A director like Tyrone Guthrie commented quite rightly that "Dramatic criticism of the classics, certainly, is nearly always conducted on the assumption that there exists, probably in the mind of the critic, an ideal performance which completely realizes the intention of Shakespeare or Molière or Eugene O'Neill or whoever else" (in Wills, 1976:88). A. Ubersfeld is much more prudent in her estimate of the link between text and performance, and she is careful to grant to the *mise en scène* the possibility of adding autonomous stage signs. Her formulation "in control" is a happy one since it suggests that the text is a language act addressed to the stage practitioners: "The status of the *written* text (text, canvas, scenario, score, etc.) is that of being in control of the performance signs (although there are of necessity autonomous signs in the performance which are produced with no direct relationship to the text)" (1977:256). It is now my turn to suggest an explanation for the dialectic T/P. Instead of reducing one term to the other, it seems preferable (and methodologically more elegant) to consider *mise en scène* the establishment of a dialectical opposition between T/P which takes the form of a *stage enunciation* (of a global discourse belonging to *mise en scène*) according to a *metatext* "written" by the director and his team and more or less integrated, that is established in the enunciation, in the concrete work of the stage production and the spectator's reception.

STAGE ENUNCIATION

Despite their diversity, the conceptions of *mise en scène* enumerated above have one idea in common: the work on stage is always somehow *separate* from the text. We find the proof of this in that obsessive question posed in theatre criticism: how is one to establish a stylistics or a typology of all possible *mises en scène* of a single text? What stage variations are possible? How can we attribute several interpretations and *mises en scène* to a text while making sure that we do not ascribe to them an erroneous interpretation? (cf. Jansen, 1980:11). In fact, it is futile to hope we can produce a stable typology of the potential *mises en scène* of a text, since it would require that we take into account all of a reader's critical positions at various points in time on the basis of diverse critical interests—a utopian task. Instead of looking for those future "correct" *mises en scène* of a text, it would be more profitable to explain how the performance, in the *mise en scène* made of it, throws light on, that is contradicts, approves, comments on, or counterbalances the dramatic text. The *mise en scène* not only presents one particular version of the text, it re-presents it to be read (this might be the source of the fashionable expression used in the Parisian salons "In this *mise en scène* I *heard* the text"). So the T/P relationship is not one of implication or inclusion; it is not symmetrical, but , rather, dialectical.

It might be worthwhile to recall the obvious: in order to read a dramatic text, we must create a "representation" of it (even if it is simply an imaginary one); of course this is not specific to dramatic texts, it is true of every other fiction or figurative work. But for theatre, a certain knowledge of the conditions of *mise en scène* and acting are, if not essential, at least extremely useful in understanding the text. So when we read a classical text, and if we want to understand it in its historical context, then it is absolutely indispensable to know something about performance conditions at that time, to know in just what scenographic, material, and social context the author offered his plays to the theatre. In fact what the author wrote was no doubt influenced by his knowledge of concrete performance conditions, of which today we retain only that which remains in the text. This historical parenthesis serves as a forceful reminder of the fact that the *mise en scène* becomes concrete in the dialectical relationship T/P, as a global enunciation of a potential textual utterance.

This is an appropriate point to introduce the utterance/enunciation (*énoncé/énonciation*) dichotomy, which itself comes from the celebrated Saussurian distinction between language and speech (*langue/parole*). Speech (or discourse) is the individual concrete use in a given situation of language by a user (through whom speak several intermingled subjects). The *discourse of the mise en scène* is the manner in which the *mise en scène* (the director's metatext, as we shall see) organizes, in space and time, the fiction conveyed by the text, making use of a series of enunciators: actors, decor, objects and all those indices of the way in which text and fable are recounted on stage (verbally by the text, and, at the same time, visually by all the signs of the performance). This discourse thus transcends the opposition between the spoken and the visual, since it organizes the fable into a sequence of verbal and stage actions according to a global and dialectical meaning established between T and P. This is the very source of the production of theatrical meaning, the consonance of telling and doing.

I have still to show how the enunciation (*mise en énonciation*) of the text through the stage and of the stage through the text comes about. In order to respond to this challenge one must enter the terrain upon which the construction of the fictional world in theatre space takes place.

From the very first the *mise en scène* provides a framing device, a modality, and a key to the reading of the fictional world; that is why scenographic and gestural space (i.e., proxemic relationships) supply the canvas indispensable to the writing of every performance text. But these spaces are there to be filled by an action or a word; they only spring to life when provided with the sonoric background of speech, of action or of a stage event. In the theatre, enunciating the text always means creating tension between it and what is shown on the stage, polarizing it between various sources of enunciation, spatializing the spoken word and conflicts—individual or collective—in a polyphony of sources of emission.

This polyphony is assured, furthermore, by the attitudes of the speakers towards what they have to utter: here the speakers are not just the actors, but all of those scenic means which can indicate a certain standpoint: agreement, refusal, humor, passion, etc., *vis-a-vis* whatever is said. The *mise en scène* adopts a stance with regard to the specific attitude of the enunciators towards their utterances; once that is done, those utterances are decoded according to the appropriate modal or affective key. In practice, distinguishing between what belongs to the utterance and its enunciation is therefore a matter of some delicacy; the enunciation, in a work of art, immediately (as soon as it is proferred) becomes an utterance (*énoncé*); it becomes concretized as a standpoint with regard to the *dictum*.

A whole system of modalities of the spoken underpins the *mise en scène*, as though the text were "located" through modal adverbs. This is the level on which we can best grasp the ideological foundations of the text, insofar as it is expressly supported by the director's critical metatext, or on the contrary, concealed and rendered commonplace. The *mise en scène* is fundamentally a modalization of the *dictum* by the theatrical term. It is at this level that the director's metatext is uttered, either directly, clearly, almost over-insistently, as a commentary laminated to the text of characters and stage, or, on the contrary, uttered "in filigree" or even left to the spectator's own free search for meaning, if he is unable to detach such a metatext from the global discourse of the *mise en scène* and from what the text seems to be saying on the surface.

So the *mise en scene* decides who will speak and how, thereby modulating the meaning of the spoken text. But, just as understanding and describing an utterance means describing it by specifying "the roles of its possible speakers and receivers," casting "them in the theatrical sense of this word" (Ducrot, 1978:108), so one must decide, for every *mise en scène* not only *who* speaks but *to whom*: who is it hidden there behind the apparent addressee of the discourse (the other character)? How does the performance make itself accessible to the public? What is the role of each set of lines as a speech act in the language game between the protagonists, and how does it form a segment in the story to be shown? What pre-suppositions and innuendos does each verbal and stage utterance entail and in what way is a dialectic established between the protagonists or between the components of the performance? These are some of the questions that the linguistics of discourse helps us to formulate and invites us to transfer to theatre.

Finally, there is always a certain choice made by the stage enunciation concerning the relationships between stage systems, their interaction and hierarchy in what was precisely termed the *mise en scène* by Copeau: "the design of a dramatic action, the ensemble of movements, gestures and attitudes, the matching of physiognomies, voices and silences; it is the total stage performance, emanating from one unique thought, which conceives it, rules over and harmonizes it" (in Veinstein, 1976:65). Once again, we are back to the writing of the performance text, to the necessary decisions regarding its coherence (as in Copeau's statement) or its diversity, or its openness. Here too, it is not sufficient to arrest critical reflection at the point of recognizing the structuring of utterances; we have to ask according to what principles the discourse of the *mise en scène* was made. Here the notion of the *metatext of the mise en scène* becomes unavoidable.

THE METATEXT OF THE *MISE EN SCÈNE*

It seems quite evident—although this depends on how successfully I have refuted the traditional conceptions of *mise en scène* as an act of fidelity—that the director has a "closely watched" freedom to interpret the text according to his *a priori* aesthetic and ideological stance and that we cannot fail to find traces of his commentary in his work. It is not too hard to imagine, furthermore, that this commentary will vary according to the moment in history at which it is enunciated. Here we are once again confronted with the ideological aspect of the *mise en scène*: the nature and norms of the metatext cannot in fact be prescribed. It is therefore essential to distinguish between two notions: the *metteur en scène* (director), the autonomous and individual subject of his own discourse, and the *mise en scène*, a collective activity bringing together such diverse practices as literary hermeneutics, stage figuration, and the actor's interpretation of his role. It seems unlikely that the director can entirely dominate all of these languages, so he often only stands at the crossroads of paths that he himself has not trod, or that he has not fully controlled. Therefore he too is subject to prevailing ideology—to the current attitude toward the classics, for example, thus, there is an important sociological component that he shares broadly with his era, and which gives him, just as it gives contemporary readers, a general view of the period staged, of the philological research relevant to the author and, in particular, of the degree of development of critical methods—psychoanalysis, the history of discursive forms, structuralism, formalism. Finally, he depends as well and even more so on the political stance of the director (even when the latter is not conscious of or denies this position). The debate about how to produce classical texts—which deserves to be developed at length—conveniently reminds us that reading and showing a text obliges us to show its historicity and at the same time to indicate what use we want to make of it today.

As with enunciation, the task of reconstituting the area of the *mise en scène* into which the metatext is incribed is a delicate one, since it is always cunningly integrated into the textual enunciation and since it is always artificial (but nonetheless essential) to extract it in the form of a coherent aesthetico-ideological system. This can legitimately be done only if one can indicate just what concrete form this system takes in the performance.

The metatext of the *mise en scène* does not need to be written as a linguistic text composed by the director and presented to the actors to be read. It takes the form of a commentary, a key to the stage options of the performance, a specific enunciation of all those materials made use of in the performance: text, music, gesture, images, etc.

Furthermore, the metatext of those who enact the performance is always constituted in comparison with the *metatext of the spectators* which arises from the reception of the theatre object as an artistic system. The dialectic of these two metatexts unfolds as follows: the former is first constituted when it is *received* by the spectator as a key capable of explaining to him the ensemble of the text and his understanding of it. There is no metatext of the *mise en scène* without its being received and identified by a spectator. One might well ask how we can speak of a metatext when the director rejects even the idea of his own systematic intervention in the form of a commentary. We might answer that 1) metatext and *intention* should not be assimilated, and that 2) the metatext is a structural notion; it is the dialectical and productive relationship of the materials used. Thus it always exists, not really in the form of a written and definitive text, but as a system which can be constituted, i.e., as a system of interpretation of the stage by the spectator. The metatext is nothing other than the system (commentary) supplying the key to the *performance text* with which the spectator is confronted.

This brings us back again to the discussion begun somewhat earlier concerning whether or not we can distinguish between what belongs to the text and what to the personal contribution of the *mise en scène*. Contrary to the usual belief which opposes the *text to be spoken* and the *stage metatext* (often called the text of the *mise en scène*), it would be preferable to see how text and stage metatext are embedded in each other, each of them informs and relativizes the other. The metatextual enunciation of the director does not stand apart from the utterances of the actors. It is only thanks to the spectator's and critic's efforts to extract the discourse of the *mise en scène* (i.e., the metatext) that we can artificially, and in the interests of clarity, disassociate these two texts. Only the perspicacious spectator can carry out such a dissociation—the spectator, in fact, proposes a certain interpretation of the text. We need to remember that the text does not exist ready-made, with its own structure and meaning; it has to be seen from the outside (and it can be seen from many different angles) to be *constituted* as a text. Each interpretative metatext suggests a specific constitution. We, as spectators, perceive in a *mise en scène* the director's reading of the author's text; thus, through the performance, we do not have direct access to the text which is being staged. Of course we can propose our own metatext in lieu of that of the *mise en scène* (provided that we possess a degree of knowledge about the author, the era, and particularly about our own era and its ideological and cultural codes); we always have the means of criticizing the reading imposed on us by the director, as long as we are able to demonstrate the incoherence and the contradictions in the work of the *mise en scène* and criticize the suggested reading of the text. Therefore, if it is true that as spectators we always perceive within the *mise en scène* the embedded vision of the *metteur en scène* "reading" the author, it is also true that we can separate the two views. It is one thing to read a director's reading; it is quite another—and illusory—to believe that this reading exhausts and immobilizes the text. Consequently I cannot subscribe to Hornby's conclusion that the "right" *mise en scène* is a point by point transformation of the text: "a good production is script-into-performance, an intimate point-to-point transformation that moves us only in its wholeness" (1978:109) (. . .) "in a good production, there is no distinction between text and performance. The audience should be unable to tell which parts of the production were in the original text and which came from the director, designer, or actors, because performance is not something added to a text" (1978:104). What Hornby does not see is that *mise en scène* is not the attempt to produce an *ideal interpretation* (that does not exist) but instead aims at harmonizing a *dramaturgical reading* of the text (which takes into account the historicity of the work and its reception) with a concrete performance utilizing all of the theatrical means at its disposal.

The *raison d'être* of *mise en scène* has been discussed at length, especially with regard to its appearance in the second half of the nineteenth century: the need to harmonize text and performance. However this does not mean, as Hornby seems to think, that the text becomes the *mise en scène* or that the two can be confused. As B. Dort remarks, the advent of *mise en scène* corresponds to the moment when the mediation by the director consecrated the dialectic between T and P.: "The director's work is no longer that of adjustment, prettying-up, or ornamentation. It goes beyond illustrating or making a frame for a text. It becomes the fundamental element in the theatrical performance, the essential mediation between text and performance. Previously, this mediation was, so to speak, kept in parenthesis, ignored if not suppressed: either the performance is only here for the sake of the text or the text is only here for the sake of the performance; one dissolves into the other in a "reciprocal relationship" (1971:55-56).

We might ask ourselves how our ancestors could "survive" before the "invention" of the *metteur en scène* and his metatext. As a matter of fact, a metatext of the *mise en scène* has always existed whenever a text was performed, even though it was not produced by one individual who took sole charge and thought it lacked the coherence and the systematization that the centralizing eye gets out of the text; it was left pretty much to chance (to a leading actor, a master of ceremonies, an acting tradition, highly codified and known by everyone) and, at the same time, this metatext only became apparent *after* the fact, in the communal reception by the public. Indeed, the metatext as interpretation of the *mise en scène* is never a notion which belongs exclusively to one person (the director); it is co-produced by the audience in terms of its knowledge and expectations. If a metatext has become almost indispensable, has definitely been forced upon us since the advent of *mise en scène*, it is because the classical text—that of the seventeenth or eighteenth centuries, for example—has moved further and further away from our own horizon and an *intermediary* (that organizer and "production editor," the director), has to "create the screen through which we can see." The metatext imposed on a single work will vary with time and distance, and (important corollary), the further from us in time and space and the stranger to us the text consequently is, the more necessary is the metatext to our understanding of that work when performed. If the text is too distant from us, all that remains for us is the metatext which stands in lieu of the work itself, which has been definitively absorbed into the operation of reconstitution and making the work relevant.

This is an extreme example aimed at making clear the importance of the structuring and textual reading in the *mise en scène*. If it is clear that the *mise en scène* is not the translation of a pre-existing text, but rather presents for viewing and perusal the ensemble T/P, then we can go on to ask at what moment the meaning of that *mise en scène* is produced. Ideally, the meaning would be produced not as the *expression* of the text by the *mise en scène*, but as a *signifying practice* (Kristeva) brought about by the united effort of the director and of the "productive spectator." But this can only come about if the metatext of the *mise en scène* is sufficiently open and available to the spectator so as to be constituted into a coherent metatext. In this context we occasionally come upon the argument, notably among the theoreticians of *signifying practices*, according to which the *mise en scène* is *not* the "reading (interpretation) of the text, the discovery of a meaning, and finally its stage translation" (Rivière, 1971:IV), but an open text which has no meaning at all before the interpretation of the spectator. According to D. Kaisergruber, this is how Vitez directs. His *mises en scène* belong to this type of reading/practicing: "No productions of a single meaning and yet no dispersing of the text and, therefore of the spectator, into an infinity of exploded meanings" (1976:10). But does there really exist in this type of *mise en scène* a "withholding" of meaning and a refusal of interpretations? It is difficult to see how, even in the case of an open and ambiguous metatext which does not clearly suggest one interpretation, one could avoid the production of meaning. I am afraid meaning is always produced and not always the best! It seems equally utopic on the other hand, to propose a pure play of signifiers, and thereby to hope to escape from interpretation. A hermeneutic engagement with the text—and even between the text and the stage—is equally inevitable: How can any message be delivered, without a stance, even a negative one, being taken? The alternative favored by the adepts of signifying practices seems to be either not to produce any meaning at all in the *mise en scène*, or to generate for the text "a maximum of meanings in the time and space of a theatrical performance" (Kaisergruber, 1976:15). Can one thus—within the framework of this openness to signifying practices—postpone meaning and refuse interpretation by opposing to it a semiotic reading? (cf. Kaisergruber, 15). Is it not to step back farther in order to jump better?

But we seem to have moved away slightly from the problem of how *mise en scène* is evolved, and I still have to explain how a *mise en scène* becomes a metatext. It is not necessary to return to the false debate on originality, individual or collective conception of the metatext, but simply to explain the genesis of the metatext through a theory of fiction. This will perhaps bring us one step nearer to solving the problem of textual interpretation and the resultant link between text and stage.

THE THEORY OF FICTION

There might be something surprising in this return to fictional reality, to a possible world sketched by an author, relayed by a director and received by a spectator. Does not this necessitate the reintroduction of the problem of authorial intention, the re-emergence of a reality which can be represented, although we have no direct access to it and although the text is a structure of signs which produce a system of signifieds without our having access to the signs' referents? I am not trying to reconstitute the ''realities'' suggested by the text, or focus strictly on the text's signifieds, instead, I want to suggest how a literary work is received and symbolized. It is obvious that many studies inspired by the speech act theory have made the error of searching for the intention of the author of the speech act and have thereby returned to the old debate about a creator's intentions and the success of their realization in the work. (On this danger, see the warnings of Dolezel, 1979:523-524.)

The fundamental hypothesis of the work of *mise en scène* is that the passage from text to performance is mediated by a fictional universe, one first of all structured by a *reading*, then reproduced by a stage figuration. The ideological presupposition for such a conception of *mise en scène* is that there must be (theoretically and in all probability) a connection between T and P, not in the form of translation, but rather of a mediation and a displacement of certain signifieds. Therefore we can say something about the organization of the fiction (no longer declaring it an unknowable ''magma''). This does not signal a return to the type of criticism which constructed fables around the fictional world of the characters; instead, this point of view proposes that fiction is a type of discourse which obeys certain laws of composition. This mediation T/P which occurs by means of the intermediary of fiction does not introduce, as has often been claimed, an actualizable referent which is then actualized on stage; on the contrary it passes through a possible world which is structured in a fictional discourse that can be analyzed formally, and the passage of which can be followed between text and performance. Steen Jansen best defines this phenomenon of fictional transcodification: "It is difficult to establish a direct connection between text and stage which might permit (beyond particular instances) a clear distinction to be made between what 'comes from' the text and what is 'added' by the director. If there is a connection, it passes through a fictional universe constructed in a reading of the text, but by the reader, who becomes the director and re-writes [his conception of] the fictional universe by means of the performance" (1980:10-11). Jansen's other hypothesis, which seems perfectly correct, is that we pass from the text to its representation thanks to an understanding of the structuring of the fictional universe, and not because of its *figuration*, that varies from one *mise en scène* to another.[5]

Before I establish just how the structuration of the fictional universe operates, I need to clarify this theory of fiction, and in particular to see in what way the fictional discourse has need of a real discourse in order to exist, i.e., elements or "effects of reality" which the reader locates in the text and which permit him to orient himself and to find his position with regard to the fiction.

The great merit of philosophy of language, and in particular of the theory of *speech acts*, is that it has made the pragmatic value of every utterance clear and has removed it from the problematic of truth (defined as the equivalence between language and the world) in order to demonstrate its use in social practice. Thus fictional discourse is not to be defined by content, but by the attitude of the speaker (the artist) towards his utterances. Whereas literature is instituted by the reader's decision to accept it as such, fiction is instituted by the speaker's attitude with regard to the truth/falsehood of his utterance: "whether or not a work is a work of literature is for the readers to decide, whether or not it is fiction is for the author to decide" (Searle, 1975:320). The fictional discourse is *instituted* (even *institutionalized*) by the illocutionary attitude of the author who "pretends to perform a series of illocutionary acts, normally of the representative type" (325). This is only possible if the fiction writer replaces both habitual and real conventions between language and reality by new conventions which break the widely accepted real conventions: "the pretended illocutions which constitute a work of fiction are made possible by the existence of a set of conventions which suspend the normal operation of the rules relating illocutionary acts and the world" (326). The consequence of Searle's definition of fiction is that in this type of discourse conventions of real-life communication and fictional conventions, by their very opposition, are intermingled. Far from excluding each other, these two types of conventions reinforce each other. And all the more so in that fiction must, if we are really to believe it, contain reality (real names, authentic spatio-temporal indications, ideological effects of meaning already experienced by us, etc.). It is this reality effect which cements the fictional structure together for us, and every critical reflection on a text begins by trying to disentangle the fictional from the real, by examining how one discourse secretes the other.

The *fictional discourse* and the *reality* of our world and the world represented are in a dialectical relationship. In order that fiction take on meaning for the receiver, it is indispensable that the world of fiction which is closed upon itself (the closed structure of signs) open out onto the world outside, i.e., the real world of our experience. In fact, in order to pass as acceptable in the eyes of the receiver, fiction calls on a reality known to it, more precisely on an ensemble of accepted knowledge, of presuppositions and maxims which constitute a foundation on which the fictional structure is erected: how could we believe in the story of Rodrigue if the text had not first of all persuaded us that one must always "avenge one's father." If by chance the ideological bait no longer works the *fiction* will have great difficulty "taking off" and we shall keep a suspicious eye on this discourse which we now recognize to be ideological and thus suspect.

Such is the constitution of the work of art: at once autoreferential (closed upon itself) and referential (open onto the outside world), what S. Skwarczynska thus sums up: "with theatrical 'language,' we are in the presence of a referentiality which works: in the direction of its own internal world, and at the same time in the direction of objective reality which gives way to the artistic world" (1974:354).

THE STRUCTURING OF THE FICTIONAL WORLD

As soon as we try to establish a connection, not of cause and effect, but of structural homology between stage, fiction, and textual fiction, we confront the problem of the structuring of the fictional world by *mise en scène*. The structural designs which we can discern in the textual work are not always *necessarily* those of the *mise en scène: if the text proposes, the stage disposes!*

It is around the trilogy of space, time and action that the fiction is structured. I would therefore simply like to note a few general rules concerning their passage from T to P.

1. *Space*: the basic spatial relationship is the one which describes stage/audience rapport, the *performance space*. This relationship indicates that space from which the spectator receives the performance, and thus it reveals the *perspective*—in both the concrete and abstract meanings of the word—from which we are invited to live out the theatrical event. Reading a classical text therefore obliges us, for example, to investigate the conception and practice of scenography at the text's moment of origin. In the case of Marivaux, it would be important to know for what type of stage and what style of acting, the author "encoded" the spatial indications of his plays—whether the performance space was closed upon itself or opened out onto the audience space. These are not simply technical questions of a stage set more or less

adapted to a specific dramaturgy, but rather, questions which are profoundly involved with the conception of theatre and of its faculty for representing the world through the spoken word. Thus one might show that the structuring of space which is "pronounced" in the text and shown on stage undergoes a profound mutation in Marivaux' era and through his particular example. Whereas, prior to Marivaux—in classical theatre, for example—language *states* the world with no difficulty (there is even a coincidence between world and language), with Marivaux the mode of representation starts to vacillate, language no longer faithfully reproduces the structures of psychological and social reality. Language is no longer used by the characters to represent the world, but instead as a means of acting upon it. Language is experienced as a trap, a game which acquires new conventions, different from the usual conventions between word and world. Searle would call the old conventions vertical and the new ones horizontal (1975:326). This new conception of language has repercussions for social relationships and for the way space is depicted by the text. In fact, the whole of the performance at this point relies on the global conception of the space and how it represents the world and social relations.

Without prolonging this sort of philosophical debate, we can state that every reading of the theatre text imposes choices of spatial structuring, as soon as one has to decide *who* is speaking and according to what proxemic relationships. Space is organized as much within the scenographic framework as it is by the actors' bodies and the individual and social distances to be observed between them.

A reading of the text does not impose a single precise stage representation of the symbolized space, even when the stage directions or spatiotemporal precisions of the text are explicit. On the other hand, it seems unavoidable that we respect certain semantic oppositions of place or types of space, inasmuch as such structuring organizes paradigms of opposition between characters or actions. Thus the opposition between interior and exterior spaces seems sufficiently pertinent for it to be maintained in any staging of a text in which these two types of space feature.

In the same way, the contrast between space shown in a concrete situation, and space evoked by the spoken word, is a sufficiently clear criterion for it to be signaled in the stage/offstage duality.

Finally, *mise en scène* always makes a choice of the objects to be shown on stage: even though there is not the slightest obligation to represent these objects or even abstractly evoke them, we can all agree that the text suggests an *isotopy*, i.e., a series of relationships between these objects (whether by opposition, similarity, or spatial contiguity), and that the stage often finds its inspiration in that isotopy by transcribing it in terms of visual oppositions.

2. *Time*: the fiction also obeys a temporal development and its concrete

stage version cannot altogether escape this structure as found in the text. In addition to the different periods of the play—which can be translated without difficulty into compact temporal units on stage—the text suggests a certain rhythm of action. As J.L. Styan writes, we can always "take the measure of the play's stageworthiness . . . Movement, tempo and mood are not the qualities in a play that are most readily recognized from the printed text, but they are the elements without which the drama would not hold" (1971:3). A whole school of semiotics (Serpieri, 1978; Gulli Pugliati, 1976; Elam, 1980) studies the deictic and performative structure of the text to see how text becomes performance in structures bound up with stage enunciation. The central element in this study of temporal structures is incontestably the rhythm according to which the characters' discourse and the presentation of visual elements leave their mark on the *mise-en-scene*.

3. Action and actants: the action of a play is sketched on a spatio-temporal background, whether or not the action is carried out, as in most cases, by the characters or by impersonal actants (objects, lighting, music, etc.) is not really important. What we read in the text is always the course through a certain time and a certain space of one or more protagonists. This is why, in the theatre, the characters are "quite naturally" incarnated by the actors, so strong is the referential illusion and so necessary does it seem to the director, as a physical anchoring on stage of the fictional characters (already individualized, true enough, by their discourse). Current theatre practice, when it involves the regrouping, doubling, or suppression of characters suggested by the text, serves as convincing enough proof of the stage's ability to avoid the unequivocal translation of T into P, at least where actants are concerned.

Perhaps it is at the level of stage action that the passage between T and P undergoes the greatest transformation, despite the reality effect of characters immediately embodied by the actors. As soon as the linear dramatic text is staged, the linearity seems disjointed, projecting and scattering itself among the varied and spatio-temporally distinct sources of enunciation. Pieces of information coming from successive moments in the play are grouped together and "inscribed" on the actors and on the set: they remain ever-present in the mind of the spectator, though the text has long since "gone on." Thus, as soon as an action is staged, its structure undergoes a basic mutation, the scenic consequences of which are difficult to foresee. The only frame of reference is the integration of every actant and every action into a plan of meaning, a particular direction given to the Story—the role of dramaturgical analysis is to reveal the play of the action and the story proposed by the text, which the director can manipulate, in order to give it concrete expression or to transform it by his stage work.

In the end, the results of a theory of fictional structuring and of the transference of the fiction from T to P might well appear slight. If we want to avoid making normative statements and defining the *mise en scène* as a certain type of relationship between text and performance (fidelity, deviation, identification), we should not expect to see a substantial inventory of the structural traits of the fictional world. All we can point out are the general limits within which fiction is transposed from T to P. If we want to go further, to declare just what a "good" *mise en scène should do*, we get into the area of normative and ideological judgments. In that game the answers are all known in advance. One can say of the *mise en scène* either that it "corresponds" to the text, that it replaces the text which it obscures, that it "neutralizes" the text, making it visible, that it presents a new ideological conviction or, on the contrary—and this is the ideological and aesthetic choice that I personally would aim for—that it establishes a gap between text and stage, which then contradict and constitute each other by means of a collision of the fictional worlds each reveals. This gap between written text and stage text which J.L. Rivière called "the pantomime of the text" (1971), is a gap which "does not come from a difference instituted between two series, the textual series and the stage series (no displacement is 'stuck onto' the text), but is constituted by successive shifts, leaps from one to the other of these two series to transform the text, a set of words, into a gesture (a movement accentuated by the detailed diction of each alexandrine) which, in the same manner as the bodily gesture of the actor, and in his displacement (and in a dialectical 'play' relationship with it) contributes to the writing of this new text which is the performance" (1971:V).

The theory of fiction brings us back to our point of departure—the writing of the performance text by the *mise en scène* and the urgent need which exists for a theory of reception to be developed.

In this game of Chinese boxes that I have been playing, it seems that the theory of reception supplies the largest box and therefore encloses other approaches. In fact, the performance text, the metatext of the *mise en scène*, just like the theory of fiction, can only be understood in the light of the different mechanisms (perceptional, emotive, textual and ideological) of reception. Every metatext of a *mise en scène* and every choice of structuring a fiction is over-determined by the social practice which governs—today and for the spectator of today—the relationship between a director and a text. I quite agree with Dort's historical explanation that the advent of the director coincided with a time when one could witness a "profound transformation in the demands of the theatre audience and the introduction into the theatre performance of an historical consciousness" (1971:64). The next step is to understand the present demand of the audience, its "reception desire" in the current ideological context. One of the paradoxes of the hypertrophy of the director's function is that he is, at least in avant-garde practice, obliged both to deconstruct and recreate the play for us, and that at the same time we are invited to "practice" *mise en scène* by inventing "our own" (or "his"?) own mode of using it—paradox of an era in which we give ourselves up, bound hand and foot, to the director who *pretends* (as part of the global fictional discourse) to let us decipher and rewrite the performance. Certain performances, like those of Schechner or Kirby or of the *Théâtre du Soleil* are even based on the desire to change the audience's perspective and on the fragmentation of the performance.

THE SEMIOLOGY OF *MISE EN SCÈNE* and the *MISE EN SCÈNE* OF SEMIOLOGY

And so after examining the text/performance relationship as mediation of the *mise en scène*, we end up with a double identity crisis: 1. Are *we*, the performance receivers, the real director, navigating between text and stage, writing our own performance text? Is reading the performance nothing other than an exercise in "signifying practice?" 2. Is the director not himself involved in this game of mirrors between text and performance and, thus, a semiologist in action and in disguise? At this point we arrive at a paradox: if we want to understand the work of *mise en scène*, then we shall have to turn the traditional formula, "leave the *mise en scène* to produce its own work," inside out. Everything leads us to believe, in fact, that the director, half semiologist and half "sorceror's apprentice," makes up his own performance text. The fundamental restriction in the case of the classical text envisaged here is that the text's fiction commands and determines (if we still want to talk about the *mise en scène* of text X) certain structural choices of the work on stage. I cannot accept, in the staging of classical texts, the idea of a *mise en scène* which would be nothing but a pure signifying practice, without a trace of the original text in it. After all, what interest would there be in weighing oneself down with a classical text if it meant denying any possibility of agreement on its meaning because of its being wide open to the play of significance? This does not mean that I have finally returned to the thesis of eternal truths in a text and a necessary fidelity in the *mise en scène*. The director's metatexts are quite numerous enough and the paths of meaning dense enough for the *mise en scène* to provide play which is varied and *also* says something about the text that it claims to interpret.

Finally, the work of *mise en scène* (and, I might add, of semiology) can never be an end in itself, a high-powered exercise before which the public has only to prostrate itself. It must also (another and last normative demand) permit us to rediscover a text, to judge the coherence and the value of the *mise en scène*, and thus keep for ourselves some of the perverse emotions of the deconstruction of the artistic text.

Translated by Susan Melrose

Footnotes

[1]I would like to be sure that there is no misunderstanding of the closely related concepts in-

volved in this essay:

Dramatic text: the text composed by the author that the director is responsible for staging. This is only the text that is heard (pronounced by the characters), and excludes that stage directions (or didascalia)(see note 3).

Theatrical text: the text in a concrete situation of enunciation in a concrete area before an audience.

Performance: the ensemble of stage systems used, including the text, considered prior to the examination of the production of meaning through their interrelationships.

Mise en scène: the interrelationship of the systems of performance, particularly, in this essay, the link between text and performance.

Theatre event: the totality of the unfolding production of the *mise en scène* and of its reception by the public, and the exchanges between the two.

Performance text: the *mise en scène* of a reading and any possible account made of this reading by the spectator.

²On the history of the concept of the *mise en scène,* see: Veinstein, 1955, 1976; Dort, 1971; Wills, 1976.

³The status of the stage directions is radically different from that of the text spoken on stage. The failure to define the dialogue text (primary text, according to Ingarden's terminology) sometimes leads to their being regarded as a single entity (under the pretext that they are both written by the same author), although their status in the performance and in the reception of the theatre event is very different: one is essentially "heard," the other is the advice given to the director of which we will not necessarily find traces in the stage interpretation. In the example given by Searle, there is also some confusion between didascalia and the dialogue text. It is clear that the *directions* given by the author are especially in the stage directions rather than in the dialogue. Furthermore, these *directions* are neither absolute *directives,* nor authorial intentions, but "friendly counsel," "recipes" which are more or less tested and fixed in writing.

⁴It is surprising to find that this demand for a faithful transposition is still formulated by some semiologists and by avant-garde authors like Sam Shepard: "For me, the reason a play is written is because a writer receives a vision which can't be translated in any other way but a play. It is not a novel or a poem or a short story or a movie but a play. It seems to me that the reason someone wants to put that play together in a production is because they are pulled to its vision. If that is true then it seems they should respect the form that vision takes place in and not merely extrapolate its language and invent another form which isn't the play. It may be interesting theatre but it's not the play and it can never be the play" (quoted from Schechner, 1973:12). Other directors, on the contrary, try not to imitate or to contradict the text through the performance, but to open a gap between them. Thus, according to A. Vitez, "theatrical pleasure, for the spectator, lies in the difference between what is said and what is shown . . . otherwise what interest could he find in the theatre? It's the difference which is interesting . . . What seems to me to be exciting for the spectator depends on this idea: not showing what is said" (1974:50 and 42).

⁵This hypothesis about the structuring of fiction construed as a mediation which authorizes the transposition of T and P seems to be confirmed in this remark by R. Schechner: "I assume that plays 'present' themselves to their authors as scenes, that this scening is coexistent with playwriting . . . The act of playwriting is a translation of this internal scening into dialogue + stage directions. The stage directions are vestiges and/or amplifications of the internal scening . . . The work of those doing the production is to re-scene the play not as the writer might have envisioned it but as immediate circumstances reveal it . . . Re-scening is inevitable because the socio-cultural matrix of the play-as-envisioned soon changes" (1973:13). The aim of this essay was to determine just what is involved in this process of "scening/re-scening."

Bibliography

Artaud, Antonin (1964) *Le Théâtre et son double,* Gallimard, Paris.

Craig, Edward Gordon (1976) *The Art of the Theatre* (appeared in 1911), in Wills, 1976.

Doležel, Lubomir (1979) "In Defence of Structural Poetics," in *Poetics,* v. 8, no. 6.

Dort, Bernard (1971) *Théâtre réel,* Seuil, Paris

Ducrot, Oswald (1978) "Le structuralisme, énonciation, sémantique," in *Poetique*, no. 33.

Elam, Keir (1980) *The Semiotics of Drama and Theatre*, Methuen, London.

Gulli-Pugliati, Paola (1976) *I segni latenti*, d'Anna, Florence.

Guthrie, Tyrone (1976) "Directing a Play," in Wills, 1976.

Hornby, Richard (1977) *Script into Performance: A Structuralist View of Play Production*, University of Texas Press, Austin and London.

Jansen, Steen (1980) "L'Espace scénique dans le spectacle dramatique et dans le texte dramatique," paper presented at the Conference of Cosenza, September 1979.

Kaisergruber, David (1976) "Théorie/pratique théâtrale," in *Dialectique*, no. 14.

Metz, Christian (1975) " L'etude sémiologique du langage cinematographique," in *Revue d'Esthétique* (republished in 1978).

Pavis, Patrice (1981) "Dire et faire au theatre. L'action des stances du Cid," in *Etudes littéraires*, Montréal, vol. 13 no. 3, decembre 1980.

Pratt, Marie-Louise (1978) *Towards a Speech Act Theory of Literary Discourse*, Indiana University Press, Bloomington.

Ricoeur, Paul (1974) "Metaphor and the Main Problem of Hermeneutics," in *New Literary History*, no. l.

Rivière, Jean-Loup (1971) "La pantomime du texte," in *L'autre scène*, no. 3.

Roumette, Sylvain (1974) "Images de textes, textes en images," in *Langue francaise*, no 24.

Searle John (1975) "The Logical Status of Fictional Discourse," in *New Literary History*, v. VI, no. 2.

Schechner, Richard (1973) "Performance and the Social Sciences," in *The Drama Review*, v. 17, no. 3 (T59).

Serpieri, Alessandro et al. (1978) *Come Comunica il teatro*, Formichiere, Milano.

Skwarczyńska, Stefania (1974) "Anmerkungen zur Semantik der theatralischen Gestik," in W. Kroll and A. Flaker, *Literaturtheoretische Modelle und kommunikatives System*, Scriptor Verlag.

Ubersfeld, Anne (1977) *Lire le théâtre*, Paris, Editions Sociales.

Veinstein, Andre (1976) "La Mise en scène," in *Le Théâtre*, encyclopoche, Larousse, Paris.

Vitez, Antoine (1974) "Ne pas montrer ce qui est dit," in *Travail théâtral*, v. , no.

Wills, John Robert (1976) *The Director in a Changing Theatre*, Mayfield, Palo Alto.

IV. EXAMPLES OF SEMIOTIC ANALYSIS

A Semiotic Approach to *Disparitions*

This essay was first published in *The Drama Review*, vol. 23, no. 4 (T84).

There is no question, in these few pages, of presenting methods of semiotic analysis applied to the theatre or even of completely describing a performance and its structural principles. Rather, beginning with some theoretical concepts and a montage of photographs I simply would like to develop some thoughts on a performance and its semiotic analysis and to try to find a middle ground between concrete description and abstract semiotic theory: an approach, therefore, determinedly practical *and* theoretical that could contribute to a new phase of theatrical semiotics. Following some indispensable epistemological reflections on the justification of an approach derived from linguistics and structuralism, and following the examination of general models of theatrical functioning, it is imperative that the facts and the hypotheses be verified by comparison with precise analyses and practical observations of theatrical production.

The example chosen for this comparison is *Disparitions (Disappearances)*, a work written by Richard Demarcy, directed by the author and Teresa Motta, performed in Paris at the Centre Pompidou, then at the Théâtre de la Tempête in March and April 1979. The piece is a free adaptation of texts by Lewis Carroll; in particular, *The Hunting of the Snark*. Besides being very original, this production lends itself easily to semiotic experimentation, not only because Demarcy is one of the first theatrical theoreticians to be interested in semiotics (cf. his *Eléments d'une sociologie du spectacle*, 1973) and it is always extremely interesting to look for traces of his thought in his productions, but especially because a purely narrative or dramaturgical analysis would take into account neither the specific nature of this performance nor its plastic and musical composition.

Photographs courtesy of Benjamin Danon

Photo 1

The Scenic Space

Seated frontally in tiers, the audience looks down onto the performance space, which contains a large expanse (230 m²) of shallow water. This aquatic surface is not a mimetic representation of a river or a lake but an artificial pond with clearly defined limits that is used as a performance surface. The objects (tents, car, table, chairs, desks) are not at all nautical: they seem to signify chiefly by their deceptively random geometrical arrangement. This surface creates an impression of frightening emptiness, the emptiness of the white sheet of paper before the creative act, an emptiness that the performers do not try to fill with situationally motivated movements and activities. The reflections from this sheet of water are projected onto the three walls, which have been broken up into innumerable screens, positioned in different directions in order to catch the images of the reflections and the shadows. (Photographs 3 and 4). This space, flattened out in three dimensions, immmediately suggests the metaphor of a space to be filled with visual impressions, of a polymorphous space that will have to be occupied, and of a musical score/partition into which the performance is going to flow. This musical metaphor is very quickly confirmed by the spatial arrangement of the six performers. Under the direction of the Captain, *"metteur en scène"* (director) and *"metteur en abyme"* (condenser of images) of the story, they position themselves in front of their respective implements. In a semicircle, from left to right, there are: the Baker, in front of an old sewing machine; the Butcher, sharpening his knife at a bench; the Beaver, conscientiously watering the pool of water; the Captain moving from one "musician" to another and organizing the snark hunt. The text, especially when it touches on the leitmotif of the snark, passes from one character to another, and in each case it is delivered according to a specific mode of diction, gesture or action. As in the poem by Lewis Carroll, the text is divided into eight fits ("crises") that recount the misadventures of the crew. The same mathematical division of the whole space produces the effect of a puzzle made up of words, gestures and images. Whenever the *mise en scène* centers on it, each element, visible from the beginning, merely "pushes aside" the others. Two points function as poles of attraction—the tent and the car: everything takes place as though these two objects draw all the other objects and all the action into their magnetic fields.

No performance description is ever without subjective elements that influence the fundamental understanding of the work. In attributing to the scenic space, as I have just done, the function of a *basic system* onto which the other signifying systems (text, gestures, lighting, music, etc.) are grafted *a posteriori*, I am guiding the reading of the *mise en scène* toward what seems to me to correspond to the general *composition* of the *mise en scène* in the sense that S.M. Eisenstein gave to this term: "the construction which, in the first place, serves to embody the author's relation to the content while at the same time compelling the spectator to relate himself to the content in the same way" (Eisenstein, "*La non-indifférente nature*," p. 81). This compositional principle (the grafting of all the systems onto a *space-score/partition*) is justified by the fact that the Carroll/Demarcy text does not "make up" an exterior referent and visualize it in the space; rather, it is the production of images that channels the energy of the performance and integrates the text as one of the scenic "accessories." The space or, more precisely, the water, functions as a mode-effector (*modalisateur*) and as a reading code; it becomes a means for the interpretation of the other scenic systems. Although, like a musical key, this spatial system remains in effect throughout the whole performance, it is not always the basic system. It is replaced at times by music, by an ensemble of gestures or by a monologue. In general, a theatrical performance presents as a perpetual dialectic of the various systems, a more or less stable *hierarchization* of these different elements. In addition to this organizing and structural principle of the space as *score/partition* (segmentation and support of the writing), there is the thematic value of the water and its capacity to produce a hypersign of which the signifier will be "water" and the signified "hunt." In all its possible forms, the signifier "water" generates an infinity of signifieds: the water becomes the place of reflections, of monsters, of the elusive, of fantasy, of writing, etc.

The Theatrical Sign

We are almost at the end of the voyage. In spite of the energetic leadership of the Captain, the snarkers disappear (the Baker), take flight (the Bar-

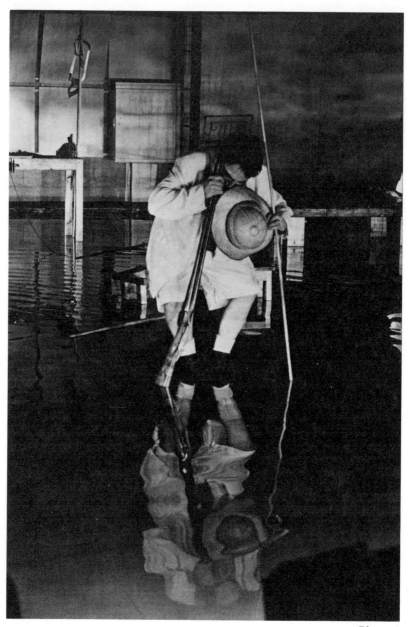

Photo 2

rister), die (the Banker) or, like the Butcher in photograph 2, collapse. In this moment of prostration, it is possible to discern the mechanisms for the construction/destruction of a theatrical character as well as the character's potential as a *carrier of signs*.

But, in the theatre, what is it exactly that *constitutes* a sign? At first, the semiotics of performance explained the formation of meaning by the accumulation of minimal signs (or units) that were defined as the shortest segments endowed with meaning and isolable in the scenic continuum. Currently, attention is moving away from this theoretical search for the minimal unit (too fragmenting), toward the grouping of signs according to a shared semiotic objective (or signifying function). In this way, in order to isolate the signified "explorer," it is enough here to add up the signifier "rifle," "helmet," "shorts," "whiteness," etc. Every performance reading proceeds by a back-and-forth motion between translation of the signifiers and the signifieds and attempts to find signifiers with which to corroborate the signifieds already identified. This rapid reading is done all the more easily when the spectator is put in a position where he need only pay attention to relevant signs and can group them according to a semiotic objective which is closely related to dramaturgical ends. (Here the explorer comes immediately to mind as he is identified with the narrative and thematic development of the hunt.)

To reintroduce the dimensions of its referent into the sign, it has sometimes been tempting to go beyond Saussurianism (where the emphasis is on the relationship between the signifier and the signified) into a three-term system such as Pierce's model (sign, object, interpretant) and by a trichotomy based on the relationship between the sign and the object (icon, index, symbol). The theoretical debate is far from being over, and it is futile to try to reduce the Saussurian model to that of Pierce. It is possible, however, to integrate the two semiotics in the following opposition:

> 1) *Indexical function*: this function depends upon the place of the sign in the message, on the enunciation, on the stage and the performer as sources of ostension and physical presence—in all, on the *use* of the sign in the geneeral discourse of the stage. In the example of the explorer, this indexical function clarifies the necessity and the situation of this episode in the total story.
>
> 2) *Iconic and symbolic function*: this function is related to the object that the sign refers to in the story. The relationship to the object is more or less mimetic, it produces an effect of variable reality and fluctuates between a communication by conventional means and by referential illusion. This function is that of the structure and the nature of the sign: in the example above, it indicates the identity of the character and the reason for this metaphor of the disheartened explorer.

Photo 3

Metamorphoses And Networks of Signs

Here we are in the midst of the action during the second fit: Under the anxious gaze of the Captain, the Beaver, the Butcher and the Judge have just changed into pigs. This metamorphosis is one of the gestural highlights of the performance; it is the first time that the characters come into direct contact with the water. Apart from the pleasure of watching them flounder about in the water, this episode has an additional impact that stems from its placement at the intersection of several isotropies (that is, thematic and signifying conductor threads). The signification of the scene rests on a series of semantic oppositions: water-surface of the Captain/water-element of the pigs; humanity/animality; sleep/hyperactivity; uncontrollable movements/tense orchestral direction; furniture for grown-ups/children's objects; closed and protected spaces/open spaces (water). These oppositons belong to several sign systems that come together and result in a kind of synthesis or tying-up of meaning. Another example: when a fish tank full of water and heteroclite objects comes down from the ceiling toward the Beaver, several sign systems are reiterated and summarized (rectangular shape; oppositions between full/empty, dry/wet) and this ordinary object functions "*en abyme*" (a condensed image within an image) as the concentration and the emblematic image of the performance.

Here we have an essential characteristic of *Disparitions* and, more generally, of every performance where there is a concern with signs. Every visual sign is part of one or several networks of oppositons; it is transformed and produces new signs; its presence and its "sting" vary at different moments of the *mise en scène*, depending on the rhythm and the dynamics of the stage action. (In contemporary productions, the function of objects becomes all the more important when they are no longer related mimetical-ly to their referent but have a syntagmatic value within the signifying systems.) With this type of image-production, the spectators have a great deal of freedom to reorganize these isotopies and to reconnect the disparate elements. Some spectators will respond to the system—water and movement—while others, for example, will follow the thematic chain of the *bird* (sea-gull, Beaver-swan, Judge-raptor, Captain-parrot, blood-red feathers, which denote the death of the Banker . . .). Throughout the per-formance, the accumulation of these scenic images and signs constitutes a sort of *visual discourse* that circulates beneath the surface of the play. Separated from the plot (moreover, quite loosely structured) and from the logical continuity of the action, this visual discourse finally becomes a visual current that captivates the attention because it is detached from linguistic-discursiveness and connected with the structure of fantasy and imagination.

Citations

After the mad chase comes a lull. Fallen asleep in uncomfortable posi-tions, the snarkers are quite deaf to the encouragements of their Captain, as he urges them not to give up and as he holds forth on the "five un-mistakable marks" by which to recognize a genuine snark ("Fit the Se-cond: The Bellman's Speech"). This seems like a rather unexceptional se-quence but only if one fails to perceive the signifying work of the image: its capacity to comment, to repeat, to parody—in short, to *cite*.

The citation is a technique that brings together two discourses, one of which lets the other speak in order to confirm its own text. However subtle a citation may be, it must always somehow suggest the fine line that separates the original text and the text quoted. In *Disparitions* the visual citations are more like collages than montages: they bring together in-congruous elements, heterogeneous materials, antagonistic styles. On the other hand, the plot of the piece is closer to a *montage*—repeated or parallel sequences, the development of tensions in spite of the fragmentary struc-ture, epic progression toward the "last word" of the story. The most effec-tive examples of citations are the *portmanteau-word* and the *portmanteau-image*.

Portmanteau-Image

The Judge is dining in the trunk of a very official and ominous, black Peugeot 404 with the registration plate *Snark 161*. The Banker is fiddling around with the engine. This image of the car-snark constitutes the pro-totype of what could be called a *portmanteau-image* if we apply to it Lewis Carroll's conception of *portmanteau-words*. This theory of Carroll brilliantly foreshadows the work of Freud, Jakobson and Lacan on *condensation* (*Ver-dichtung*) and *displacement* (*Verschiebung*), metaphor and metonymy. The portmanteau word is a verbal creation from two words which, when put

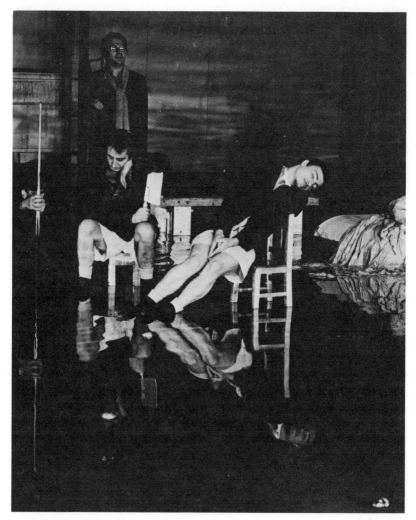

Photo 4

together, produce a new sign and a new concept (Snark = snake + shark). We know, since Freud, that the process of dreaming proceeds either by the condensation of two dream elements (by metaphorization) or by displacement of one sign toward the other (by metonymy). In their theatre work, Demarcy and Motta have developed this practice (without, of course, always doing so consciously or systematically), and if note were taken of all the rhetorical figures of the performance, they would show very many condensed images, extremely fertile for the interpretation of symbols. (For example, the world of birds-men, of the Beaver-swan are obtained by the condensation of a horserider, a cyclist, a child and a lively small animal). This principle of condensation is especially valuable for the production of images and for experimental work with words, gestures and new rhythms.

As for the stage image created by *displacement*, it is much more rare and seems to be utilized especially in the arrangement of the plot elements. In effect, the play is conceived on a metonymic basis, a metonymy of verbal and theatrical creation. The sounds of typewriting machines that are heard at the beginning of the play, and with which the performance ends, relate to the original work now translated into text and image. These sound effects *displace* the attention from the creative act to the creation itself. In the same way, as object and as auditory leitmotif, the *snark* continually resists identification, and resists finally, therefore, our apprehension of a definitive meaning.

Considering the stage as a producer of more or less conscious images, and still trying to find a formal method with which to apprehend its signifying functions, semiotics has recourse to ancient rhetoric, to the study of dreams and the unconscious, to the analysis of the networks of images in the *performance text*.

Action, Text, Gesture: Correspondence

No matter how structured and dynamic they may be, the networks of signs, visual citations and portmanteau-images will not hold together without a cementing element to bind them. This cementing element is the *action*—not action in the sense of plot progression or the development of situations, but as a current that "unifies word, actor, costume, scenery and music, in the sense that we could then recognize them as different conductors of a single current that either passes from one to another or flows through several at one time"(Honzl). In *Disparitions,* the action is more scenic even than plot; it is not wholly dependent on the text but uses it as one of its components. Apart from functioning as a support for the plot, the Carroll/Demarcy text works in two diametrically opposed ways: on the one hand, as a metatextual commentary on the language (for example, the Baker's monologue of portmanteau-words, photograph 6); and, on the other hand, as a play on sounds, a verbal and poetic creation that has no obvious referent. These are two extreme limits of all theatrical discourse: a commentary external to the director and the spectator that is intimately connected with the words of the characters; a complete absence of meaning that leaves the stage open to every critical interpretation of the audience. These two extremes of theatrical discourse are both present in *Disparitions*. Sometimes a character will philosophize on his own speech act. More often yet, the text as rewritten by Demarcy seems to be concerned only with its own signifying materiality: it becomes a poetic play on linguistics and sound patterns, an extended onomatopoeia. This kind of discourse seems to be propelled by the all-engulfing oral energy of the characters, who take delight in swallowing the text, in gargling with rich, repetitive sounds, in

Photo 5

giving in with pleasure to this verbal gluttony, to these calisthenics of the mouth. The boundaries between gesture, body, diction and text are done away with, as though the whole performance—or at least those sequences where portmanteau-words flourish—tended, under the sign of *Gestus*, toward the discovery of correspondences.

When the Baker is reciting his poem of portmanteau-words, his accompanying gestures are not an imitation of the object of the discourse (which, moreover, has no definite referent), neither are they an accompanying phatic movement. The performer creates gestures that, by their fullness, their intensity, their halts, suggest the action of his discourse in a plastic manner. He brings back to the text a phrasing and a *Gestus* that tries to find a correspondence for the linguistic rhythm, the physical action and the plastic image. Discourse becomes physical action, and the body can be read like a text. Here we touch on the concept of correspondences. (Is there a unification of the scenic arts in the work, as in a *Gesamtkunstwerk*, or rather autonomy and reciprocal distancing of the stage systems?) It is unquestionable that a fixed code of equivalence between a sound, a color, a word and a gesture does not exist. But in spite of that, we sense that in a good *mise en scène* there is a relationship between the rhythm—or the *Gestus*—of all the theatrical elements. (Cf. the research of Eisenstein or of Adorno and Eisler in "Composing for the Film.")

This experimentation with systems of gestures is part of the more extensive framework of research into "plastic music" (Eisenstein), the relationships between pictorial composition, music and text. Many sequences of the performance are essentially nothing more than attempts to constitute signifying correspondences between several scenic systems. Even if there is never a true organic fusion of sound and meaning, image and text, we are deeply moved by some scenes precisely because they do come near to this organic fusion (the Beaver, dressed as a ballerina, riding a bicycle, accompanied by a very lyrical and exhilarating song by Neil Diamond; or the delirious Barrister taking off, physically and lyrically, to a piece of music by Purcell, etc.) The placement of the performers in the scenic space gives a clear view of the focusing, the exchanges of eye contact, the composition of the characters through the interplay of looks, glances and attitudes (Photo 6). Each performer makes all his movements according to his own given system of gestures; each actor complements the other, creating an impression of rhythmical balance.

The Discourse of the Mise en Scène

The most difficult aspect of the semiotic approach to performance is that of not only pointing out signs but of demonstrating their evolution and their syntagmatic arrangement, of describing the rhythm of the *mise-en-scene* and the "flow" of the movement from one sequence to the next. Often, semioticians fail to take into account the question of tempo (of rhythm, and even, as we have seen, of *Gestus*)—at least those semioticians who are too intent on static descriptions of a few different scenic systems or fixed moments. And yet, every theatre lover is well aware that the rhythm and the phrasing of the scenic discourse are very closely associated with the elaboration of meaning, especially in a piece like *Disparitions*, where the whole composition is so "musical." The *discourse* of the *mise en scène* is punctuated by silences, narrative breaks, changes in the mode of gesture, and, especially in this piece, by musical interludes.

The music does more than add emotional illustration to a scene, it also segments and articulates the narrative, and indicates the movement from one word to another. The eclecticism of the music (Purcell, Mahler, Neil Diamond, musical comedy, Genesis, Barry Lyndon, sound effects, etc.) suits the very variable rhythmical style, while the precision of its associational codes, including the leitmotif, functions as a sort of automatic pilot for the spectator and brings about a perception of the performance at a nonverbal, subconscious level.

To describe the discourse of the *mise en scène* is also to define the mediating structure of the *performance text* and to become aware of the networks and the forms of signs. At the level of the story, the spectator follows the articulations of the narrative as well as the extratextual elements that are part of the plot structure. In *Disparitions* the discourse is structured around each fit, with one of the six performers as the organizer of his own narration and his own story. Each mini-plot includes and goes beyond the others, and in the story of the Captain-*Metteur en scène*-Author, all the narrative material is brought together and recomposed.

Photo 6

The scenic discourse also influences the parallel arrangement of the scenic systems: how they are brought together during the performance, the structuring design of each of the individual systems and, in particular, their reciprocal relationships of divergence and reconciliation.

Very often, it is the *out of sync*, the absence of harmony between parallel scenic systems, that brings about the greatest aesthetic pleasure and produces meaning. The delay or the advance of one stage element in relation to the others always indicates an aesthetic intention. The "tying up of meaning" happens at a focal point when a signifying system unites several isotropies (narrative, thematic, visual), or when the network of sign transformation no longer opens up into something new. In practice, fortunately, this end state is never reached because the spectator always has the capacity of combining other elements, of picking out new signs and of developing new signifying relationships. In this way, semiotics has a means of avoiding the frequent accusation that it freezes the actor, the performance space and the event into a system where everything is foreseen, where every element is semiotized—trapped in the grip of an infernal signifying machine. But in the theatre there are always those elements that are unpredictable, that happen by chance, that are non-signifying. The body of the actor, the rhythm of the diction, and—in a *mise en scène* as open as that of *Disparitions*—the interpretive participation of the spectator, vary from one evening to another. Any preconceived system where every sign is marked in advance would be quite useless. If semiotics wants to do justice to the *event-structure* of theatrical performance, it must be open to hermeneutics and to the aesthetics of audience participation. Semiotics must integrate the act of reception into an interpretive circuit and allow the interpreters the freedom to make mistakes and to manipulate the signs according to their own conscious and unconscious desires. The task, however, is far from being simplified. From now on, in addition to the precise methods of linguistics, the semiotician of the theatre must develop an understanding of rhetorical stage movements, a flexible critical model that takes into account the subjectivity of the spectator, and finally, the capacity to apply the semiotic approach to the mechanisms of cognition and ideology. This is an extensive project but one that attracts and challenges us, especially when a work of the quality of *Disparitions* formulates—in practice—both the questions and the answers. It is an enormous prey, also, which could easily attract all the snarks in the semiotic waters.

Translated by Marguerite Oerlemans Bunn

Avant-Garde Theatre and Semiology: A Few Practices and the Theory Behind Them

This essay was first published in *Performing Arts Journal,* vol. V, no. 3 (PAJ 15), 1981.

Avant-garde theatre and semiology perform a curious ballet: they avoid each other at first, for want of being acquainted, as if they were going through an identity crisis, not quite knowing how to define themselves and, *a fortiori*, how to behave *vis-a-vis* each other. It is certain that the artistic avant-garde in no way resembles a domain precisely marked out in time, space, style or method; as for semiology, even if its place in theatre studies is no longer in dispute, it still hesitates between a theoretical model, abstract and often difficult to put into practice, and a concrete, but too descriptive, application.

Let us therefore not ask semiology if it can be applied to the avant-garde and what it enables us to discover about it; this would be a naive question rendered false from the outset: one can always apply a method to one's subject, even if it is with a very mixed success, and there is no reason why the semiologist should not tackle contemporary theatre events and describe certain signifying systems of the performance. It is much more productive to turn the question and the perspective about and to examine how the avant-garde uses or disqualifies certain semiotic practices in its creative work.

In this way we can better understand the characteristic union of avant-garde art and theory, at a time when the artistic subject is very often called upon to formulate its own theory and to integrate this metalanguage into its very content, and when establishing a theory very much resembles an artistic operation, since it takes a lot of imagination to create explanatory models more or less adapted to their subject. Nothing, however, has been decided as regards the type of semiology which would be the best suited to the avant-garde, and it is by examining the use or the rejection of semiotic tools in avant-garde theatrical art that we can appreciate the integration of the avant-garde and semiology.

It is obviously not the first time that an artistic movement and a theory have met and enriched each other. One only has to think of futurism and formalism in Russia, Czech structuralism and the art of the thirties, the *nouveau roman* and the theory of narration, structuralism and the rereading of the classics, etc. What seems to be new, in the relationship between theatrical practice and theory, is a willingness not to separate and oppose approaches and to check the validity of the one against the other. Thus *mise en scène* becomes the stake of semiotic practice, and a reading of the *mise en scène* no longer takes place except through the discovery of contrasts, isotopies and textual and visual exchanges. Now—is this the sign of over exaggerated abstraction and theorizing?—it is certain that the notion of *mise en scène* which for a century, ever since the official birth of the historical avant-garde in 1887,[1] has been the end result of a centralizing and controlled conception of meaning in the theatre, is today in a state of crisis. Perhaps because the spectator's role has become too rigid (the *mise en scène* being considered the source of and key to the meaning furnished by the author of the performance), he is wrongly expected to find a continuity and a centering in what is, on the stage, but a multitude of performance practices and texts. To replace the structural notion of *mise en scène* by that of an author of the performance or director, is thus to fall back into a problematic situation that the avant-garde had indeed resolved to transcend: that of an autonomous subject who is the source of meaning and who controls the totality of signs, as did formerly the playwright or actor. Thus meaning is not assumed in advance, it emerges from the bringing into view (*la mise en regard*), by the stage practices, of the different signifying systems always out of steps in relation to one another, and which necessitate, in order to be recentered, the intervention of the perception of a "spectator-director," for a while disconcerted: the end of his disconcertion is always the end of the avant-garde.

In order to understand this outcome, but also this premature end of an avant-garde theatre sick because of the director rather than as a result of *mise en scène,* we should consider how the notions of *sign* and *theatrical language,* used by both the avant-garde and semiology, are necessary but at the same time insufficient to describe the theatre of today and its critical analysis. These are notions that were useful for a first theorization and a first semiology, but that today, by being identified with space and visuality, could easily hamper both theoretical advance and contemporary practice.

The Death of the Sign?

The avant-garde distrusts and tries to free itself from the sign, but always succumbs to it in the end: such is the attraction-repulsion movement that was best personified by Artaud in his criticism of the theatre founded on the text and psychology. Artaud wanted to create "a new physical language based on signs and no longer on words" (1964:81). But the signs, "stage images" (p. 91) or animated hieroglyphs, were unable to form a veritable language, since that would have frozen the theatre by reducing it to a dessicated and codified language, as limited, in the long run, as the alphabet and the sounds of articulate language. Faced with this contradiction inherent in any "artistic language" seeking to form a semiological system having its own units and its own specific way of functioning, the avant-garde had to choose between two solutions and two diametrically opposed aesthetics: (1) entirely give up the idea of the sign and the codification of the *mise en scène* or (2) multiply signs and units until the signifying structure degenerates into an infinite series of identical patterns.

(1) In the first case, a whole trend of research into improvisation tries to escape from the constraint of re-petition or re-presentation; it refuses the idea of a separation between sign and thing, stage and life. The perfect example is that of The Living Theatre and their search for an expression freed from all prior codification, for an original and spontaneous language. This trend is the direct descendant of Artaud's research. Analyzing contemporary theatre (that of the thirties, which is still so close to the present-day output), Artaud was quick to diagnose its "dessication," (p. 17) its inability to take hold of life in the theatrical and gestural event; he proposed to replace it by a "directly communicative language" (p. 162), composed of gestures, incantation, gesticulation and scenic rhythm, a "new physical language based on signs and no longer on words" (p. 81). But this new language, even if it goes beyond dialogue and the discursive, could not come into being outside of a system of signs, i.e., a codification that, sooner or later, is likely to become solidified in a system as rigid as that of speech.

This was a phenomenon, moreover, of which Artaud was wholly aware, since as early as the Preface to *The Theatre and Its Double,* he pointed out the limits of this new language: "And the fixation of the theatre in a language: written words, music, light, noises, very soon indicates its downfall, the choice of a language proving the taste that one has for this language; and the dessication of this language accompanies its limitation" (p. 17). This double movement of Artaud—the search for and rejection of a specifically theatrical language—is characteristic of the avant-garde: driven by the desire to create its own units without lapsing for that very reason into the codification of language, it hesitates between the indefinable *expressiveness* of the artistic language and the dessicating *codification* of a too mechanical semiology.

(2) On the other hand, the "serial" trend has reacted in a manner apparently opposed to this fossilization of the sign: by multiplying the sign *ad infinitum,* by repeating it to satiety or by varying it very slightly. The series has become the privileged avatar of structure and even of myth. We know, ever since Walter Benjamin (1955), that in the era of mechanical reproduction the work of art acquires a completely new meaning and that it ceases to

be founded on the ritual to enter straight away the domain of the politic: "The reproduced work of art becomes more and more the reproduction of a work of art conceived for its character of reproductability" (p. 375). For a serial work of art, this new context, in which everything is multipliable and repetitive, becomes one of the constituent principles of its creation. Thus, in the fifties, the theatre of the absurd turned the repetition of a situation or *leitmotiv* into the symptom of its blind submission to the series principle, admitting its inability to recount a unique and original story in which the meaning—moral, lesson, argument—could no longer refer to a stable and exemplary analysis of reality. In the same formal manner, the "theatre of everyday life" (*"Théâtre du Quotidien"* of Franz Xaver Kroetz, Michel Deutsch, Jean-Paul Wenzel, etc.) chooses to retell a "story without a story" or a banal news item, stereotyped formulas that ideology and its sounding-boards drum into our ears all day long. Thus a play like Maria Irene Fornes's *Evelyn Brown (A Diary)*[2] copies indefinitely the identical sentences of the personal diary of a charwoman in which are recorded everyday household tasks, while the actresses perform unceasingly these "scenes of housework" (washing the floor, sweeping, dusting the furniture, etc.). An author such as Michel Vinaver delights in hunting down the typical and banal phrases of a conversation between office workers (*Les Travaux et les Jours* [Work and Days]) or business executives (*A la Renverse* [Backwards]). In all these examples, the repetitions are the scarcely emphasized parody of the classical tragic play whose hero performs in the myth a liberating and meaningful action. These plays and this dramaturgy indicate that the basic *myth* or more simply the tale to be told are relayed by the *series* and thematic variation. This is the moment of the degradation of structure, admirably described by Claude Lévi-Strauss:

> The structrural content (of these narratives) is dispersed. For the vigorous transformations of genuine myths we now find feeble ones substituted. . . . The sociological, astronomical and anatomical codes whose functioning hitherto observed out in the open now pass beneath the surface; and structure sinks into seriality. This degradation begins when oppositions turn into mere duplications: episodes succeeding each other in time, but all formed in the same pattern. It is complete when reduplication itself takes the place of structure. The form of a form, reduplication receives the dying breath of structure itself. Having nothing more, or so little, left to say, myth survives only by repeating itself. (1968:105)

Whatever the trends of the present-day theatre of research, whether these be the negation of the sign or its parodic affirmation, the relationship between the sign and the thing appear profoundly disturbed. The sign seems to have lost its stable relationship between signifier and signified and to have lapsed into two extreme avatars: (1) the *hieroglyph* (a motivated "sign" that refers to the thing by pointing to it rather than by signifying it:

this is the case of spontaneous or improvised theatre); (2) the *serial* form in which the sign has no more than a syntactical value for "serial theatre." Avant-garde theatre has brought about a crisis in the semiotic and referential relationship of the sign with the world. It has lost all confidence in a mimetic reproduction of reality by the theatre, without having invented a semiological system and an autonomous theatrical language capable of taking its place. Semiology doubtlessly owes its rapid development to this calling into question of the mimetic nature of art and the refusal of the stage to presume to imitate a pre-existent exterior world.

It is amusing to note that this crisis in mimetism and representation dates back to the end of the nineteenth century, when naturalism and symbolism combined forces under the aegis of the director. Theatre, and in a similar manner literary theory, decided to depend no longer, in order to define themselves, on the exterior world, but to elaborate their own semiotic units and to concentrate on their different possibilities of combination rather than on their meaning. If they have not succeeded, however, up to the present day, in defining a semiological system and an autonomous theatrical language, it is because they have proved to be too ambitious and dogmatic, hoping to find (like Artaud) a universal language and a specificity that practice and the continual invention of new forms do not cease to refute. What one could term "avant-gardes of specificity" are all those experiments that try to define theatre by a criterion judged necessary and self-sufficient: the actor, space, *mise en scène*, spectator participation, etc. However, none of these criteria is tenable in the long run, with the result that it is becoming impossible to found a semiology based on such specific criteria.

Curiously enough, this has had repercussions on theatrical practice, since a reversal in the relationship between theatrical expression and exterior reality has taken place. Formerly, when the sign was innocent, art was conceived of as the imitation of an objective exterior fact, and the success of the artistic act was measured according to the affinity between sign and thing. Today art no longer seeks to be mimetic, it tries to take the scope of the work of art as its starting point, as its first reality, and is only interested in the referent as a trace in the sign. This is the case of the verbal frescoes of Vinaver (1979, 1980): the referent is a stock of stereotypes and stylistic devices that the plays use as raw material, without bothering about the global and realistic reconstitution of the business enterprise or capitalist society. If it so happens that these fragments of ideology and jargon reconstitute a fictional universe closely resembling our own world, this could only be by "pure coincidence" . . . or as a result of the productive work of the spectator.

If the concept of language, sign or specificity is thus in a state of crisis, crystallizing, but also blocking avant-garde thought, this is probably because it has linked its fate too closely to the notions of *mise en scène* and spatiality. Indeed everything indicates that it is the encounter between *mise en scène* and artistic language, conceived of as the bringing into view and into space (*mise en vue et en espace*) of meaning, that dominates avant-garde research today, a domination that *another* avant-garde, that of time, rhythm and voice, is seeking to break. Perhaps one should see in this mutation the failure or at least the limits of a semiology based solely on a Cartesian examination, measurable, geometric and, in a word, *spatial*, of the theatrical performance.

It has so often been repeated that theatre has nothing to do with literature, that it is a visual and scenic art that spatiality and the geometric and visual measurement of signs have been made, a trifle hastily, the only specific criterion of theatre, thus dismissing all too quickly the temporal, continuous and pulsational aspect of the theatrical performance, the furtive event that is the meeting of an actor and a spectator, all that Jerzy Grotowski and a whole unofficial avant-garde have made into the profound token of the theatre.

Jean-Francois Lyotard has come in time to remind us of the limited and paralyzing nature of such an artistic and semiotic vision by locating the semiological block in the undertaking of the man of space that Artaud was. According to Lyotard, Artaud, wanting "to destroy not the theatrical system termed *Italian,* that is European, but at least the predominance of articulate language and the effacement of the body," stopped halfway, since he

> turned towards the construction of a "tool," which was to be yet another language, a system of signs, a grammar of gestures, hieroglyphs [. . .] It is thus that the mutilation felt by Artaud came back in the form of the Balinese hieroglyph. Silencing the body through the theatre of the *playwright,* a form of theatre dear to middle-class Europe of the nineteenth century, is nihilistic; but making it speak in a vocabulary and a syntax of mime, songs, dances, as does the Noh, is another way of annihilating it: a body "entirely" transparent, *skin* and *flesh* of the bone that is the spirit, intact from any pulsational movement, event, opacity. (1973:100)

Artaud's failure was his wanting to counter the fossilization of the theatre by putting in its place a vision of the theatre that was too spatial and not sufficiently inner and pulsational, his searching for an impossible scenic and gestural language, his forming an idea likewise too specific, in this case too spatial and visual, of the theatrical event.

If today the avant-garde transcends the exclusively spatial, geometric and content-orientated vision of the theatre, it is obviously not through a return to the text, to psychology on linear narrativity. It is a transcendence toward other repressed components of the stage: voice, rhythm, inner duration, the absence of hierarchy between sign systems, the semiological creativity of the spectator, the part played by chance and event in any theatrical performance.

Two Semiologies for One Theatre?

We therefore have to ask ourselves if the two ways, that of space and that of temporal event, are necessarily opposed and exclusive, and whether they condemn any semiological theory to be split up into two discourses foreign to each other. According to this schema we would have, on the one hand, a *semiology of space*: starting off from an "empty space" (Peter Brook) to be filled within a predetermined framework (a three-dimensional scenographic space, a framework susceptible to scenographic modifications but fundamentally stable and limited, hence reassuring), and on the other hand, a *semiology of time*, which no longer starts off from units that are foreseeable (visible in advance), which neither measures nor divides space, but creates it as needed, using as its starting point the play event. The latter semiology organizes an experience of the actor and the spectator in a non-structured series of discourses, rhythms, verbal exchanges, relays between image and word—all elements of stage enunciation.

The semiology of space and the theatrical practice it describes are well known because ever since the recognition of *mise en scène* they have reigned supreme over theory and the stage. From the time of naturalism and symbolism up to Brechtian critical realism, space has been considered the frame of reference within which lie *mise en scène* and meaning. For naturalism, space is the only environment in which man moves and where he finds his place according to social determinisms. With Brecht, we reach another peak of spatialization, since *mise en scène* is entrusted with making visual the social relations of the characters by emphasizing their *Gestus* or the basic arrangement of the scenic figures. The alienation-effect theory is proof of the takeover by space of the production of meaning in the theatre, for it makes visible the character behind the apparent character, the "processes behind the processes," inscribing the signs on the stage as the typographer spaces the letters on the paper (a metaphor of Benjamin regarding the Brechtian alienation-effect).

Even if space has lost all sense of direction and unity, meaning continues to be more or less readable in it. Thus in Brook's film version of Peter Weiss's *Marat/Sade*, the camera relativizes space by multiplying the viewpoints of the prison-baths of the Asylum of Charenton. However, a movement backwards of the camera shows, on several occasions, the director of the institution outside the place of action, separated from the public by a row of bars. This ironic zoom movement re-establishes immediately the boundary between inside and outside, and situates the discourse on liberty in a visual counter-discourse on imprisonment. Even fragmented and disorganized, this type of space so characteristic of the present-day avant-garde still has meaning; it puts the pieces together again and reassures the spectator who can project himself into it. This kind of avant-garde and semiology are based on the clear perception of the borderline between signs, spaces, the dramatic work and the outside world. The border line even becomes the criterion of distinction and of the production of meaning, according to the Saussurian principle of language in which "there are only differences, without specific terms."

On the contrary, the semiology and practice founded on time no longer have an expanse to fill, but a duration and rhythm to maintain. Space no longer exists except in reference to the whereabouts of the actor; it is often not pertinent to the production of meaning (Pavis, 1980: *Espace*). To define the theatrical experiments that correspond to this "event" where dimension is much more problematic, for they are often still in the planning stage and in the form of counter-propositions to the dominant ideology of staged space (*l'espace mise en scène*). This is the case of the *energetic theatre* that Lyotard dreams of without being able to define it other than by what it is not: a theatre where one can feel the "domination of the dramatist + director + choreographer + set designer over the alleged signs and also over the alleged spectators" (p. 103). Of this theatre we can catch a few "glimpses" or, rather "sounds," through a rhythm (as in the *Sprechstücke* of Peter Handke), a voice (those of the "immaterial" characters of Marguerite Duras), a hackneyed repetition of ideological speech (that of Vinaver's garrulous heroes), or a narrative presence of a "performer."

The present success of *performances* can be explained by the rediscovery of the temporal "event" aspect unique to the theatre. After all, the theatre is always the presence of a living being in front of me, the actor who lives in a time and a space that are also mine. Instead of re-presenting and playing an exterior situation and a stable referent, the *performer* admits to being a fugitive and elusive being, willing to go "a little way" with the spectator. In all these examples, there is no longer a referential space doubling and illustrating the text, no longer a visible and foreseeable functioning of the spectacle/theatre event that the spectator has to encompass with his gaze and mind. It is a question of the listener letting himself be borne by the rhythm of the enunciation and concentrating on his task as structurer of materials delivered pell mell, hence the insistence on the process of the elaboration of meaning, more than on meaning itself. "The result is a high degree of focus on process. How one sees is as important as what one sees" (Marranca, 1977: XII). In these theatrical practices, the boundary line between sense and nonsense, work of art and life, is ceaselessly being moved back, so that any limit seems conventional and capable of being repressed.

Numerous texts thus play on the experience of limits. Vinaver repeats the same stereotypes until an aesthetic nausea is reached which should make us feel physically the ever-growing power of ideology. Brook pretends to intimate that the madness and the revolt of the inmates could easily take over the social space of the asylum and of the theatre auditorium. But this is only to remind us all the better in the end that any psychological, social or artistic excess is in fact controlled by the frontiers of the institution or the work of art. Scenic space and the screen protect us from this overflowing of life, the boundary is not wiped out, but its very mobility indicates the impossibility of counting on fixed units and a stable semiological system. Thus structure and spatial form have become a dynamic force linked to the continuous changing of time. The frontier between art and life, actor and spectator, sign and referent has thus become fluid as if this displacement were transcribing into incessant drift the clear boundaries of a theatre and a semiology founded on space.

Other more radical theatrical experiments play still more systematically on the frontier between gesture and word, total improvisation and fixed repetition. For example, the *Théâtre de l'Immédiat* of Nicole Sauvagnac and Nicole Random[3] proposes a series of "calculated improvisations." Starting off from a gestural impulse, from a movement first bodily felt, varied and elaborated little by little, they attempt to shift into a vocal impulse, then into a production of words and phrases induced by the gestural and vocal event. The interest of these experiments is to make one feel the moment of drift or of capsizing between gesture and word, to show how the text (even very rudimentary) can be the result of a gestural "trying out." There is nothing surprising in the fact that it is the voice that serves as mediation between these two heterogeneous elements: the body (supposedly improvisable and therefore liberated) and the text (supposedly repeatable and fixed). At a time when technology and Western civilization have attained a perfection in writing and in space conquered by the gaze and by signs, there no longer remains but the invisible refuge, difficult to locate and to notate, of the voice, of which we are incapable of grasping visually, thus systematically the "grain" (Barthes) or the pulsion. By insisting on the vocal signifier, on the orality dimension in the theatrical message, artistic and theoretical practice is less interested in the utterances (visible, comprehensible and made concrete in a scenic space) than in the enunciation (place of the enunciating subjects, noises and failures of their production). Theatre thus has a *voice at court.*

What avant-gardes?

It is easy to propose a typology of the avant-garde in the theatre according to this space/time dichotomy. It should suffice to give two opposing examples: that of Artaud's writings, the productions of the *Théâtre du Soleil* or Roger Planchon's *mises en scène,* all of which work in accordance with the principle of a place to be invested or a fable to be materialized scenically; that of Vinaver's dramatic works or the *mises en scène* which are also *mises en espace* (spacings) of Jacques Lassalle and his stage designer Y. Kokhos, who play on the ear's sensitivity to textual exchanges and on the economy of the image in contrast to the richness of what is left unsaid in the text. Such a typology would, however, have only a limited interest, since it would help deepen the gulf that divides the two avant-gardes by assimilating space to exuberant theatricality and scenic writing, and time to an aural theatre (*théâtre d'écoute*) and a theatricality inherent in dramatic language. Artaud represents the extreme result of the first tendency: "And it seems to me that on stage, which is above all a space to be filled and a place where something happens, the language of words must give way to the language of signs whose objective aspect is what strikes us most strongly" (p. 162).

As for aural theatre, Vinaver is today its most brilliant exponent: "a theatrical performance is for me an oral projection of a written text, an incitement to listening . . . I would like it [the decor] to be the most effective machine for saying a text, and to be as such unremarkable. I would almost go as fas as saying that it should be invisible" (1980:8).

Today one could take these two tendencies as the standard-bearers of two kinds of theatre. Though they describe it theoretically, they are not, however, distinct and necessarily contradictory categories. There would, moreover, be a certain danger (from which semiology might even fail to recover) in dividing theatrical production and analyzed spectacle into space and time; it would be the same danger (and the same theoretical and practical impossibility) that exists in separating and isolating utterance and enunciation, content and form, fable and recounting discourse (*story* and *discourse* according to Benveniste [1966:237-250]). It would in fact be wrong, on the pretext of establishing a typology and a classification, to consider utterance and space as the domain of the visible, the structurable and the signifier, while reducing enunciation to the level of the invisible, the superfluous, the pulsional and the affective—everything experienced individually and of which no social trace remains.

Any analyst of a spectacle knows full well that scenic or gestural space, even very well structured, can only be read in a process and a putting into discourse (*une mise en discours*): that of the *mise en scène* and of the scanning effect of the spectator's gaze. Even Artaud, whom I have made the archetype of space as guardian of theatricality, suspects the presence of "undreamt-of riches" behind space: "In this theatre, to create space, a new notion of space that one multiplies by tearing it apart, one undoes it thread by thread, one digs down to the core, and underneath appear undreamt-of riches" (1964, vol. IV, p. 312). Conversely, the process of the scenic event (the putting into discourse [*la mise en discours*] of the text and the actors by the scenic work) always ends in being organized into a system of regularities, repetitions and contrasts, with the result that an image and a spatial inscription force themselves on the mind. Moreover, certain practices (such as those of Bob Wilson or Richard Demarcy) are timely reminders that a "theatre of images" plays simultaneously "on both panels" and according to the two rhythms peculiar to each system, and particularly that such a theatre needs music and the voice to "cement" the images.

Semiological practice would once again do well to follow this reflex of theatrical practice: instead of replacing classical semiology based on the sign and on observable space by a "generalized desemiotics" (Lyotard, 1973:99), founded on a theatre of events, semiology wishes to establish a circuit between the structuring principle (codifying) and the destructuring principle (of events) and to join together again what has been only artificially separated: utterance and enunciation, writing and orality, meaning and sound, signifier and signified. One can only appeal for a semiology that takes all the dimensions of theatre into account, that neglects none of the *Voices and Images of the Stage*.[4]

In all these examples, the avant-garde plays with semiology and its theoretical position is far from certain; it questions and contests the fact that the sign can be considered a minimal unit, even the spatial and representative base of the scenic event; it postpones, however, the death of the sign, in the same way as does the deconstruction undertaking of Jacques Derrida, which also refuses the metaphysics of the sign, without for all that being able to go beyond it: "The sign and divinity were born at the same time and in the same place. The era of the sign is essentially theological. It will perhaps never end. Its historical end is, however, designated" (1967:25). Like philosophy, the avant-garde and semiology are still in the age of the sign and the performance/representation (*la représentation*). We have not yet reached the post-avant-garde, but are still in the period of avant-postmodernism. Theatre finds in these labels and borderline cases, not its end, but its very substance.

Translated by Jill Daugherty

Footnotes

[1] 1887 is the year that *Théâtre Libre* of Antoine and *Théâtre d'Art* of Paul Fort were founded.
[2] A performance presented in April, 1980, at Theatre for the New City, New York City.
[3] *Le plein du délié* was presented in 1981 in Paris.
[4] Title of my book to be published by the Presses Universitaires de Lille, 1982.

Bibliography

Artaud, Antonin (1964). *Le Théâtre et son double*, Paris, Gallimard.
Benjamin, Walter (1955). "Das Kunstwerk im Zeitalter seiner Reproduzierbarkeit," in *Schriften*, Frankfurt, Suhrkamp (vols. I & II).
Benvéniste, Emile (1966, 1974). *Problèmes de linguistique générale*, Paris, Gallimard.
Derrida, Jacques (1967). *De la Grammatologie*, Paris, Minuit.
Lévi-Strauss, Claude (1968). *L'origine des manières de table*, Paris.
Lyotard, Jean-Francois (1973). "La dent, la paume," *Des dispositifs pulsionnels*, Paris, UGE-10-18.
Marranca, Bonnie (1977). *The Theatre of Images*, New York, Drama Book Specialists.
Pavis, Patrice (1980). *Dictionnaire du théâtre: Termes et concepts de l'analyse théâtrale*, Paris, Editions sociales.
Pavis (1980). "Lire et faire au théâtre l'action parlée dans les stances du cid," *Etudes Littéraires*, Decembre 1980.
Ubersfeld, Anne (1977). *Lire le théâtre*, Paris, Editions sociales.
Vinaver, Michel (1979). *Le Travaux et les jours*, Paris, L'Arche.
Vinaver (1980). *A la Renverse*, Lausanne, Editions de L'aire.

POSTFACE

Interrogation:
An Exercise in Self-Exorcism

INTERROGATION
(An exercise in self-exorcism)

What is the use of semiology? Is it not just one more technology to be added to the already very advanced technologization of stage arts and theatre studies, a pedantic and tortuous method of weighing obvious facts that every man of the theatre knows instinctively?

Semiology in no way resembles a machine or a technique meant to *produce* ready-made discourses about a text or the stage. It is necessary in fact to *construct* this analytical machine which is not preconceived and which has to be built up according to the theatrical subject studied. To analyze the codes and signifying systems of a performance is not to rediscover what the author and director had previously established secretly, once and for all. It is to organize the performance and the text as a possible circuit of meaning whose productivity and coherence are more or less great according to the theatre event in question, but also according to the analyst.

DISCUSSION
I, ii

By speaking of the theatre with such a scientific *or even, as you would say,* epistemological *fervor, are you not destroying at the same time this artistic object, imposing on it a conceptual framework of which neither the author nor the average spectator is aware?*

NOTATION
III, iii

Perhaps, but without this analysis, what exists of the performance? Am I not obliged to become involved and to situate myself in relation to this aesthetic object, still shapeless and meaningless as long as I have not grasped a few principles about the way it functions?

And, so with your semiology or your semiotics, you claim to replace the traditional ways of approaching the text and the performance? You throw overboard twenty-five centuries of poetics and one century of mise en scène?

CRITICISM
III, ii

Do not worry, theatrical semiology is not trying to take the place of any existing discipline; it does not claim to be a prophetic discovery or a religion for the use of the initiated. It is not even a new science or domain, an enclave in the heart of theatre studies but a methodological principle which facilitates the interaction of several aims and discourses of criticism. This reflection on the production of the meaning(s) of the text or of the performance obliges it to take into

DISCUSSION
I, ii

account the teachings of poetics, dramaturgy, the technique of the actor, as well as the history of the different theatrical genres. To classify and evaluate for each particular case these partial (in both senses of the word) approaches is no mean matter: not every theory of knowledge is both propaedeutic and epistemological.

By stressing this propaedeutic value of semiology and your own hermeneutic commitment vis-a-vis textual and stage signifiers, are you not returning to a traditional and subjective interpretation of criticism?

Not necessarily, if research into the signifying systems is seen as a possible construction of meaning which occurs when an objective analysis of the performance data (observation and description of the signifiers) is joined to a more flexible attempt to take into account the audience's freedom of association and maneuver. It is a matter of explaining how we construct meaning from the signifiers, and how in return the latter determine our perception.

In this country of pragmatism and efficiency, what use can we find for a theory borrowed from linguistics—abstract,

weighed down by jargon and far removed from human realities?
How will it improve the training of the actor, the production of
a show or the historical knowledge of the theatrical tradition?

RECEPTION
III, i

You could be answered with the same vigor: how does the mixture of psychology, humanism and letters that one hears in dramatic discussions, seminars and lectures help the actor to acquire an overall view of drama, and not to be simply content with a technique of reproducing a meaning spoon-fed to him by virtue of one or another mystery?

CRITICISM
III, ii

But are you not crushing under the weight of the semiological
apparatus (which is far from being ''the simple apparatus of a
beauty recently awakened''—Racine) the creativity and
humanity of the theatre event, that holy place where the
transmutation of actor into character takes place? Are you not
needlessly concealing under an esoteric vocabulary something
that we experience daily in the flesh?

I beg of you: do not give me that old story about the unexplainable Romantic artist. Spare me the inevitable quotation from the *Bourgeois-Gentilhomme* about Mr. Jourdain's prose, if it is to tell about expressiveness, humanism and the 'things in life' that are immediately accessible. Do not remind me of the obvious fact that we all practice semiology without knowing it, in order to prove to me that it does not exist. I doubt whether you would have the satirical talent of the playwright Dubillard: "What, when I say Nicole, bring me my slippers, the recurrence of my two slipper units every evening means that I am talking in isotopies? Well, to think that I have been making isotopies for forty years without knowing it." To which it would be necessary to reply in the words of a Marivaux character (*Fausses Confidences*, III, v): "So for fifty years you haven't known what you have been saying."

But why do you want to explain everything? What are the
limits of semiological curiosity?

They include domains and questions suppressed for too long: the connection between the work and history defined at last in a way other than by a theory of reflection and sociological simplification; the places where ideological contradictions and ruptures in the text occur, where we manipulate it and where we are manipulated by it. Thus semiology is in no way a formal game closed upon itself as is often imagined. Strangely enough, today a whole school of criticism, which formerly derided structuralism, New Criticism and "classical semiology," has climbed onto the semiological bandwagon the better to defend the autonomy of its domain, the work of literature, human activity, in short the academic career: these are hard times. However, to read the sign is not only to understand its function in the aesthetic or fictional ensemble to the exclusion of the outside world, it is to seek the link between the sign and the referer, the aesthetic and the political, delirium and deliverance.

It does not seem possible to get you to explain clearly your project as far as theatre is concerned, and the position from which you claim to deliver your discourse.

That is so, I'm afraid: it moves, I move, it moves me. This brings us to the question of the institution that orders all these discourses. Was not the famous question of the seventies: "Tell me where you are speaking from and I will tell you. . . ." Today it is changed, wherever one may be, into: "Tell me where you are speaking from and what your professional status is. . . ," "Tell me if you can make your semiological discourse into the forms to be filled out for the governmental plans or for requests for grants from research organizations. . . ." Petty questions, but, epistemologically speaking, quite radical in order to situate oneself. In these pages, I have not ceased to move from the iconic to the symbolic, from text to stage, from gesture to discourse, from classicism to the avant-garde, from space to time, from the production of the *mise-en-scene* to its reception by the audience.

Do these constant shifts of position not indicate an uneasiness or an instability inherent in semiology, the impossibility of embracing in one critical gaze the whole of the semiological adventure?

Probably, at any rate they indicate that one should hardly believe nowadays in the universality of a model if this prevents a lively and illustrated clarification of the performance or text, of the actor or spectator. They also indicate that semiology, instead of retreating into a linguistic model or universal logic (whether this be a logical square, an actantial model or a theatrical genre), must necessarily classify the problems that puzzle the lover of theatre and organize the levels of critical intervention, without *a priori* excluding any discourse or attitude.

Exactly: classical semiology claimed that the sign was a minimal unit, whereas you seem today to be turning away from an approach that, inspired by researchers such as Saussure or Benveniste, primarily defined the sign as a unit combining a signifier and a signified. Moreover, was not semiology, from which you claim to descend, constructed on the Saussurian model, and therefore on the pattern of language and linguistics, which makes it inadequate for the theatre where speech is only one of the components among many others? Are you not applying a literary and logocentric grid to an object that, particularly today, is trying precisely to escape from logocentrism?

MISE EN SCÈNE
III, iv

This argument, which one often hears on the other side of the Atlantic (seen from Europe), does not take into account the fact that, if semiology was indeed elaborated by a linguist, it certainly does not follow that it must be logocentric or limited to the study of the literary text. In fact, the model of the sign (signifier/signified) can be applied to any system of communication or art as soon as one can make out a plan of expression or a plan of content. One could perfectly well use this model for an avant-garde kind of theatre consisting only of gesture or lighting or space effects. In the analysis of a performance involving a text, great care is taken—contrary to certain studies which claim to be semiological—not to make the text the signified of the sequence and the stage elements the signifier (*le signifiant*). Or, one should rather say, the non-signifier (*l'insignifiant*) of this "theatrical sign," wrongly defined as the bringing together (or *mise en presence*) of a text and a stage image. The semiology of performing arts does *not apply* a linguistic model, it plays at finding possible correspondences between signifier and signified, rather than at determining in this object the hierarchical or simply concurrent relationship of the elements, investigating this bringing into relationship (or *mise en relation*) which is the *mise en* scène.

But do you not continue to cling to the sign as to a buoy in the semiotic shipwreck and in the relativity of meanings? Since you no longer limit it or distinguish from the outset between its two sides (signifier and signified), how will you manage to avoid its assimilation to the word, to the literarity or narrativity of the fable?

The sign in the theatre does not exist only when it possesses a clear *semantic* value (when it represents mimetically an exterior reality). It is just as valid, and sometimes exclusively so (1) as a relational value in a *syntactical* order: it then combines with other signs. Lighting (spotlight) only has meaning, for example, in relation to the lighting effect (night) that preceded it; (2) as a *pragmatic* dimension, as soon as its impact on the receiver is clearly apparent.

RECEPTION III, i

If you are no longer looking for a constant or for a clearly defined correspondence between signifier and signified, in what way can the sign still be of interest to you?

Simply as a marker to determine and examine in depth the signifiers of the performance. It is relatively easy to ramble on about the signified, once it has been more or less identified. It is *much* more problematic to examine the signifier before "translating" it directly into a signified; an effort will thus be made to examine the composition of the signifier, its organization and the logic of its evolution and its mutations in the text or on the stage. A signifier is what best holds out against the immediate and conclusive establishing of a meaning: the texture of a voice, the resonance of music, the construction of a stage image—as many materials worked on by the theatrical artist and working according to their own logic. Moreover, the distinction between iconic (analogical) communication and symbolic (digital) communication remains important when one first takes into account the form of theatrical meaning. But it is not enough to oppose these two communications. One must examine the dialectical elucidations that take place during the work of the *mise en scène*: codification of the image and the analogical into a discourse of the *mise en scène*, *iconization* of the text produced by the voice and the presence of the actor.

But even supposing you go beyond this narrow definition of the sign, combining in exemplary fashion one signifier and one signified, do you not still remain dependent on a theatre that is founded on the linear, even literary development of a text subject to the unfolding of a story? How can you apply this semiological grid to an avant-garde theatre that tells no story, has no fable and escapes from the linearity of discourse and text?

MIME
II, ii

You are confusing text and narrativity, literary, linguistic and narrative traits. Even in the case of the most abstract mime, dance, or a succession of lighting effects, there is narrativity—a placing into sequence (into discourse) of scattered and consecutive elements. Narrativity can be read as a theoretical model which accounts for the passage from one utterance to another. It is not at all necessary for this narration to take the form of a linguistic narration; any text is narrative, but all narrativity is not necessarily textual. One must therefore carefully distinguish between various systems: the *textual* (a system which uses a spoken or heard or readable text), the *narrative* (which tells a story, gives the phrases of a narration), the *fictional* (a type of discourse that, due to its own conventions, is distinguishable from a real discourse about the world), the *logocentric* (which stresses the primacy of the verbal in relation to the visual).

MISE EN SCÈNE
III, iv

But then, how can avant-garde theatre escape from literature, from narrativity, from logocentrism?

To say that the avant-garde fears the text like the plague, going as far as to totally eliminate it, is one thing. This does not mean that it gets rid of narrativity as easily; the image always recounts something, even silence or darkness have a meaning which is "extended" in a fable, or in more or less clear utterances, or in the process of enunciation. As for logocentrism, who can pride himself on escaping it, since it has been established that we see the world through the framework of language? We read the image according to the segmentation imposed by language, and the social world, as Benveniste pointed out, is embodied and informed by language.

However, the models elaborated by semiology tend to favor exactness, as far as components and universality are concerned, at the expense of an analysis which particularizes and historicizes the objects to which they are applied. The actantial model inspired by Greimas admittedly replaces the traditional psychological analysis, but by a totally abstract model, which introduces eternal categories: Eros, the People, Desire, Death, etc. Whereas the work of Propp and that of Souriau were at least based on a corpus of existing texts, the actantial models of Greimas completely "smooth out" historical bumps and ideological irregularities in support of a universal, logical and ideological schema.

It is true that this difficulty pointed out by you has considerably hindered the development of the study of character or of action, and that these grids have overshadowed other specifically dramatic or theatrical approaches. Therefore we are at present turning toward other kinds of formalization: textual grammar, the mechanism of discourse, the rhetoric of patterns and images, etc. What we still lack is a model—whether it be actantial, discursive or textual—that takes into account the stage forms of theatricality and also the work of the actor and the director. We are now moving away from an actantial code to return to a study of the character considered as the sum of his discourses or stage events, and no longer as the ideologically neutral site of human action.

But will these new models you promise us be concrete enough to furnish a key to the creativity of the author, the stage designer, the actor and the director?

Only if we are careful to examine through them the practical function of semiology in theatre work. Should we not point out to the actor how the miming, gestural and linguistic signs he emits will be received? Suggest to the stage designer that the space in which the actor's path is traced will circumscribe and influence the reception of the event or text? Remind the director that his reading of the story, his dramaturgical choices, must be given concrete form in an interplay of actor, space and time made "readable" for the spectator?

You are trying to make meaning visible. That is all very well, but is that not one particular ideological choice, among other possible choices, insofar as you postulate that meaning is a product of space, of visualization, of geometric perception as a measurable exterior fact?

Perhaps we have indeed let ourselves become too confined by this measurable spatial dimension, which has resulted in our ignoring the temporal dimension of the theatre event, a dimension which is rhythmic, interior and driving. This is no doubt the reason why, in a series of record actions, the sign has exploded, the code has become nothing more than a provisional convention to be dismantled, and the performance resists being reduced to an ensemble of purely spatial signs. What we now have to rediscover, in our updating of semiology, is the temporal perspective, the perception of rhythmic patterns, the dynamics peculiar to any work of the actor, of temporal flow, of the voice and of affect. A whole theatrical movement, from Bob Wilson to the *Théâtre du Quotidien* (Theatre of the Everyday), encourages by diverse means the latter approach. This will lead to our questioning the ideological founding of our discipline on arguments that have favored space, measurement, the visible paradoxically. The survival of the semiological enterprise depends on the sign, on meaning and on the origin of meaning being continuously challenged. Ever since Artaud, there has been a ceaseless insistence on the necessity "of making space talk, of nourishing and furnishing space." Today there is every reason to believe that it is in time, in silence and in the body, that the sign is made and unmade.

How can one be sure of the meaning of the performance, how can one know whether the mise en scène *has been done according to the* right *meaning? Have you not reached a total relativism of the meaning of text and performance? Why should I retain such-and-such a semiological schema rather than any other, and what attention is paid, amid all this, to the intentions of the creator?*

RECEPTION
III, i

"Alas, poor Yorick!" Alas, poor creator! How could you accuse me of being unfaithful to your intentions, since I have no means of knowing them? Even if, by some misfortune, you took the naive precaution of noting them down in the margin of your text, what informs me that *this* is the only true way of reading your text? Haven't you not only moved away from, but also turned away from what you have just written? The creator, like the semiologist, can only intervene afterwards, searching in the work for signs which give an *outline* or *rhythm* to a possible structure.

Under the pretext of a freedom of reading and a "discovery" of the creativity of the spectator, are you not transferring to the receptor the belief in unlimited creativity, subjectivity and relativism? Are you not shifting the source of meaning the better to conceal what determines its production, and through what institutions or powers it can be exercized?

That is indeed a reversal risk of which we must remain aware, and this transfer of creativity is often a potential maneuver to evade the explanation of the ideological foundations of taste, subjectivity and the formalization of sign systems. Through this side-stepping of meaning and the refusal to locate the aesthetic and ideological discourse, one senses the difficulty our era experiences in identifying the subject in his relationship with social forces, the discourses which pass through him and which are caught in the net of his conscious or unconscious strategy. It is clear that the semiologist is part of a whole philosophical and aesthetic movement, and that he must take this into account or be submerged and annihilated by it.

Is this warning not also the acknowledgement of your inability to fix the meaning of a text and, what is still more complex, of a text confronted with a stage enunciation? So far, if I understand you correctly, you recommend a plural and open reading, an easy way of not committing yourself to an interpretation.

MISE EN SCÈNE III, iv   Unfortunately, yes. Semiology is not a fairy godmother who offers recipes for and solutions to the problem of the reading and the *mise en scène* of a text. Just as there is not a finite number of possible *mises en scène* for the dramatic text, so the semiologist, doubled by the hermeneutic, never reaches the end of his pursuit of analysis and meaning. One always wants to write, as at the end of a somewhat lazy student's composition: "making progress, but can do better." It is this dynamic and provisional situation which appeals to me.

And what do you intend doing with this anarchy of mean-

ings?

Declare that it exists and give it two or three good reasons to carry on doing so.

I imagine that you must feel very close to many modern directors who profess the same casual attitude toward the text.

Most certainly, my feeling for them is one of admiration mingled with envy: the director too is someone who plays hide-and-seek with the text he claims to "serve." He was smart enough to seize his chance at the end of the nineteenth century, when the theatre was opened to an hetergeneous public that needed to be guided, when literature began, with Mallarmé notably, to ponder over its meaning and to feed on its own substance, when logocentrism appeared as an inevitable, but ungainly flow of Western civilization. Ever since then, the director has not relinquished his hold on the text, he spends his time bringing out of the text personal accents and directions, the better to conceal others. He is the man of the sign *par excellence*, because he has complete power to draw from the text, through the intervention of the stage, potentialities, possibilities or even (sometimes) impossibilities. He plays the "modest" role of servant to the text, yet never loses on opportunity of recalling the providential nature of his appearance.

GESTUS
II, i

However, he knows full well that *mise en scène* is basically a relative, historical notion and that it lasts only as long as we believe in the obviousness and singularity of the meaning. If he was able, at the start of his career, to pass as the one who opposed King Text and logocentrism—fighting against the text's pretension to control the whole performance—he is revealed today as belonging to a "neo-logocentrism" just as radical as the old, since he aims, through his *stage discourse*, to control entirely the theatre event, and therefore also the text rewritten by the magic baton of this conductor of the stage. If such a director tends to exercise power secretly and to systematize, he will turn the *mise en scène* into a tool which can be analyzed and summarized in a discourse on the text to be played in his reaction to this testing of the stage. This will result in that hybrid and disturbing being: the semiological director.

I am beginning to see what you are getting at. So allow me one final question to close the debate: what if you really detested the theatre? What if you could not bear multiplicity and if semiology were only a desperate search for the lost unity of meaning and of the text, a unity the theatre squanders in a thousand gambols?

And you, what if you were incapable of going beyond the stage of childish pleasure to be had in watching a puppet show where all the rules are known in advance, but behind which you could not help but see, unless you were dishonest, the operator. To every man his own pleasure: the bare puppet or the concealed operator.

Let us end on a less aggressive note: in short, for you the semiologist is but an artist in disguise, he who "plays with signs as with a conscious decoy, whose fascination he savors and wants to make others savor and understand" (Barthes, Lecture, p. 41).

I am afraid that you are right and that this decoy is what lets him go on living and working. There again, Barthes had felt and propagated this fascination; he always understood everything ten years in advance. It seems to me that henceforth the avant-garde and theory will have a warmed-up and bitter taste.

Kaliky; 8-13 February 1981

Translated by Jill Daugherty